W9-ALV-585

LIMITED INC

JACQUES DERRIDA

Northwestern University Press
Evanston, IL

Northwestern University Press
Evanston, Illinois 60208

"Signature Event Context" copyright © 1972 by Les Editions de Minuit. English translation by Samuel Weber and Jeffrey Mehlman first published in *Glyph* 1, 1977. Copyright © 1977 by The Johns Hopkins University Press and Editions de Minuit. "Signature Event Context," translated by Alan Bass, appears in *Margins of Philosophy* by Jacques Derrida, published 1982 by the University of Chicago Press.

English translation of "Limited Inc a b c . . . " by Samuel Weber first published in *Glyph* 2, 1977. Copyright © 1977 by The Johns Hopkins University Press. Used by permission of The Johns Hopkins University Press.

Afterword copyright © 1988 by Jacques Derrida. Translation copyright © 1988 by Samuel Weber. Editor's Foreword and Summary of "Reiterating the Differences" copyright © 1988 by Northwestern University Press. All rights reserved.

Printed in the United States of America

First published 1988
Second paperback printing, 1990
Third paperback printing, 1993

Library of Congress Cataloging-in-Publication Data

Derrida, Jacques.
    Limited Inc/Jacques Derrida.
       p. cm.
    Translated from the French.
    Two essays herein appeared in Glyph v. 1 & 2, 1977.
    Contents: Signature event context—Summary of "Reiterating
the differences"—Limited Inc a b c—Afterword: toward an ethic of discussion.
    ISBN 0-8101-0787-2   ISBN 0-8101-0788-0 (pbk.)
    1. Deconstruction   I. Title
PN98.D43D45 1988
801'.95—dc19

88-28322
CIP

LIMITED INC

Contents

Editor's Foreword

Limited Inc collects, in one volume for the first time, the two essays that constitute Jacques Derrida's most sustained engagement with Anglo-American speech act theory. In a new Afterword, "Toward an Ethic of Discussion," Derrida responds to questions (submitted to him in written form) about the two essays and the criticisms they have received, as well as other controversial aspects of Derrida's work.

The opening essay, "Signature Event Context," has a somewhat complicated publishing history. In its first version, the essay was written for a conference on the theme of "Communication" held by the Congrès international des Sociétés de philosophie de langue francaise (Montreal, August, 1971) and was published in French in the Congres's *Proceedings.* The essay was then collected in Derrida's *Marges de la Philosophy,* published by Editions de Minuit in 1972. The first English translation, by Samuel Weber and Jeffrey Mehlman, appeared in volume 1 of the serial publication *Glyph* in 1977. It subsequently appeared in a translation by Alan Bass in *Margins of Philosophy* (University of Chicago Press, 1982).

In its second volume (1977), *Glyph* published a response to Derrida's essay by John R. Searle entitled "Reiterating the Differences: A Reply to Derrida." It was this "Reply" that drew Derrida's rejoinder, the essay "Limited Inc abc. . .," translated by Samuel Weber. When Professor Searle declined to have his essay included in the present book, we decided to insert a brief summary of its main points in an editorial note between Derrida's two essays. With this summary and Derrida's comprehensive quotation of Searle's "Reply," readers should be able to reconstruct the dispute between Derrida and Searle. But they are advised to consult the full text of Searle's essay in *Glyph* 2.

Because Searle's "Reply" and Derrida's rejoinder in "Limited Inc" make extensive reference to passages in the Weber-Mehlman translation of "Signature Event Context," we have chosen to use that translation here.

On behalf of the Northwestern University Press, I want to extend my warmest thanks to Samuel Weber for initially suggesting this project, helping it along in innumerable ways, and translating the Afterword under considerable deadline pressure. And of course we thank Jacques Derrida for giving us the honor of making his texts available in book form, and for enhancing them with his most recent thoughts.

GERALD GRAFF

Signature Event Context

> "Still confining ourselves for simplicity to *spoken* utterance."
> Austin, *How to Do Things with Words*

Is it certain that to the word *communication* corresponds a concept that is unique, univocal, rigorously controllable, and transmittable: in a word, communicable? Thus, in accordance with a strange figure of discourse, one must first of all ask oneself whether or not the word or signifier "communication" communicates a determinate content, an identifiable meaning, or a describable value. However, even to articulate and to propose this question I have had to anticipate the meaning of the word *communication:* I have been constrained to predetermine communication as a vehicle, a means of transport or transitional medium of a *meaning,* and moreover of a *unified* meaning. If *communication* possessed several meanings and if this plurality should prove to be irreducible, it would not be justifiable to define communication a priori as the transmission of a *meaning,* even supposing that we could agree on what each of these words (transmission, meaning, etc.) involved. And yet, we have no prior authorization for neglecting *communication* as a word, or for impoverishing its polysemic aspects; indeed, this word opens up a semantic domain that precisely does not limit itself to semantics, semiotics, and even less to linguistics. For one characteristic of the semantic field of the word *communication* is that it designates nonsemantic movements as well. Here, even a provisional recourse to ordinary language and to the equivocations of natural language instructs us that one can, for instance, *communicate a movement* or that a tremor [*ébranlement*], a shock, a displacement of force can be communicated—that is, propagated, transmitted. We also speak of different or remote places communicating with each other by means of a passage or opening. What takes place, in this sense, what is transmitted, communicated, does not involve phenomena of meaning or signification. In such cases we are dealing neither with a semantic or conceptual content, nor with a semiotic operation, and even less with a linguistic exchange.

1

We would not, however, assert that this non-semiotic meaning of the word *communication,* as it works in ordinary language, in one or more of the so-called natural languages, constitutes the *literal* or *primary* [*primitif*] meaning and that consequently the semantic, semiotic, or linguistic meaning corresponds to a derivation, extension, or reduction, a metaphoric displacement. We would not assert, as one might be tempted to do, that semio-linguistic communication acquired its title *more metaphorico,* by analogy with "physical" or "real" communication, inasmuch as it also serves as a passage, transporting and transmitting something, rendering it accessible. We will not assert this for the following reasons:

1) because the value of the notion of *literal meaning* [*sens propre*] appears more problematical than ever, and

2) because the value of displacement, of transport, etc., is precisely constitutive of the concept of metaphor with which one claims to comprehend the semantic displacement that is brought about from communication as a non-semio-linguistic phenomenon to communication as a semio-linguistic phenomenon.

(Let me note parenthetically that this communication is going to concern, indeed already concerns, the problem of polysemy and of communication, of dissemination—which I shall oppose to polysemy—and of communication. In a moment a certain concept of writing cannot fail to arise that may transform itself and perhaps transform the problematic under consideration.)

It seems self-evident that the ambiguous field of the word "communication" can be massively reduced by the limits of what is called a *context* (and I give notice, again parenthetically, that this particular communication will be concerned with the problem of context and with the question of determining exactly how writing relates to context in general). For example, in a philosophic *colloquium* on philosophy in the *French language,* a conventional context—produced by a kind of consensus that is implicit but structurally vague—seems to prescribe that one propose "communications" concerning communication, communications in a discursive form, colloquial communications, oral communications destined to be listened to, and to engage or to pursue dialogues within the horizon of an intelligibility and truth that is meaningful, such that ultimately general agreement may, in principle, be attained. These communications are supposed to confine themselves to the element of a determinate, "natural" language, here designated as French, which commands certain very particular uses of the word *communication.* Above all, the object of such communications is supposed, by priority or by privilege, to organize itself around communication qua discourse, or in any case qua signification. Without exhausting all the implications and the entire structure of an "event" such as this one, an effort that would require extended preliminary analysis, the conditions that I have just recalled seem to be evident; and those who doubt it need only consult our program to be convinced.

But are the conditions [*les réquisits*] of a context ever absolutely determinable? This is, fundamentally, the most general question that I shall endeavor to elaborate. Is there a rigorous and scientific concept of *context?* Or does the notion of context not conceal, behind a certain confusion, philosophical presuppositions of a very determinate nature? Stating it in the most summary manner possible, I shall try to demonstrate why a context is never absolutely determinable, or rather, why its determination can never be entirely certain or saturated. This structural non-saturation would have a double effect:

1) it would mark the theoretical inadequacy *of the current concept of context* (linguistic or nonlinguistic), as it is accepted in numerous domains of research, including all the concepts with which it is systematically associated;

2) it would necessitate a certain generalization and a certain displacement of the concept of writing. This concept would no longer be comprehensible in terms of communication, at least in the limited sense of a transmission of meaning. Inversely, it is within the general domain of writing, defined in this way, that the effects of semantic communication can be determined as effects that are particular, secondary, inscribed, and supplementary.

Writing and Telecommunication

If we take the notion of writing in its currently accepted sense—one which should not—and that is essential—be considered innocent, primitive, or natural, it can only be seen as a *means of communication*. Indeed, one is compelled to regard it as an especially potent means of communication, *extending* enormously, if not infinitely, the domain of oral or gestural communication. This seems obvious, a matter of general agreement. I shall not describe all the *modes* of this extension in time and in space. I shall, however, pause for a moment to consider the import [*valeur*] of *extension* to which I have just referred. To say that writing *extends* the field and the powers of locutory or gestural communication presupposes, does it not, a sort of *homogeneous* space of communication? Of course the compass of voice or of gesture would encounter therein a factual limit, an empirical boundary of space and of time; while writing, in the same time and in the same space, would be capable of relaxing those limits and of opening the *same field* to a very much larger scope. The meaning or contents of the semantic message would thus be transmitted, *communicated,* by different *means,* by more powerful technical mediations, over a far greater distance, but still within a medium that remains fundamentally continuous and self-identical, a homogeneous element through which the unity and wholeness of meaning would not be affected in its essence. Any alteration would therefore be accidental.

The system of this interpretation (which is also, in a certain manner, *the* system of interpretation, or in any case of all hermeneutical interpretation), however currently accepted it may be, or inasmuch as it is current, like common sense, has been *represented* through the history of philosophy. I would even go so far as to say that it is the interpretation of writing that is peculiar and proper to philosophy. I shall limit myself to a single example, but I do not believe that a single counterexample can be found in the entire history of philosophy as such; I

3

know of no analysis that contradicts, essentially, the one proposed by Condillac, under the direct influence of Warburton, in the *Essay on the Origin of Human Knowledge (Essai sur l'origine des connaissances humaines)*. I have chosen this example because it contains an *explicit* reflection on the origin and function of the written text (this explicitness is not to be found in every philosophy, and the particular conditions both of its emergence and of its eclipse must be analyzed) which organizes itself here within a philosophical discourse that, in this case and throughout philosophy, presupposes the simplicity of the origin, the continuity of all derivation, of all production, of all analysis, and the homogeneity of all dimensions [*ordres*]. Analogy is a major concept in the thought of Condillac. I have also chosen this example because the analysis, "retracing" the origin and function of writing, is placed, in a rather uncritical manner, *under the authority of the category of communication.*[1] If men write it is: (1) because they have to communicate; (2) because what they have to communicate is their "thought," their "ideas," their representations. Thought, as representation, precedes and governs communication, which transports the "idea," the signified content; (3) because men are *already* in a state that allows them to communicate their thought to themselves and to each other when, in a continuous manner, they invent the particular means of communication, writing. Here is a passage from chapter XIII of the Second Part ("On Language and Method"), First Section ("On the Origins and Progress of Language") (Writing is thus a modality of language and marks a continual progression in an essentially linguistic communication), paragraph XIII, "On Writing": "Men in a state of communicating their thoughts by means of sounds, felt the necessity of imagining new signs capable of perpetuating those thoughts and of making them *known* to persons who are *absent*" (I underscore this value of *absence,* which, if submitted to renewed questioning, will risk introducing a certain break in the homogeneity of the system). Once men are already in the state of "communicating their thoughts," and of doing it by means of sounds (which is, according to Condillac, a second step, when articulated language has come to "supplant" [*suppléer*] the language of action, which is the single and radical principle of all language), the birth and progress of writing will follow in a line that is direct, simple, and continuous. The history of writing will conform to a law of mechanical economy: to gain or save the most space and time possible by means of the most convenient abbreviation; hence writing will never have the slightest effect on either the structure or the contents of the meaning (the ideas) that it is supposed to transmit [*véhiculer*]. The same content, formerly communicated by gestures and sounds, will henceforth be transmitted by writing, by successively different modes of notation, from pictographic writing to alphabetic writing, collaterally by the hieroglyphic writing of the Egyptians and the ideographic writing of the Chinese. Condillac continues: "Thus, the imagination will represent to them only the very *same* images that they had already expressed through actions and words, and which had, from the very beginning, rendered language figural and metaphorical. *The most natural means* was thus to depict [*dessiner*] images of things. *To express the idea* of a man

4

or of a horse, one represented the form of the one or of the other, and the first attempt at writing was nothing but a simple painting" (my emphasis—J.D.).

The representational character of the written communication—writing as picture, reproduction, imitation of its content—will be the invariant trait of all progress to come. The concept of *representation* is here indissociable from those of *communication* and of *expression* that I have emphasized in Condillac's text. Representation, of course, will become more complex, will develop supplementary ramifications and degrees; it will become the representation of a representation in various systems of writing, hieroglyphic, ideographic, or phonetic-alphabetical, but the representative structure which marks the first degree of expressive communication, the relation idea/sign, will never be either annulled or transformed. Describing the history of the types of writing, their continuous derivation from a common root that is never displaced and which establishes a sort of community of analogical participation among all the species of writing, Condillac concludes (in what is virtually a citation of Warburton, as is most of this chapter): "Thus, the general history of writing proceeds by simple gradation from the state of painting to that of the letter; for letters are the final steps that are left to be taken after the Chinese marks which, on the one hand, participate in the nature of Egyptian hieroglyphics, and on the other, participate in that of letters just as the hieroglyphs participate both in Mexican paintings and Chinese characters. These characters are so close to our writing that an alphabet simply diminishes the inconvenience of their great number and is their succinct abbreviation."

Having thus confirmed the motif of economic reduction in its *homogeneous and mechanical* character, let us now return to the notion of *absence* that I underscored, in passing, in the text of Condillac. How is that notion determined there?

1) It is first of all the absence of the addressee. One writes in order to communicate something to those who are absent. The absence of the sender, of the receiver [*destinateur*], from the mark that he abandons, and which cuts itself off from him and continues to produce effects independently of his presence and of the present actuality of his intentions [*vouloir-dire*], indeed even after his death, his absence, which moreover belongs to the structure of all writing—and I shall add further on, of all language in general—this absence is not examined by Condillac.

2) The absence of which Condillac speaks is determined in the most classic manner as a continuous modification and progressive extenuation of presence. Representation regularly *supplants* [*supplée*] presence. However, articulating all the moments of experience insofar as it is involved in signification ("to supplant," *suppléer,* is one of the most decisive and most frequent operational concepts in Condillac's *Essay²*), this operation of supplementation is not exhibited as a break in presence but rather as a continuous and homogeneous reparation and modification of presence in the representation.

I am not able to analyze, here, everything presupposed in Condillac's philosophy and elsewhere, by this concept of absence as the modification of presence. Let us note only that this concept governs another operational notion (for the sake of convenience I invoke the classical opposition between *operational* and *thematic*) which is no less decisive for the *Essay*: *tracing* and *retracing*. Like the concept of supplanting [*suppléance*], the concept of trace would permit an interpretation quite different from Condillac's. According to him, tracing means "expressing," "representing," "recalling," "rendering present" ("Thus painting probably owes its origin to the necessity of tracing our thoughts in the manner described, and this necessity has doubtless contributed to preserving the language of action as that which is most readily depictable" ["On Writing," p. 128]). The sign comes into being at the same time as imagination and memory, the moment it is necessitated by the absence of the object from present perception [*la perception présente*] ("Memory, as we have seen, consists in nothing but the power of recalling the signs of our ideas, or the circumstances that accompanied them; and this power only takes place by virtue of the *analogy of the signs* [my emphasis—J. D.: the concept of analogy, which organizes the entire system of Condillac, provides the general guarantee of all the continuities and in particular that linking presence to absence] that we have chosen; and by the order that we have instituted among our ideas, the objects that we wish to retrace are bound up with several of our present needs." [1, 11 ch. iv, # 39]). This holds true for all the orders of signs distinguished by Condillac (arbitrary, accidental, and even natural, distinctions that Condillac qualifies and, on certain points, even calls into question in his letters to Cramer). The philosophical operation that Condillac also calls "retracing" consists in reversing, by a process of analysis and continuous decomposition, the movement of genetic derivation that leads from simple sensation and present perception to the complex edifice of representation: from ordinary presence to the language of the most formal calculus [*calcul*].

It would be easy to demonstrate that, fundamentally, this type of analysis of written signification neither begins nor ends with Condillac. If I call this analysis "ideological," I do so neither to oppose its notions to "scientific" concepts nor to appeal to the dogmatic—one might also say ideological—usage to which the term "ideology" is often put, while seldom subjecting either the various possibilities or the history of the word to serious consideration. If I define notions such as those of Condillac as "ideological" it is because, against the background [*sur le fond*] of a vast, powerful, and systematic philosophical tradition dominated by the prominence of the *idea* (*eidos, idea*), they delineate the field of reflection of the French "ideologues," who in the wake of Condillac elaborated a theory of the sign as representation of the idea which itself represented the object perceived. From that point on, communication is that which circulates a representation as an ideal content (meaning); and writing is a species of this general communication. A species: a communication admitting a relative specificity within a genre.

If we now ask ourselves what, in this analysis, is the essential predicate of this *specific difference,* we rediscover *absence.*

I offer here the following two propositions or hypotheses:

1) since every sign, whether in the "language of action" or in articulated language (before even the intervention of writing in the classical sense), presupposes a certain absence (to be determined), the absence within the particular field of writing will have to be of an original type if one intends to grant any specificity whatsoever to the written sign;

2) if perchance the predicate thus introduced to characterize the absence peculiar and proper to writing were to find itself no less appropriate to every species of sign and of communication, the consequence would be a general shift; writing would no longer be one species of communication, and all the concepts to whose generality writing had been subordinated (including the *concept* itself qua meaning, idea or grasp of meaning and of idea, the concept of communication, of the sign, etc.) would appear to be noncritical, ill-formed, or destined, rather, to insure the authority and the force of a certain historical discourse.

Let us attempt, then, while still continuing to take this classical discourse as our point of departure, to characterize the absence that seems to intervene in a specific manner in the functioning of writing.

A written sign is proffered in the absence of the receiver. How to style this absence? One could say that at the moment when I am writing, the receiver may be absent from my field of present perception. But is not this absence merely a distant presence, one which is delayed or which, in one form or another, is idealized in its representation? This does not seem to be the case, or at least this distance, divergence, delay, this deferral [*différance*] must be capable of being carried to a certain absoluteness of absence if the structure of writing, assuming that writing exists, is to constitute itself. It is at that point that the *différance* [difference and deferral, *trans.*] as writing could no longer (be) an (ontological) modification of presence. In order for my "written communication" to retain its function as writing, i.e., its readability, it must remain readable despite the absolute disappearance of any receiver, determined in general. My communication must be repeatable—iterable—in the absolute absence of the receiver or of any empirically determinable collectivity of receivers. Such iterability—(*iter,* again, probably comes from *itara, other* in Sanskrit, and everything that follows can be read as the working out of the logic that ties repetition to alterity) structures the mark of writing itself, no matter what particular type of writing is involved (whether pictographical, hieroglyphic, ideographic, phonetic, alphabetic, to cite the old categories). A writing that is not structurally readable—iterable—beyond the death of the addressee would not be writing. Although this would seem to be obvious, I do not want it accepted as such, and I shall examine the final objection that could be made to this proposition. Imagine a writing whose code would be so idiomatic as to be established and known, as secret cipher, by only two "subjects." Could we maintain that, following the death of the receiver, or even of both partners, the mark left by one of them is still writing? Yes, to the extent that, organized by a code, even an unknown and nonlinguistic one, it is constituted in its identity as mark by its iterability, in the absence of such and such a person, and hence ultimately of every empirically determined "subject." This implies that there is no such thing as a code—organon of iterability—which could be structurally secret. The possibility of repeating and thus of identifying the marks is implicit in every code, making it into a network [*une grille*] that is communicable, transmittable, decipherable, iterable for a third, and hence for every possible user in general. To be what it is, all writing must, therefore, be capable of functioning in the radical absence of every empirically determined receiver in general. And this absence is not a continuous modification of presence, it is a rupture in presence, the "death" or the possibility of the "death" of the receiver inscribed in the structure of the mark (I note in passing that this is the point where the value or the "effect" of transcendentality is linked necessarily to the possibility of writing and of "death" as analyzed). The perhaps paradoxical consequence of my here having recourse to iteration and to code: the disruption, in the last analysis, of the authority of the code as a finite system of rules; at the same time, the radical destruction of any context as the protocol of code. We will come to this in a moment.

What holds for the receiver holds also, for the same reasons, for the sender or the producer. To write is to produce a mark that will constitute a sort of machine which is productive in turn, and which my future disappearance will not, in principle, hinder in its functioning, offering things and itself to be read and to be rewritten. When I say "my future disappearance" [*disparition*: also, demise, *trans.*], it is in order to render this proposition more immediately acceptable. I ought to be able to say my disappearance, pure and simple, my nonpresence in general, for instance the nonpresence of my intention of saying something meaningful [*mon vouloir-dire, mon intention-de-signification*], of my wish to communicate, from the emission or production of the mark. For a writing to be a writing it must continue to "act" and to be readable even when what is called the author of the writing no longer answers for what he has written, for what he seems to have signed, be it because of a temporary absence, because he is dead or, more generally, because he has not employed his absolutely actual and present intention or attention, the plenitude of his desire to say what he means, in order to sustain what seems to be written "in his name." One could repeat at this point the analysis outlined above this time with regard to the addressee. The situation of the writer and of the underwriter [*du souscripteur*: the signatory, *trans.*] is, concerning the written text, basically the same as that of the reader. This essential drift [*dérive*] bearing on writing as an iterative structure, cut off from all absolute responsibility, from *consciousness* as the ultimate authority, orphaned and separated at birth from the assistance of its father, is precisely what Plato condemns in the *Phaedrus*. If Plato's gesture is, as I believe, the philosophical movement par excellence, one can measure what is at stake here.

Before elaborating more precisely the inevitable consequences of these nuclear traits of all writing—that is: (1) the break with the horizon of communication as communication of consciousnesses or of presences and as linguistical or semantic transport of the desire to mean what one says [*vouloir-dire*]; (2) the disengagement of all writing from the semantic or hermeneutic horizons which, inasmuch as they are horizons of meaning, are riven [*crever*] by writing; (3) the necessity of disengaging from the concept of polysemics what I have elsewhere called *dissemination*, which is also the concept of writing; (4) the disqualification or the limiting of the concept of context, whether "real" or "linguistic," inasmuch as its rigorous theoretical determination as well as its empirical saturation is rendered impossible or insufficient by writing—I would like to demonstrate that the traits that can be recognized in the classical, narrowly defined concept of writing, are generalizable. They are valid not only for all orders of "signs" and for all languages in general but moreover, beyond semio-linguistic communication, for the entire field of what philosophy would call experience, even the experience of being: the above-mentioned "presence."

What are in effect the essential predicates in a minimal determination of the classical concept of writing?

1) A written sign, in the current meaning of this word, is a mark that subsists, one which does not exhaust itself in the moment of its inscription and which can give rise to an iteration in the absence and beyond the presence of the empirically determined subject who, in a given context, has emitted or produced it. This is what has enabled us, at least traditionally, to distinguish a "written" from an "oral" communication.

2) At the same time, a written sign carries with it a force that breaks with its context, that is, with the collectivity of presences organizing the moment of its inscription. This breaking force [*force de rupture*] is not an accidental predicate but the very structure of the written text. In the case of a so-called "real" context, what I have just asserted is all too evident. This allegedly real context includes a certain "present" of the inscription, the presence of the writer to what he has written, the entire environment and the horizon of his experience, and above all the intention, the wanting-to-say-what-he-means, which animates his inscription at a given moment. But the sign possesses the characteristic of being readable even if the moment of its production is irrevocably lost and even if I do not know what its alleged author-scriptor consciously intended to say at the moment he wrote it, i.e. abandoned it to its essential drift. As far as the internal semiotic context is concerned, the force of the rupture is no less important: by virtue of its essential iterability, a written syntagma can always be detached from the chain in which it is inserted or given without causing it to lose all possibility of functioning, if not all possibility of "communicating," precisely. One can perhaps come to recognize other possibilities in it by inscribing it or *grafting* it onto other chains. No context can entirely enclose it. Nor any code, the code here being both the possibility and impossibility of writing, of its essential iterability (repetition/alterity).

3) This force of rupture is tied to the spacing [*espacement*] that constitutes the written sign: spacing which separates it from other elements of the internal contextual chain (the always open possibility of its disengagement and graft), but also from all forms of present reference (whether past or future in the modified

9

form of the present that is past or to come), objective or subjective. This spacing is not the simple negativity of a lacuna but rather the emergence of the mark. It does not remain, however, as the labor of the negative in the service of meaning, of the living concept, of the *telos,* supersedable and reducible in the *Aufhebung* of a dialectic.

Are these three predicates, together with the entire system they entail, limited, as is often believed, strictly to "written" communication in the narrow sense of this word? Are they not to be found in all language, in spoken language for instance, and ultimately in the totality of "experience" insofar as it is inseparable from this field of the mark, which is to say, from the network of effacement and of difference, of units of iterability, which are separable from their internal and external context and also from themselves, inasmuch as the very iterability which constituted their identity does not permit them ever to be a unity that is identical to itself?

Let us consider any element of spoken language, be it a small or large unit. The first condition of its functioning is its delineation with regard to a certain code; but I prefer not to become too involved here with this concept of code which does not seem very reliable to me; let us say that a certain self-identity of this element (mark, sign, etc.) is required to permit its recognition and repetition. Through empirical variations of tone, voice, etc., possibly of a certain accent, for example, we must be able to recognize the identity, roughly speaking, of a signifying form. Why is this identity paradoxically the division or dissociation of itself, which will make of this phonic sign a grapheme? Because this unity of the signifying form only constitutes itself by virtue of its iterability, by the possibility of its being repeated in the absence not only of its "referent," which is self-evident, but in the absence of a determinate signified or of the intention of actual signification, as well as of all intention of present communication. This structural possibility of being weaned from the referent or from the signified (hence from communication and from its context) seems to me to make every mark, including those which are oral, a grapheme in general; which is to say, as we have seen, the nonpresent *remainder* [*restance*] of a differential mark cut off from its putative "production" or origin. And I shall even extend this law to all "experience" in general if it is conceded that there is no experience consisting of *pure* presence but only of chains of differential marks.

Let us dwell for a moment on this point and return to that absence of the referent and even of the signified meaning, and hence of the correlative intention to signify. The absence of referent is a possibility easily enough admitted today. This possibility is not only an empirical eventuality. It constructs the mark; and the potential presence of the referent at the moment it is designated does not modify in the slightest the structure of the mark, which implies that the mark can do without the referent. Husserl, in his *Logical Investigations,* analyzed this possibility very rigorously, and in a two-fold manner:

1) An utterance [*énoncé*] whose object is not impossible but only possible can very well be made and understood without its real object (its referent) being

present, either to the person who produced the statement or to the one who receives it. If while looking out the window, I say: "The sky is blue," this utterance will be intelligible (let us say, provisionally if you like, communicable) even if the interlocutor does not see the sky; even if I do not see it myself, if I see it badly, if I am mistaken or if I wish to mislead my interlocutor. Not that this is always the case; but the structure of possibility of this utterance includes the capability to be formed and to function as a reference that is empty or cut off from its referent. Without this possibility, which is also that of iterability in general, "generable," and generative of all marks, there would be no utterance.

2) The absence of the signified. Husserl analyzes this as well. He judges it to be always possible even if, according to the axiology and teleology that governs his analysis, he judges this possibility to be inferior, dangerous, or "critical": it opens the phenomenon of the *crisis* of meaning. This absence of meaning can take three forms:

A) I can manipulate symbols without animating them, in an active and actual manner, with the attention and intention of signification (crisis of mathematical symbolism, according to Husserl). Husserl insists on the fact that this does not prevent the sign from functioning: the crisis or the emptiness of mathematical meaning does not limit its technical progress (the intervention of writing is decisive here, as Husserl himself remarks in *The Origin of Geometry*).

B) Certain utterances can have a meaning although they are deprived of *objective* signification. "The circle is squared" is a proposition endowed with meaning. It has sufficient meaning at least for me to judge it false or contradictory (*widersinnig* and not *sinnlos*, Husserl says). I place this example under the category of the absence of the signified, although in this case the tripartite division into signifier/signified/referent is not adequate to a discussion of the Husserlian analysis. "Squared circle" marks the absence of a referent, certainly, as well as that of a certain signified, but not the absence of meaning. In these two cases, the crisis of meaning (nonpresence in general, absence as the absence of the referent—of the perception—or of the meaning—of the intention of actual signification) is still bound to the essential possibility of writing; and this crisis is not an accident, a factual and empirical anomaly of spoken language, it is also its positive possibility and its "internal" structure, in the form of a certain outside [*dehors*].

C) Finally there is what Husserl calls *Sinnlosigkeit* or agrammaticality. For instance, "the green is either" or "abracadabra" [*le vert est ou;* the ambiguity of *ou* or *où* is noted below, *trans.*]. In such cases Husserl considers that there is no language any more, or at least no "logical" language, no cognitive language such as Husserl construes in a teleological manner, no language accorded the possibility of the intuition of objects given in person and signified in *truth*. We are confronted here with a decisive difficulty. Before stopping to deal with it, I note a point that touches our discussion of communication, namely that the primary interest of the Husserlian analysis to which I am referring here (while precisely detaching it up to a certain point, from its context or its teleological and metaphysical horizon, an operation which itself ought to provoke us to ask how and why it is always possible), is its claim rigorously to dissociate (not without a certain degree of success) from every phenomenon of communication the analysis of the sign or the expression (*Ausdruck*) as signifying sign, the seeking to say something (*bedeutsames Zeichen*).[3]

Let us return to the case of agrammatical *Sinnlosigkeit*. What interests Husserl in the *Logical Investigations* is the system of rules of a universal grammar, not from a linguistic point of view but from a logical and epistemological one. In an important note to the second edition,[4] he specifies that his concern is with a pure *logical* grammar, that is, with the universal conditions of possibility for a morphology of significations in their cognitive relation to a possible object, not with a pure grammar in *general*, considered from a psychological or linguistic point of view. Thus, it is solely in a context determined by a will to know, by an epistemic intention, by a conscious relation to the object as cognitive object within a horizon of truth, solely in this oriented contextual field is "the green is either" unacceptable. But as "the green is either" or "abracadabra" do not constitute their context by themselves, nothing prevents them from functioning in another context as signifying marks (or indices, as Husserl would say). Not only in contingent cases such as a translation from German into French, which would endow "the green is either" with grammaticality, since "either" (*oder*) becomes for the ear "where" [*où*] (a spatial mark). "Where has the green gone (of the lawn: the green is where)," "Where is the glass gone in which I wanted to give you something to drink?" [*"Où est passé le verre dans lequel je voulais vous donner à boire?"*] But even "the green is either" itself still signifies an *example of agrammaticality*. And this is the possibility on which I want to insist: the possibility of disengagement and citational graft which belongs to the structure of every mark, spoken or written, and which constitutes every mark in writing before and outside of every horizon of semio-linguistic communication; in writing, which is to say in the possibility of its functioning being cut off, at a certain point, from its "original" desire-to-say-what-one-means [*vouloir-dire*] and from its participation in a saturable and constraining context. Every sign, linguistic or nonlinguistic, spoken or written (in the current sense of this opposition), in a small or large unit, can be *cited*, put between quotation marks; in so doing it can break with every given context, engendering an infinity of new contexts in a manner which is absolutely illimitable. This does not imply that the mark is valid outside of a context, but on the contrary that there are only contexts without any center or absolute anchoring [*ancrage*]. This citationality, this duplication or duplicity, this iterability of the mark is neither an accident nor an anomaly, it is that (normal/abnormal) without which a mark could not even have a function called "normal." What would a mark be that could not be cited? Or one whose origins would not get lost along the way?

Parasites. Iter, of Writing: That It Perhaps Does Not Exist

I now propose to elaborate a bit further this question with special attention to—but in order, as well, to pass beyond—the problematic of the *performative*. It concerns us here for several reasons:

1) First of all, Austin, through his emphasis on an analysis of perlocution and above all of illocution, appears to consider speech acts only as acts of communication. The author of the introduction to the French edition of *How To Do Things With Words,* quoting Austin, notes as much: "It is by comparing *constative* utterances (i.e., classical 'assertions,' generally considered as true or false 'descriptions' of facts) with *performative* utterances (from the English 'performative,' i.e., allowing to accomplish something through speech itself) that Austin is led to consider *every* utterance worthy of the name (i.e., intended to communicate—thus excluding, for example, reflex-exclamations) as being primarily and above all a speech act produced in the *total* situation in which the interlocutors find themselves" (*How To Do Things With Words*, p. 147, G. Lane, Introduction to the French translation, p. 19).

2) This category of communication is relatively new. Austin's notions of illocution and perlocution do not designate the transference or passage of a thought-content, but, in some way, the communication of an original movement (to be defined within a *general theory of action*), an operation and the production of an effect. Communicating, in the case of the performative, if such a thing, in all rigor and in all purity, should exist (for the moment, I am working within that hypothesis and at that stage of the analysis), would be tantamount to communicating a force through the impetus [*impulsion*] of a mark.

3) As opposed to the classical assertion, to the constative utterance, the performative does not have its referent (but here that word is certainly no longer appropriate, and this precisely is the interest of the discovery) outside of itself or, in any event, before and in front of itself. It does not describe something that exists outside of language and prior to it. It produces or transforms a situation, it effects; and even if it can be said that a constative utterance also effectuates something and always transforms a situation, it cannot be maintained that that constitutes its internal structure, its manifest function or destination, as in the case of the performative.

4) Austin was obliged to free the analysis of the performative from the authority of the truth *value*, from the true/false opposition,[5] at least in its classical form, and to substitute for it at times the value of force, of difference of force (*illocutionary* or *perlocutionary force*). (In this line of thought, which is nothing less than Nietzschean, this in particular strikes me as moving in the direction of Nietzsche himself, who often acknowledged a certain affinity for a vein of English thought.)

For these four reasons, at least, it might seem that Austin has shattered the concept of communication as a purely semiotic, linguistic, or symbolic concept. The performative is a "communication" which is not limited strictly to the transference of a semantic content that is already constituted and dominated by an orientation toward truth (be it the *unveiling* of what is in its being or the *adequation-congruence* between a judicative utterance and the thing itself).

And yet—such at least is what I should like to attempt to indicate now—all the difficulties encountered by Austin in an analysis which is patient, open, aporetical, in constant transformation, often more fruitful in the acknowledgment of its impasses than in its positions, strike me as having a common root. Austin has not taken account of what—in the structure of *locution* (thus before any illocutory or perlocutory determination)—already entails that system of predicates I call *graphematic in general* and consequently blurs [*brouille*] all the oppositions which follow, oppositions whose pertinence, purity, and rigor Austin has unsuccessfully attempted to establish.

In order to demonstrate this, I shall take for granted the fact that Austin's analyses at all times require a value of *context*, and even of a context exhaustively determined, in theory or teleologically; the long list of "infelicities" which in their variety may affect the performative event always comes back to an element in what Austin calls the total context.[6] One of those essential elements—and not one among others—remains, classically, consciousness, the conscious presence of the intention of the speaking subject in the totality of his speech act. As a result, performative communication becomes once more the communication of an intentional meaning,[7] even if that meaning has no referent in the form of a thing or of a prior or exterior state of things. The conscious presence of speakers or receivers participating in the accomplishment of a performative, their conscious and intentional presence in the totality of the operation, implies teleologically that no *residue* [*reste*] escapes the present totalization. No residue, either in the definition of the requisite conventions, or in the internal and linguistic context, or in the grammatical form, or in the semantic determination of the words employed; no irreducible polysemy, that is, no "dissemination" escaping the horizon of the unity of meaning. I quote from the first two lectures of *How to Do Things with Words*:

> Speaking generally, it is always necessary that the *circumstances* in which the words are uttered should be in some way, or ways, *appropriate*, and it is very commonly necessary that either the speaker himself or other persons should *also* perform certain *other* actions, whether 'physical' or 'mental' actions or even acts of uttering further words. Thus, for naming the ship, it is essential that I should be the person appointed to name her, for (Christian) marrying, it is essential that I should not be already married with a wife living, sane and undivorced, and so on; for a bet to have been made, it is generally necessary for the offer of the bet to have been accepted by a taker (who must have done something, such as to say 'Done'), and it is hardly a gift if I *say* 'I give it you' but never hand it over.
>
> So far, well and good. (pp. 8-9)

In the Second Lecture, after eliminating the grammatical criterion in his customary manner, Austin examines the possibility and the origin of failures or "infelicities" of performative utterance. He then defines the six indispensable—if not sufficient—conditions of success. Through the values of "conventional procedure," "correctness," and "completeness," which occur in the definition, we necessarily find once more those of an exhaustively definable context, of a free consciousness present to the totality of the operation, and of absolutely meaningful speech [*vouloir-dire*] master of itself: the teleological jurisdiction of an entire field whose organizing center remains *intention*.[8] Austin's procedure is rather remarkable and typical of that philosophical tradition with which he would like to have so few ties. It consists in recognizing that the possibility of the negative (in this case, of infelicities) is in fact a structural possibility, that failure is an essential risk of the operations under consideration; then, in a move which is almost *immediately simultaneous*, in the name of a kind of ideal regulation, it excludes that risk as accidental, exterior, one which teaches us nothing about the linguistic phenomenon being considered. This is all the more curious—and, strictly speaking, untenable—in view of Austin's ironic denunciation of the "fetishized" opposition: *value/fact*.

Thus, for example, concerning the conventionality without which there is no performative, Austin acknowledges that *all* conventional acts are exposed to failure: "it seems clear in the first place that, although it has excited us (or failed to excite us) in connexion with certain acts which are or are in part acts of *uttering words*, infelicity is an ill to which *all* acts are heir which have the general character of ritual or ceremonial, all *conventional* acts: not indeed that *every* ritual is liable to every form of infelicity (but then nor is every performative utterance)" (pp. 18-19, Austin's emphasis).

In addition to the questions posed by a notion as historically sedimented as "convention," it should be noted at this point:

1) that Austin, at this juncture, appears to consider solely the conventionality constituting the *circumstance* of the utterance [*énoncé*], its contextual surroundings, and not a certain conventionality intrinsic to what constitutes the speech act [*locution*] itself, all that might be summarized rapidly under the problematical rubric of "the arbitrary nature of the sign," which extends, aggravates, and radicalizes the difficulty. "Ritual" is not a possible occurrence [*éventualité*], but rather, *as* iterability, a structural characteristic of every mark.

2) that the value of risk or exposure to infelicity, even though, as Austin recognizes, it can affect a priori the totality of conventional acts, is not interrogated as an essential predicate or as a *law*. Austin does not ponder the consequences issuing from the fact that a possibility—a possible risk—is *always* possible, and is in some sense a necessary possibility. Nor whether—once such a necessary possibility of infelicity is recognized—infelicity still constitutes an accident. What is a success when the possibility of infelicity [*échec*] continues to constitute its structure?

The opposition success/failure [*échec*] in illocution and in perlocution thus seems quite insufficient and extremely secondary [*dérivée*]. It presupposes a general and systematic elaboration of the structure of locution that would avoid an endless alternation of essence and accident. Now it is highly significant that Austin rejects and defers that "general theory" on at least two occasions, specifically in the Second Lecture. I leave aside the first exclusion.

> I am not going into the general doctrine here: in many such cases we may even say the act was "void" (or voidable for duress or undue influence) and so forth. Now I suppose some very general high-level doctrine might embrace both what we have called infelicities *and* these other "unhappy" features of the doing of actions—in our case actions containing a performative utterance—in a single doctrine: but we are not including this kind of unhappiness—we must just remember, though, that features of this sort can and do constantly obtrude into any case we are discussing. Features of this sort would normally come under the heading of "extenuating circumstances" or of "factors reducing or abrogating the agent's responsibility," and so on. (p. 21, my emphasis)

The second case of this exclusion concerns our subject more directly. It involves precisely the possibility for every performative utterance (and a priori every other utterance) to be "quoted." Now Austin excludes this possiblity (and the general theory which would account for it) with a kind of lateral insistence, all the more significant in its off-handedness. He insists on the fact that this possibility remains *abnormal, parasitic,* that it constitutes a kind of extenuation or agonized succumbing of language that we should strenuously distance ourselves from and resolutely ignore. And the concept of the "ordinary," thus of "ordinary language," to which he has recourse is clearly marked by this exclusion. As a result, the concept becomes all the more problematical, and before demonstrating as much, it would no doubt be best for me simply to read a paragraph from the Second Lecture:

> (ii) Secondly, as *utterances* our performances are *also* heir to certain other kinds of ill, which infect *all* utterances. And these likewise, though again they might be brought into a more general account, we are deliberately at present excluding. I mean, for example, the following: a performative utterance will, for example, be *in a peculiar way* hollow or void if said by an actor on the stage, or if introduced in a poem, or spoken in soliloquy. This applies in a similar manner to any and every utterance—a sea-change in special circumstances. Language in such circumstances is in special ways—intelligibly— used not *seriously* [my emphasis, J. D.], but in many ways *parasitic* upon its normal use—ways which fall under the doctrine of the *etiolations* of language. All this we are *excluding* from consideration. Our performative utterances, felicitous or not, are to be understood as issued in ordinary circumstances. (pp. 21–22)

Austin thus excludes, along with what he calls a "sea-change," the "non-serious," "parasitism," "etiolation," "the non-ordinary" (along with the whole general theory which, if it succeeded in accounting for them, would no longer be governed by those oppositions), all of which he nevertheless recognizes as the possibility available to every act of utterance. It is as just such a "parasite" that writing has always been treated by the philosophical tradition, and the connection in this case is by no means coincidental.

I would therefore pose the following question: is this general possibility necessarily one of a failure or trap into which language may *fall* or lose itself as in an abyss situated outside of or in front of itself? What is the status of this *parasitism?* In other words, does the quality of risk admitted by Austin *surround* language like a kind of *ditch* or external place of perdition which speech [*la locution*] could never hope to leave, but which it can escape by remaining "at home," by and in itself, in the shelter of its essence or *telos?* Or, on the contrary, is this risk rather its internal and positive condition of possibility? Is that outside its inside, the very force and law of its emergence? In this last case, what would be meant by an "ordinary" language defined by the exclusion of the very law of language? In excluding the general theory of this structural parasitism, does not Austin, who nevertheless claims to describe the facts and events of ordinary language, pass off as ordinary an ethical and teleological determination (the univocity of the utterance [*énoncé*]—that he acknowledges elsewhere [pp. 72–73] remains a philosophical "ideal"—the presence to self of a total context, the transparency of intentions, the presence of meaning [*vouloir-dire*] to the absolutely singular uniqueness of a speech act, etc.)?

For, ultimately, isn't it true that what Austin excludes as anomaly, exception, "non-serious,"[9] *citation* (on stage, in a poem, or a soliloquy) is the determined modification of a general citationality—or rather, a general iterability—without which there would not even be a "successful" performative? So that—a paradoxical but unavoidable conclusion—a successful performative is necessarily an "impure" performative, to adopt the word advanced later on by Austin when he acknowledges that there is no "pure" performative.[10]

I take things up here from the perspective of positive possibility and not simply as instances of failure or infelicity: would a performative utterance be possible if a citational doubling [*doublure*] did not come to split and dissociate from itself the pure singularity of the event? I pose the question in this form in order to prevent an objection. For it might be said: you cannot claim to account for the so-called graphematic structure of locution merely on the basis of the occurrence of failures of the performative, however real those failures may be and however effective or general their possibility. You cannot deny that there are also performatives that succeed, and one has to account for them: meetings are called to order (Paul Ricoeur did as much yesterday); people say: "I pose a question"; they bet, challenge, christen ships, and sometimes even marry. It would seem that such events have occurred. And even if only one had taken place only once, we would still be obliged to account for it.

I'll answer: "Perhaps." We should first be clear on what constitutes the status of "occurrence" or the eventhood of an event that entails in its allegedly present and singular emergence the intervention of an utterance [*énoncé*] that in itself can be only repetitive or citational in its structure, or rather, since those two

17

words may lead to confusion: iterable. I return then to a point that strikes me as fundamental and that now concerns the status of events in general, of events of speech or by speech, of the strange logic they entail and that often passes unseen.

Could a performative utterance succeed if its formulation did not repeat a "coded" or iterable utterance, or in other words, if the formula I pronounce in order to open a meeting, launch a ship or a marriage were not identifiable as *conforming* with an iterable model, if it were not then identifiable in some way as a "citation"? Not that citationality in this case is of the same sort as in a theatrical play, a philosophical reference, or the recitation of a poem. That is why there is a relative specificity, as Austin says, a "relative purity" of performatives. But this relative purity does not emerge *in opposition to* citationality or iterability, but in opposition to other kinds of iteration within a general iterability which constitutes a violation of the allegedly rigorous purity of every event of discourse or every *speech act*. Rather than oppose citation or iteration to the noniteration of an event, one ought to construct a differential typology of forms of iteration, assuming that such a project is tenable and can result in an exhaustive program, a question I hold in abeyance here. In such a typology, the category of intention will not disappear; it will have its place, but from that place it will no longer be able to govern the entire scene and system of utterance [*l'énonciation*]. Above all, at that point, we will be dealing with different kinds of marks or chains of iterable marks and not with an opposition between citational utterances, on the one hand, and singular and original event-utterances, on the other. The first consequence of this will be the following: given that structure of iteration, the intention animating the utterance will never be through and through present to itself and to its content. The iteration structuring it a priori introduces into it a dehiscence and a cleft [*brisure*] which are essential. The "non-serious," the *oratio obliqua* will no longer be able to be excluded, as Austin wished, from "ordinary" language. And if one maintains that such ordinary language, or the ordinary circumstances of language, excludes a general citationality or iterability, does that not mean that the "ordinariness" in question—the thing and the notion—shelter a lure, the teleological lure of consciousness (whose motivations, indestructible necessity, and systematic effects would be subject to analysis)? Above all, this essential absence of intending the actuality of utterance, this structural unconsciousness, if you like, prohibits any saturation of the context. In order for a context to be exhaustively determinable, in the sense required by Austin, conscious intention would at the very least have to be totally present and immediately transparent to itself and to others, since it is a determining center [*foyer*] of context. The concept of—or the search for—the context thus seems to suffer at this point from the same theoretical and "interested" uncertainty as the concept of the "ordinary," from the same metaphysical origins: the ethical and teleological discourse of consciousness. A reading of the connotations, this time, of Austin's text, would confirm the reading of the descriptions; I have just indicated its principle.

Différance, the irreducible absence of intention or attendance to the performative utterance, the most "event-ridden" utterance there is, is what authorizes me, taking account of the predicates just recalled, to posit the general graphematic structure of every "communication." By no means do I draw the conclusion that there is no relative specificity of effects of consciousness, or of effects of speech (as opposed to writing in the traditional sense), that there is no performative effect, no effect of ordinary language, no effect of presence or of discursive event (speech act). It is simply that those effects do not exclude what is generally opposed to them, term by term; on the contrary, they presuppose it, in an asymmetrical way, as the general space of their possibility.

Signatures

That general space is first of all spacing as a disruption of presence in a mark, what I here call writing. That all the difficulties encountered by Austin intersect in the place where both writing and presence are in question is for me indicated in a passage such as that in Lecture V in which the divided instance of the juridic signature [*seing*] emerges.

Is it an accident if Austin is there obliged to note: "I must explain again that we are floundering here. To feel the firm ground of prejudice slipping away is exhilarating, but brings its revenges" (p. 61). Shortly before, an "impasse" had appeared, resulting from the search for "any *single simple* criterion of grammar and vocabulary" in distinguishing between performative or constative utterances. (I should say that it is this critique of linguisticism and of the authority of the code, a critique based on an analysis of language, that most interested and convinced me in Austin's undertaking.) He then attempts to justify, with nonlinguistic reasons, the preference he has shown in the analysis of performatives for the forms of the first person, the present indicative, the active voice. The justification, in the final instance, is the reference made therein to what Austin calls the *source* (p. 60)* of the utterance. This notion of *source*—and what is at stake in it is clear—frequently reappears in what follows and governs the entire analysis in the phase we are examining. Not only does Austin not doubt that the source of an oral utterance in the present indicative active is *present* to the utterance [*énonciation*] and its statement [*énoncé*] (I have attempted to explain why we had reasons not to believe so), but he does not even doubt that the equivalent of this tie to the source utterance is simply evident in and assured by a *signature:*

> Where there is *not,* in the verbal formula of the utterance, a reference to the person doing the uttering, and so the acting, by means of the pronoun 'I' (or by his personal name), then in fact he will be 'referred to' in one of two ways:
> (a) In verbal utterances, *by his being the person who does* the uttering—what we may call the utterance-*origin* which is used generally in any system of verbal reference-co-ordinates.

---

*Austin's term is "utterance-*origin*"; Derrida's term (*source*) is hereafter translated as "source."—Trans.

19

(b) In written utterances (or 'inscriptions'), *by his appending his signature* (this has to be done because, of course, written utterances are not tethered to their origin in the way spoken ones are). (pp. 60–61)

An analogous function is attributed by Austin to the formula "hereby" in official documents.

From this point of view, let us attempt to analyze signatures, their relation to the present and to the source. I shall consider it as an implication of the analysis that every predicate established will be equally valid for that oral "signature" constituted—or aspired to—by the presence of the "author" as a "person who utters," as a "source," to the production of the utterance.

By definition, a written signature implies the actual or empirical nonpresence of the signer. But, it will be claimed, the signature also marks and retains his having-been present in a past *now* or present [*maintenant*] which will remain a future *now* or present [*maintenant*], thus in a general *maintenant,* in the transcendental form of presentness [*maintenance*]. That general *maintenance* is in some way inscribed, pinpointed in the always evident and singular present punctuality of the form of the signature. Such is the enigmatic originality of every paraph. In order for the tethering to the source to occur, what must be retained is the absolute singularity of a signature-event and a signature-form: the pure reproducibility of a pure event.

Is there such a thing? Does the absolute singularity of signature as event ever occur? Are there signatures?

Yes, of course, every day. Effects of signature are the most common thing in the world. But the condition of possibility of those effects is simultaneously, once again, the condition of their impossibility, of the impossibility of their rigorous purity. In order to function, that is, to be readable, a signature must have a repeatable, iterable, imitable form; it must be able to be detached from the present and singular intention of its production. It is its sameness which, by corrupting its identity and its singularity, divides its seal [*sceau*]. I have already indicated above the principle of this analysis.

To conclude this very *dry* discussion:

1) as writing, communication, if we retain that word, is not the means of transference of meaning, the exchange of intentions and meanings [*vouloir-dire*], discourse and the "communication of consciousnesses." We are witnessing not an end of writing that would restore, in accord with McLuhan's ideological representation, a transparency or an immediacy to social relations; but rather the increasingly powerful historical expansion of a general writing, of which the system of speech, consciousness, meaning, presence, truth, etc., would be only an effect, and should be analyzed as such. It is the exposure of this effect that I have called elsewhere logocentrism;

2) the semantic horizon that habitually governs the notion of communication is exceeded or split by the intervention of writing, that is, by a *dissemination*

irreducible to *polysemy.* Writing is read; it is not the site, "in the last instance," of a hermeneutic deciphering, the decoding of a meaning or truth;

3) despite the general displacement of the classical, "philosophical," occidental concept of writing, it seems necessary to retain, provisionally and strategically, *the old name.* This entails an entire logic of *paleonymics* that I cannot develop here.[11] Very schematically: an opposition of metaphysical concepts (e.g., speech/writing, presence/absence, etc.) is never the confrontation of two terms, but a hierarchy and the order of a subordination. Deconstruction cannot be restricted or immediately pass to a neutralization: it must, through a double gesture, a double science, a double writing—put into practice a *reversal* of the classical opposition *and* a general *displacement* of the system. It is on that condition alone that deconstruction will provide the means of *intervening* in the field of oppositions it criticizes and that is also a field of nondiscursive forces. Every concept, moreover, belongs to a systematic chain and constitutes in itself a system of predicates. There is no concept that is metaphysical in itself. There is a labor—metaphysical or not—performed on conceptual systems. Deconstruction does not consist in moving from one concept to another, but in reversing and displacing a conceptual order as well as the nonconceptual order with which it is articulated. For example, writing, as a classical concept, entails predicates that have been subordinated, excluded, or held in abeyance by forces and according to necessities to be analyzed. It is those predicates (I have recalled several of them) whose force of generality, generalization, and generativity is liberated, grafted onto a "new" concept of writing that corresponds as well to what has always *resisted* the prior organization of forces, always constituted the *residue* irreducible to the dominant force organizing the hierarchy that we may refer to, in brief, as logocentric. To leave to this new concept the old name of writing is tantamount to maintaining the structure of the *graft,* the transition and indispensable adherence to an effective *intervention* in the constituted historical field. It is to give to everything at stake in the operations of deconstruction the chance and the force, the power of *communication.*

But this will have been understood, as a matter of course, especially in a philosophical colloquium: a disseminating operation *removed* from the presence (of being) according to all its modifications; writing, if there is any, perhaps communicates, but certainly does not exist. Or barely, hereby, in the form of the most improbable signature.

(Remark: the—written—text of this—oral—communication was to be delivered to the *Association des sociétés de philosophie de langue française* before the meeting. That dispatch should thus have been signed. Which I do, and counterfeit, here. Where? There. J.D.)

J. DERRIDA.

21

NOTES

1. The Rousseauist theory of language and of writing is also introduced under the general title of *communication* ("On the diverse means of communicating our thoughts" is the title of the first chapter of the *Essay on the Origin of Languages*).

2. Language supplants action or perception: articulated language supplants the language of action: writing supplants articulated language, etc. [The word, *supplée*, used by Derrida and here by Rousseau, implies the double notion of supplanting, replacing, and also supplementing, bringing to completion, remedying—Trans.]

3. "Up to now, we have considered expressions in their communicative function. This derives essentially from the fact that expressions operate as indexes. But a large role is also assigned to expressions in the life of the soul inasmuch as it is not engaged in a relation of communication. It is clear that this modification of the function does not affect what makes expressions expressions. They have, as before, their *Bedeutungen* and the same *Bedeutungen* as in collocution" (*Logical Investigations I,* ch. I, #8). What I assert here implies the interpretation that I have offered of the Husserlian procedure on this point. I therefore refer the reader to *Speech and Phenomena (La voix et le phénomène)*.

4. "In the first edition I spoke of 'pure grammar,' a name that was conceived on the analogy of 'pure science of nature' in Kant, and expressly designated as such. But to the extent that it cannot be affirmed that the pure morphology of *Bedeutungen* englobes all grammatical a prioris in their universality, since for example relations of communication between psychic subjects, which are so important for grammar, entail their own a prioris, the expression of *pure logical grammar* deserves priority . . ." (*LI* II, part 2, ch. iv).

5. Austin names the "two fetishes which I admit to an inclination to play Old Harry with, viz. (1) the true/false fetish, (2) the value/fact fetish" (p. 150).

6. He says, for example, that "The total speech act in the total speech situation is the *only actual* phenomenon which, in the last resort, we are engaged in elucidating" (p. 147).

7. Which occasionally requires Austin to reintroduce the criterion of truth in his description of performatives. Cf., for example, pp. 50–52 and pp. 89–90.

8. Pp. 10–15.

9. Austin often refers to the suspicious status of the "non-serious" (cf., for example, pp. 104, 121). This is fundamentally linked to what he says elsewhere about *oratio obliqua* (pp. 70–71) and mime.

10. From this standpoint, one might question the fact, recognized by Austin, that "very commonly the *same* sentence is used on different occasions of utterance in *both ways,* performative and constative. The thing seems hopeless from the start, if we are to leave utterances *as they stand* and seek for a criterion." The graphematic root of citationality (iterability) is what creates this embarrassment and makes it impossible, as Austin says, "to lay down even a list of all possible criteria."

11. Cf. *La dissémination* and *Positions.*

Summary of "Reiterating the Differences"

In his "Reply to Derrida," entitled "Reiterating the Differences," John R. Searle concentrates on four interrelated aspects of Derrida's argument in "Signature Event Context": 1. Derrida's assimilation of oral speech to writing; 2. his challenge to the view that identifies the meaning of an utterance with the intentions of its speaker or writer; 3. the implications of the concept of "iterability," Derrida's word for the repeatability of the same expressions in different contexts (which for Derrida always involves transformation); 4. his critique of J. L. Austin's treatment of fictional speech acts as "parasitic" on nonfictional, normal, or "serious" ones.

Much of Searle's "Reply" responds to Derrida's critique of the classical concept of writing "as the communication of intended meaning." Searle challenges Derrida's argument that, as Searle puts it, "since writing can and must be able to function in the radical absence of the sender, the receiver, and the context of production, it cannot be the communication of the sender's meaning to the receiver" (p. 199). Searle argues that it is not, as Derrida claims, the "iterability, the repeatability of the linguistic elements," that distinguishes writing from oral speech, but the relative permanence of writing.

Searle points out that, whether written or spoken, any rule-bound system of representation must be repeatable, for "otherwise the rules would have no scope of application" (p. 199). Furthermore, written discourse is not distinguished from speech by the absence of the receiver from the sender. For "written communication can exist in the presence of the receiver, as for example, when I compose a shopping list for myself or pass notes to my companion during a concert or lecture" (p. 200). Searle concludes that "the phenomenon of the survival of the text is not the same as the phenomenon of repeatability," for the same text "can be read by many different readers long after the death of the author, and it is this phenomenon of the permanence of the text that makes it possible to separate the utterance from its origin, and distinguishes the written from the spoken word" (p. 200).

For Searle this "confusion of permanence with iterability" is central to Derrida's assimilation of speech to writing (p. 200). He argues that "the way in which a written text is weaned from its origin is quite different from the way in which any expression can be severed from its meaning through the form of 'iterability' that is exemplified by quotation" (p. 200). Since the "possibility of separating the sign from the signified" is a feature of all systems of representation as such, "there is nothing especially graphematic" about the separation (p. 201), nor anything peculiar to the classical concept of writing described by Derrida.

Thus Searle disputes what he takes to be Derrida's contention that written discourse involves a "break with the author's intentions in particular or with intentionality in general" (p. 201). Searle argues that, on the contrary, "the fact that writing can continue to function in the absence of the writer, the intended receiver, or the context of production" does not make writing any less the bearer of intentionality, which plays the same role in writing as in spoken communication. Searle concedes that we can "decide to make a radical break . . . with the strategy of understanding the sentence" as an intentional utterance, we can "think of it as a sentence of English, weaned from all production or origin, putative or otherwise. But even then there is no getting away from intentionality, because *a meaningful sentence is just a standing possibility of the corresponding (intentional) speech act*" (p. 202, Searle's italics).

Searle adds that "to the extent that the author says what he means the text is the expression of his intentions" (p. 202), and "the situation as regards intentionality is exactly the same for the written word as it is for the spoken: understanding the utterance consists in recognizing the illocutionary intentions of the author and these intentions may be more or less perfectly realized by the words uttered, whether written or spoken" (p. 202).

Searle then turns to Derrida's interpretation of J. L. Austin's theory of speech acts arguing that Derrida's version of Austin is unrecognizable. First, Derrida completely mistakes "the status of Austin's exclusion of parasitic forms of discourse from his preliminary investigations of speech acts" (p. 204). Searle argues that Austin excluded parasitic forms from consideration as a "research strategy" rather than "a metaphysical exclusion," so Derrida is mistaken to find here a "source of deep metaphysical difficulties" for the theory of speech acts (p. 205). Austin's point, in effect, was simply that "if we want to know what it is to make a promise or make a statement we had better not *start* our investigation with promises made by actors on stage" in a play or statements about characters in a novel, "because in a fairly obvious way such utterances are not standard cases of promises and statements" (p. 204).

Second, Derrida mistakenly assumes that in using the term "parasitic" Austin meant to suggest that there was "something bad or anomalous or not 'ethical' about such discourse" (p. 205), whereas Austin merely meant to indicate "a relation of logical dependence" without implying any moral judgment, "certainly not that the parasite is somehow immorally sponging off the host" (p. 205).

Third, according to Searle, Derrida mistakenly believes that, "by analyzing serious speech acts before considering the parasitic cases, Austin has somehow denied the very possibility that expressions can be quoted" (p. 206). Here Derrida has confused citationality with parasitic discourse (as well as with iterability).

In parasitic discourse, Searle argues, "the expressions are being *used* and not *mentioned*" (p. 206).

Fourth, "Derrida assimilates the sense in which writing can be said to be parasitic on spoken language with the sense in which fiction, etc., are parasitic on nonfiction or standard discourse" (p. 207). But these are different cases. The relation of fiction to nonfiction is one of logical dependency, whereas the dependency of writing on spoken language "is a contingent fact about the history of human languages and not a logical truth about the nature of language" (p. 207).

Fifth, running through Derrida's discussion is "the idea that somehow the iterability of linguistic forms (together with the citationality of linguistic forms and the existence of writing) militates against the idea that intention is the heart of meaning and communication, that indeed, an understanding of iteration will show the 'essential absence of intention to the actuality of the utterance' " (p. 207). On the contrary, "the iterability of linguistic forms facilitates and is a necessary condition of the particular forms of intentionality that are characteristic of speech acts" (p. 208).

Searle maintains that the performances of actual speech acts, written or spoken, are "datable singular events in particular historical contexts" (p. 208). Hearers are able to understand the infinite number of new things that can be communicated by speech acts because "the speaker and hearers are masters of the sets of rules we call the rules of language, and these rules are recursive. They allow for the repeated application of the same rule" (p. 208).

In conclusion, then, Searle argues that iterability—as exemplified both "by the repeated use of the same word type" and "by the recursive character of syntactical rules—is not as Derrida seems to think something in conflict with the intentionality of linguistic acts, spoken or written, it is the necessary presupposition of the forms which that intentionality takes" (p. 208).

G.G.

Limited Inc a b c . . .

d

I COULD HAVE pretended to begin with a "false" beginning, my penchant for falsity [*pour le faux*] no longer requiring special demonstration. I could have simulated what in French is called a *"faux départ"* (I ask that the translator retain the quotation marks, the parentheses, the italics, and the French). And I shall place in the margin (I ask the publishers to follow this recommendation) the following question. I address it to Searle. But where is he? Do I know him? He may never even read this question. If he does, it will be after many others, myself included, and perhaps without understanding it. Perhaps he will understand it only in part and without judging it to be *quite* serious. Others will probably read it after him. How is all that possible? What does it imply? That is precisely what interests me.

When I say that I do not know John R. Searle, that is not "literally" "true." For that would seem to mean that I have never met him "in person," "physically," and yet I am not sure of that, with all these colloquia; moreover, although I have read some of his work (more, in any case, than he seems to have read of mine—my first compliment), what I read in *"Reiterating the Differences: A Reply to Derrida,"* strikes me as being very familiar. It is as if I had known him forever. I will have occasion to return to this strange, uncanny familiarity.

Thus, I place in the margin (but why must I already repeat it? I "mets à gauche"—placing it on the left, but also putting it aside, in reserve) the question that begins with "What is the nature of the debate . . ."

What is the nature of the debate that seems to begin here? Where, here? Here? Is it a debate? Does it take place? Has it begun already? When? Ever since Plato, whispers the prompter promptly from the wings, and the actor repeats, ever since Plato. Is it still going on? Is it finished? Does it pertain to philosophy; to serious philosophy? Does it pertain to literature? The theater? Morals? Politics? Psychoanalysis? Fiction? If it takes

And I repeat (but why must I repeat again?) that I could have pretended to begin with a false start [*faux-départ*] with whatever seemed to me the "first" or "primary" utterance

29

place, what is its place? And these utterances—are they "serious" or not? "Literal" or not? "Fictional" or not? "Citational" or not? "Used" or "mentioned"? "Standard" or not? "Void" or not? All these words are, I assure you and you can verify it yourselves, "citations" of Searle.

used or mentioned—I don't know which—in the *Reply*, as I read it, "originally," in manuscript.

On top, at the left, above the title, I then read the following:

"Copyright © 1977 by John R. Searle"

And handwritten above the ©, the date: 1977. I received the manuscript short-ly before Christmas, 1976. The use of this mention (which I rediscovered in the text published by *Glyph,* this time in its proper place *at the bottom* of the first page) would have lost all value in 1976 (no one abused it then) or in another place, or between quotation marks, as is *here* the case, in the middle of a page that no normal person (except, perhaps, myself) would dream of attributing to the hand of John R. Searle.

I had, first of all, to resist the temptation of contenting myself with a commen-tary (in the American sense) on the thing. I say thing because I don't know how to name it. What kind of a performance is it, if it is one? The whole debate might boil down to the question: does John R. Searle "sign" his reply? Does he make use of his right to reply? Of his rights as author? But what makes him think that these rights might be questioned, that someone might try to steal them from him, or that there could be any mistake concerning the attribution of his original produc-tion? How would this be possible? Can the thing be expropriated, alienated? Would anyone dream of countersigning or counterfeiting his signature? Why would anyone repeat this gesture and what would such repetition signify? Why should or would it remain outside of the text, above the title or below the "nor-mal" boundary of the page? What of all the relations involved in the legal and political context of the "copyright," including the complexity of its system and of its history? Why are copyright utterances making a serious claim at truth? Had I asserted a copyright, "for saying things that are obviously false," there could have been no doubt as to its appropriateness. But that John R. Searle should be so concerned with his copyright, for saying things that are obviously true, gives one pause to reflect upon the truth of the copyright and the copyright of the truth.

Might it not be sufficient to repeat *this*

" "Copyright © 1977 by John R. Searle" "

in order to reconstitute, slowly but ineluctably, all the pieces of this "improba-ble" debate?

What is the infelicity of this—I mean, of Searle's seal? It resides in the fact that if Searle speaks the truth when he claims to be speaking the truth, the obviously true, then the copyright is irrelevant and devoid of interest: everyone will be able, will in advance *have been able,* to reproduce what he says. Searle's seal is stolen in advance. Hence, the anxiety and compulsion to stamp and to seal the truth. On the other hand, however, if Searle had the vague feeling that what he was saying was not obviously true, and that it was not obvious to everyone, then he would attempt passionately, but no less superfluously, to preserve this originality, to the point of provoking the suspicion, by virtue of his repeated and thus divided seal, that his confidence in the truth he claims to possess is a poor front for considerable uneasiness. Divided seal—is, as you can verify, a citation from *Signature Event Context* ("it . . . divides its seal." p. 20), from the section that plays with signatures and proper names.

Would it not be sufficient to repeat *this*

" " "*Copyright © 1977 by John R. Searle*" " "

in order to reconstitute, gradually but inexorably, all the pieces of this most improbable debate?

I have just said *this* in order to avoid the imprudence and haste that would be implied in calling an event such as this seal a speech act. Is it a signature? If it were a speech act, what would be its structure, its illo- or perlocutionary force, etc.? And, of course, how can I be absolutely sure that John R. Searle himself (who is it?) is in fact the author? Perhaps it is a member of his family, his secretary, his lawyer, his financial advisor, the "managing editor" of the journal, a joker or a namesake?

Or even D. Searle (who is it?), to whom John R. Searle acknowledges his indebtedness: "I am indebted to H. Dreyfus and D. Searle for discussion of these matters." This is the first note of the Reply. Its acknowledgment of indebtedness does not simply fit into the series of four footnotes since its appeal is located not in the text but in the title, on the boundary, and is directed, curiously enough, at my name—"*Reply to Derrida[1]*"—

If John R. Searle owes a debt to D. Searle concerning this discussion, then the "true" copyright ought to belong (as is indeed suggested along the frame of this *tableau vivant*) to a Searle who is divided, multiplied, conjugated, shared. What a complicated signature! And one that becomes even more complex when the debt includes my old friend, H. Dreyfus, with whom I myself have worked, discussed, exchanged ideas, so that if it is indeed through him that the Searles have "read" me, "understood" me, and "replied" to me, then I, too, can claim a stake in the "action" or "obligation," the stocks and bonds, of this holding company, the Copyright Trust. And it is true that I have occasionally had the feeling—to which I shall return—of having almost *"dictated"* this reply. "I" therefore feel obliged to claim my share of the copyright of the *Reply*.

But who, me?

e

Who, me?
Among the many elements (and they are too numerous to count) neglected

31

by the "authors" (three + n) of the *Reply to Derrida[1]*, there is at the very least this one: the "signature" of *Signature Event Context*. Or rather, the *signatures,* since it can hardly have escaped the attention of anyone that there are a great number of them and that they are curiously situated on the lower edge (within? without?) of a section entitled, precisely, *Signatures.* A great number, of varying types, which seem to cite themselves (can a signature be cited, and if so, what are the consequences?) and to constitute the *objects* of the study, the themes and examples of an analysis, no less than the seal of the analyst. Who signed *Signature Event Context?* And what if the plural subtitle, "Signatures," were to signal not only the multiplication of the signature, which takes place at the end of the text, but also that, situated *within* the text as its "object," the signature no longer simply signs, even though it does still sign, being neither entirely in the text nor entirely outside, but rather *on the edge?* Who shall decide? And if one takes into account that the end of *Signature Event Context* is also the end of the book, the book entitled *Marges,* I mean to say—the entire context of this question necessarily expands beyond the article *which* our three + n authors have extracted [*prélevé*] and *from which* they have extracted. This context is further expanded and complicated by the fact that the *same* operation is repeated *elsewhere* in *other* books that I have pretended to sign, for instance *L'écriture et la différence,* or *Glas.*

Who signed *Signature Event Context?* And who counterfeited the signature in a *Remark* between parentheses and in the margin (". . . That dispatch should thus have been signed. Which I do, and counterfeit, here. Where? There. J.D.")? Furthermore: can signatory and author be identified? And even if they can (pure hypothesis), is the signature identical with the writing, that is the *mention,* of a proper name at the bottom of a text? Where is the boundary, in this case, between *mention* and *use?* And is the proper name to be identified with the patronym (including first names or initials) registered in the official records? I abandon here these questions which, let it be mentioned in passing, I have attempted to treat elsewhere, in another fashion. To remain with the "signature" of *Signature Event Context,* the *Reply to Derrida[1]* seems to take it for granted, as though it were as clear and as certain as a copyright guaranteed by international *conventions* (up to a certain point, that is, and of relatively recent date). If, on the contrary, I recall and insist on the fact that none of this is either simple or certain, it is because these questions are not extraneous to our debate. Indeed, both common sense and traditional philosophy would say that they comprise the "central" "object" of the "apparent" "debate" between "Searle" and "me."

As the effect of an operation that can be considered *more or less* deliberate, intentional, conscious, fictional, ironic; between *use* and *mention,* undecided between citation and noncitation, *Signature Event Context* seems to conclude—apart from a *Remark* between parentheses, about which it would be difficult to know if it is in the text or outside of it—with "my" signature, handwritten (and hence, one might say, authentic), reauthenticated on several occasions by my initials in the margin (called paraph in the contractual code), and by "my" "proper name," in its official, that is conventional, form.

But: 1. The remark says that "I" (who?) "counterfeit" what I say that "I did," and this implies that I re-do (citing my signature: but can a signature be cited?) and "imitate" with a view towards deceiving (which in French, as in English, is the predominant meaning of "counterfeit" [*contrefaire*]). Naturally, the J.D. that claims to guarantee the identity of the "I" and of the signatory is itself guaranteed by nothing but the *presumed* authenticity of the handwritten signature. The latter, however, is explicitly designated as being "counterfeit" and it is reproduced, typo-photographically, in thousands of copies. Searle *himself* could easily imitate it.

2. The author of *Speech Acts* needs no lessons from me concerning the difference between mentioning one's name and using it in a signature. To write one's proper name is not the same as signing (although the American use of the signature makes it difficult to differentiate graphically between it and the writing of one's name. If I write my name at the bottom of a check, it will not have the value qua mention that it will have on the card that I fill out in an airplane or a hotel).

3. I shall not, here at least, enter into the many supplementary complications arising from the publication of *Signature Event Context* in a book, multiplying the reproduction of my signature, then in translations: can a proper name be translated? Or a signature? And how do the "common," "generic" elements, which always exist even in a proper name, withstand contamination in and by foreign languages? In order to account for all sorts of necessities which I cannot go into here, I have, in other texts, devised countless games, playing with "my name," with the letters and syllables *Ja, Der, Da*. Is my name still "proper," or my signature, when, in proximity to "There. J.D." (pronounced, in French, approximately Der. J.D.), in proximity to "Wo? Da." in German, to "Her. J.D." in Danish, they begin to function as integral or fragmented entities [*corps*], or as whole segments of common nouns or even of things? Thus, without getting into such supplementary cases of parasitism (when and where did they begin?), which repeat and deport an allegedly original "event" that is itself divided and multiple (as with an oral communication preceded by a written text, dealing with the theme of communication, chosen for a colloquium said to be philosophical—a context that the three + n authors entirely ignore), I will settle for posing a question concerning the signature, "properly" handwritten, and which, in *Signature Event Context,* is called "improbable": *improbable,* i.e. having little chance of coming to pass *and* in any case impossible to prove. This word, "improbable," which the reader has already encountered above ("improbable debate") was therefore a clandestine citation. Now, this is my question: what happens, what will happen as far as the three + n authors of the *Reply* are concerned, if I tell them (where? "here") this: I am prepared to swear that this signature is not from *my hand*. I am not speaking here of its multiplication in thousands of printed "copies," nor of the capitalized proper name that supports it, rendering it legible and capable of being authenticated, nor of the infinitely complex relations in which they are

involved, but rather of the "first," handwritten instance of the form " ⌐ *Derri'y.* , "
the reproduction of which can be read "here." Will one contend that in this case,
"my" signature will have been "imitated"? But by whom? For I imitate and
reproduce my "own" signature incessantly. This signature is imitable in its essence. And always has been. In French one would say that *elle s'imite,* a syntactical
equivocation that seems to me difficult to reproduce: it can *be* imitated, and it
imitates *itself.* This is all that I ask my interlocutors to acknowledge. And yet, as we
shall see shortly, the consequences of this very simple fact are *unlimited* and
unlimitable.

I should have to dwell on this question at length to do it justice, but among
the many contextual constraints weighing upon us there is that—economical in
nature—which concerns the spatial limits (despite the generous hospitality of
Glyph, which nonetheless has its own interest in inviting such parasites to its
table) as well as the temporal ones (the time that I can devote to this long, trans-
continental correspondence, and above all that which we can decently demand
from the readers). What I wished to mark with this allegedly false-start was, first
of all, that this *other hand,* perhaps, and none other, dictated the *Reply* to the
three + n authors. I will return to this. Second, that the question of the "copyright," despite or because of its marginal or extra-textual place (but one which is
never simply anywhere, since, were the © absolutely detached, it would lose all
value), should no longer be evaded, in any of its aspects, be they legal, economical, political, ethical, phantasmatic, or libidinal [*pulsionnel*], etc. Third, that the
word "improbable," in the first (French) version of the text, which was published
without the handwritten signature in the Proceedings of the Colloquium (*La
communication,* Montréal, 1973), is the next to the last word of the text. The last
one, which is not my signature, is "signature": "the most improbable signature."
And finally, that confronted by a *Reply* which exudes such confidence in the possibility of distinguishing "standard" from "nonstandard," "serious" from "non-
serious," "normal" from "abnormal," "citation" from "non-citation," "void" from
"non-void," "literal" from "metaphoric," "parasitical," from "non-parasitical,"
etc.,—faced with a *Reply* so serenely dogmatic in regard to the intention and the
origin of an utterance or of a signature, I wanted, before all "serious" argument,
to suggest that the terrain is slippery and shifting, mined and undermined. And
that this ground is, by essence, an underground.

f

Let's be serious.

Faced with this speech act ("let's be serious"), readers may perhaps feel authorized in believing that the presumed signatory of this text is only now beginning to be serious, only now committing himself to a philosophical discussion
worthy of the name, and is thus admitting that what he has previously been engaged in was something entirely different.

But let's be serious. Why am I having such difficulty being serious in this debate, in which I have been invited, in turn, to take part? Why did I take such pleasure in accepting this invitation? Nothing compelled me to accept, and I could have yielded to the temptation of suggesting to interested readers that they simply reread *Signature Event Context* instead of obliging myself to comment or to repeat myself more than once. Where does the pleasure I take in this repetition, in prolonging the debate, or rather the "confrontation" come from? I have just cited the *Reply*. The word "confrontation" appears twice in the first paragraph, once in each sentence, the second stating that—*at (and in the) present |au présent]*—"the confrontation" between Austin and myself "never quite takes place." Is it because the confrontation never quite takes place that I take such lasting pleasure in it? Because I, too, think as much, almost that is, almost but not quite? Or is it, on the contrary, because I am very excited, I confess, by this scene? By the speech acts of the *Reply,* by their structure composed of denial, seduction, coquettishly fascinating underneath the virile candor, initiating a "confrontation" by saying that it has not taken place and, moreover, that *at (and in the) present,* between the late Austin and myself, *it does not take place,* or at least not entirely, *not quite,* both because I have missed the point, missed him, and because he was already dead ("a theory that Austin did not live long enough to develop himself"!) when I missed him, so that in fact I did not have much of a chance. The speech acts of the *Reply* do their utmost, apparently, to insure that this confrontation will not have taken place and, moreover, that it shall not (ever) take place, or at least not quite; and yet they produce it, this confrontation that they sought to avoid, that they declare to be non-existent without being able to stop themselves from participating in it, from confirming and developing the event through the very gesture of withdrawing from it. But, it might be enjoined, it is the confrontation Austin-Derrida that is meant when the *Reply* states that it "never quite takes place." And if there is a confrontation, is it not provoked by the three + n authors of the *Reply,* who present themselves in the guise of Austin's legitimate heirs, bearing their heritage to fruition in the "general theory of speech acts" promised by the Oxford professor of moral philosophy, but which fate left to his American progeny, in the promised land, to fulfill. But would they have provoked this confrontation had it not already, in some manner, taken place? Yet, what does it mean for a "confrontation" of this type to take place (where? when? up to what point?)? And whoever claimed to be looking for a "confrontation" in the first place, in the sense of a face-to-face clash, declared, involving two identifiable interlocutors or adversaries, two "discourses" that would be identical with themselves and localizable?

This "never quite takes place," deported a bit beyond its initial, head-over-heels aggressivity (Derrida never encountered Austin and would not have encountered him even had Austin been still alive!) is one of the gayest things I have ever read in a text that presents itself as being, if not philosophical, at least theoretical, and in any event as serious: seriously supposing itself to know all about the difference between the serious and the non-serious, to know what it means for events taking the form of apparently written speech acts to take place or not to take place (where do writings take place?), writings whose presumed authors have never met each other but which circulate sufficiently to put us in the position we are in today, rereading them (how is this possible?), commenting on them, citing, questioning, translating, interpreting, while one of the participants, who died too young even to know of the debate, is represented, without his knowledge and without ever having given his consent (in a serious and "strict" sense), by a more or less anonymous company or corporation [*par une société plus ou moins anonyme*] (three + n authors) asserting the legitimacy of their lineage and sure of knowing what those "prominent philosophical traditions" are, and where they are.

Why did I say "société plus ou moins anonyme," "a more or less anonymous company or corporation"? The expression "three + n authors" seems to me to be more rigorous for the reasons I have already stated, involving the difficulty I encounter in naming the definite origin, the true person responsible for the *Reply:* not only because of the debts acknowledged by John R. Searle *before even* beginning to reply, but because of the entire, more or less anonymous tradition of a code, a heritage, a reservoir of arguments to which both he and I are indebted. How is this more or less anonymous company to be named? In order to avoid the ponderousness of the scientific expression "three + n authors," I decide here and from this moment on to give the presumed and collective author of the *Reply* the French name "Société à responsabilité limitée"—literally, "Society with Limited Responsibility" (or Limited Liability)—which is normally abbreviated to *Sarl.* I ask that the translator leave this conventional expression in French and if necessary, that he explain things in a note. If this expression does not simply translate "Limited," "Incorporated," or "Limited Inc," it is not unrelated to those terms, for it pertains to the same legal-commercial context. I hope that the bearers of proper names will not be wounded by this technical or scientific device. For it will have the supplementary advantage of enabling me to avoid offending individuals or proper names in the course of an argument that they might now and then consider, wrongly, to be polemical. And should they, perchance, see this transformation as an injurious or ironic alteration, they can at least join me in acknowledging the importance of the desires and fantasms that are at stake in a proper name, a copyright, or a signature. And, after all, isn't this the very question which, posed by *Signature Event Context,* will have involved us in this improbable confrontation? It is as a reminder of this, and not to draw the body of his name into my language by subtracting one *r* and two *e*'s, that I thus break Searle's seal (itself already fragmented or divided).

The gayest thing that Sarl has written, in the "never quite takes place," is "never quite." For this slightly too scrupulous nuance, if I haven't misunderstood it, opens a space for the very thing that should not, should never have taken place; thus, I get my foot in the door. Indeed, it has long since slipped in, and at bottom Sarl may not quite want me to pull it back, at least not too quickly. Or rather, Sarl's wishes in this regard seem rather paradoxical, caught in a kind of double bind, impelled to do everything to keep my foot there, to prolong the scene. To make it last, or at least, take place. What the *Reply* never takes into account is that the most insistent question in *Sec* (I suggest this as an abbreviation for *Signature Event Context*)[1] seeks to discover what an event—which, in the case of a speech act, is supposed to take place—might be, and whether or not the structure of such an event leaves room for certitude or for evidence. But we will have ample occasion to return to this point.

g

For Sarl—or the self-made, auto-authorized heirs of Austin—the confrontation "never quite takes place." How can they tell? Is it because the "central theses in Austin's theory of language" have been misconstrued? Or because *Sec* has "misunderstood and misstated Austin's position at several crucial points"? Let us suppose, for a moment, that this is true, simply true. I would like to pose, then, the following question: if a misunderstanding (for example, of Austin's theses) is possible, if a *mis-* in general ("mistake," "misunderstanding," "misinterpretation," "misstatement," to mention only those included in Sarl's list of accusations, from the first paragraph on) is possible, what does that imply concerning the structure of speech acts in general? And in particular, what does this possibility imply for Austin's, Sarl's or for "my own" speech acts, since, for an instant at least, in a passing phrase, this latter case is apparently not excluded entirely ("it is possible that I may have misinterpreted him as profoundly as I believe he has misinterpreted Austin")? And if the supposed misunderstanding were of such a nature (if not of such a design [*destination*]) so as to leave the auto-authorized heirs of Austin no choice but to involve themselves—passionately, precipitately —in a "confrontation" that they claim "never quite takes place," what would all that imply? What is taking place at this very moment, right here? "Where? There." Let us not exclude the possibility that the "confrontation" that so fascinates Sarl may indeed not have taken place and that it may be destined never to take place: but what, then, of this destiny and of this destination? And what is going on "here and now"? I shall not answer this question, but there can be no doubt that it is the event of this question that interests me and makes me (but why?) so light-hearted and gay.

What I like about this "confrontation" is that I don't know if it is quite taking place, if it ever will be able, or will have been able, quite, to take place; or if it does, between whom or what. Evidently, John R. Searle and "myself" do not sign here, or speak for ourselves. We are nothing more than "prête-noms," "borrowed names," straw men. In this simulated confrontation, we are "fronts": I like this word, which I encountered in the film of Woody Allen[2] dealing with events dating from the era of McCarthyism, and where I learned that it signified "prête-nom," mask, substitute for a clandestine subject. But these "fronts" do not, as Sarl suggests, represent "two prominent philosophical traditions." Because, if there is only one sentence of the *Reply* to which I can subscribe, it is the first ("It would be a mistake, I think, to regard Derrida's discussion of Austin as a confrontation between two prominent philosophical traditions"), although for reasons other than those of Sarl. I know of no one, aside from Sarl, who could have formed such an hypothesis. Nor do I know why it was formed. For I, too, consider it quite false, though for different reasons. Among the many reasons that make me unqualified to represent a "prominent philosophical tradition," there is this one: I consider myself to be in many respects quite close to Austin, both interested in and indebted to his problematic. This is said in *Sec*, very clearly; Sarl forgets to mention it. Above all, however, when I do raise questions or objections, it is always at points where I recognize in Austin's theory presuppositions which are the most tenacious and the most central presuppositions of the *continental* metaphysical tradition. I will return to this in an instant. Moreover, what these "fronts" represent, what weighs upon them both, transcending this curious chiasmus, are forces of a non-philosophical nature. They will have to be analyzed one day. Here, within the limits of this discussion, such an analysis is impossible, but the forces that exceed those limits are already implicated, even here.

I like this improbable confrontation just as others like voyages and diplomacy. There are interpreters everywhere. Each speaking his language, even if he has some knowledge of the language of the other. The interpreter's ruses have an open field and he does not forget his own interests. Most of the authors of the *Reply*, if they have read *Sec* in their fashion, do not know me either personally or, obviously, through any of the other texts that form the context of *Sec* and endow it with a certain meaning. To a certain degree, the inverse is also true. *Sec* has apparently been read, and is generally cited in English (we shall mention certain consequences of this) within a *Reply* written in English. I have read it in English but I am trying to respond in French, although my French will be marked in advance by English and destined in advance for a translation that will doubtless present certain difficulties. These problems (re-production, iterability, citation, translation, interpretation, multiplicity of codes and of parasitisms) constitute the most apparent aspect of what is at stake in this so-called "confrontation." And it will have taken place (yes or no?) on a terrain whose neutrality is far from certain, in a publication and at the initiative of professors who for the most part are Americans (more or less), but who, in their work and in their projects are second to none in their knowledge of migrations and wanderings [*déplacements*]. Their position, in terms of the political significance of the university, is highly original and their role in this debate, whether it takes place or not, decisive. This, for me, comprises the most interesting and most important aspect of the situation. Since I will not be able, here, even to outline an analysis of all this, let me say the following: that which is not quite taking place, seems to be occurring—to take geographical bearings in an area that disrupts all cartography—mid-way between California and Europe, a bit like the Channel, mid-way between Oxford and Paris. But the topology of these "fronts" and the logic of its places will have more than one surprise in store for us. For example: isn't Sarl ultimately more continental and Parisian than I am? I shall try to show why. Sarl's premises and method are derived from continental philosophy, and in one form or another they are very present in France. If I may cite myself, for the last time referring to a text other than *Sec* (hereafter I will restrict myself to the latter essay), this is what I wrote in "Avoir l'oreille de la philosophie" [To Have the Ear of Philosophy] (see footnote 1): *"Signature Event Context* analyzes the metaphysical premises of the Anglo-Saxon—and fundamentally moralistic—theory of the performative, of speech acts or discursive events. In France, it seems to me that these premises underlie the hermeneutics of Ricoeur and the archaeology of Foucault."

h

Let's be serious. I am going to try to engage myself in this confrontation without excessively prolonging the pleasure of the threshold [*limen*]. But for the sake of the record, I would still like to hazard two hypotheses. Two *types* of hypothesis. For reasons of economy, I will limit myself to underscoring the type. The interested reader can, if he wishes, multiply hypotheses of the same type.

The first type I shall baptize *set*. In French, *ensemble*, as in *théorie des ensembles*, set theory. And I say this: if this "particular debate" should develop further, the set of texts that will have been part of it (for example, *Sec*, Sarl's *Reply, Limited Inc*—but the list is not limitable either in the past or in the future) will have been not so much theoretical discourses ("constative" or "descriptive") dealing with the question of speech acts, of the performative, of illocutionary or perlocutionary acts, of iterability, of citation, of writing, speech or signature, etc.; nor will they have been discourses dominating the *ensemble* of this field and stating the truth about it. Rather, they will have constituted elements of that *ensemble*, parts of an open corpus, *examples* of events, to which all the questions and categories accredited by the theory of speech acts will still be applicable and reapplicable: whether or not they are performatives, in what measure and aspect they depend upon the per- or illocutionary, whether they are serious or not, normal or not, void or not, parasitic or not, fictional or not, citational or not, literary, philosophical, theatrical, oratorical, prophetical or not, etc. But my hypothesis does not concern all the pleasure (or pain) that one can wish to anyone who wants to attempt such analyses. Rather it concerns the essentially *interminable* character of such an analysis. For the latter will still form a part of the ensemble and will therefore raise the same questions. It will necessarily be what I will here call—parodying a French expression and challenging the translator-interpreter not to abandon at once [*aussi sec*] a copyright—a *prise de partie*, that is: *partial*. It will always be lacking the completeness of a set.

i

The second type I shall call *mis*, mistype if you like. The *Reply* teems with evaluative decrees involving *mis*. They are situated beyond, around, beneath utterances that are apparently constative, but which through their gesture of "this is so and so" tend to produce determinate effects, often quite different from those apparently intended. I shall take only one example, the first paragraph of the *Reply*. In the citation I am about to make, I shall underline all the decrees in *mis* (or related meanings). They deliver the conclusions before the demonstration has taken place, putting the reader in the proper state of mind, setting the tone or the stage, and generally aiming to produce certain effects. I shall therefore underline certain words or word-fragments (what happens when, in a citation, certain word-fragments are underlined? Does it still constitute a case of "citing," of "using," or "mentioning"?): "It would be a *mis*take, I think, to regard Derrida's discussion of Austin as a confrontation between two prominent philosophical traditions. This is not so much because Derrida has *failed* to discuss the central theses in Austin's theory of language, but rather because he has *mis*understood and *mis*stated Austin's position at several *crucial* points, as I shall attempt to show, and thus the confrontation *never* quite takes place."

I have cited at length and shall continue to, so the reader is now forewarned. I shall do so, first of all, because it gives me pleasure that I would not like to miss, even though it may be deemed perverse: a certain practice of citation, and also of iteration (which, despite what Sarl asserts, was never confused with citation, as we shall verify) is at work, constantly *altering*, at once and without delay—*aussi sec*, including *Sec*—whatever it seems to reproduce. This is one of the theses of *Sec*. Iteration alters, something new takes place. For example, here the *mis* takes place; and to account for the possibility of such *mis*ses in general is, to put it still in Sarl's code, the *crux*, the *crucial* difficulty of the theory of speech acts. Furthermore, I shall cite at length in order to limit the confusion, the denials or the selective simplifications which it seems to me the *Reply* has introduced into the debate. This may help to increase the rigor of the discussion. Finally, the citational and (more generally) iterative corpus that constitutes the object of discussion will thereby be augmented and enriched.

The overture in *mis* will have set the tone. This is then incessantly replayed throughout the *Reply*, with an insistence and a compulsive force that can hardly be simply external to the contents of the argumentation. It is as though it were imperative to recall all the *mis*takes, *mis*understandings, *mis*statements, etc. all the more loudly, nervously, regularly, to denounce and to *name* them all the more frequently, because at bottom they are not quite as evident as all that: there is always the danger of their being forgotten. It is to remind us of this less-than-evident evidence that the word *obvious, obviously* (as in "obviously false," p. 203) is so often invoked, as though to nip any doubt in the bud. But the effect produced is the reverse. For my part, wherever and whenever I hear the words "it's true," "it's false," "it's evident," "evidently this or that," or "in a fairly obvious way" (p. 204), I become suspicious. This is especially so when an adverb, apparently redundant, is used to reinforce the declaration. Like a warning light, it signals an uneasiness that demands to be followed up. Even without taking into account the fact that, given the great serenity which marks his understanding of the value of evidence, Sarl should have been able to remark that the notion of evidence, together with its entire system of associated values (presence, truth, immediate intuition, assured certitude, etc.), is precisely what *Sec* is calling into question, and that this is exemplified in the element of writing, in the narrow, if not "strict" sense of the word.

For those who may have forgotten, here are some of the reverberations, echoing interminably, of the peremptory evaluations of the first paragraph: ". . . *what is wrong* with these arguments . . ." (p. 199); "Derrida has a *distressing* penchant for saying things that are *obviously false*" (p. 203); . . . "he has *mis*understood Austin in several *crucial* ways [crucial *ways* this time, after "crucial *points*"] and the internal weaknesses in his arguments are closely tied to these *mis*understandings. In this section therefore I will *very briefly summarize* his critique and then simply list the *major mis*understandings and *mis*takes" (p. 203); . . . "Derrida's Austin is *un*recognizable. He bears *almost* [!] no relation to the original" (p. 204);. "Related to the first *mis*understanding . . . is a *mis*understanding . . ." (p. 205); ". . . what is *more than simply a mis*reading . . ." (p. 206).

I would have liked to quiet my suspicions in order to enjoy such candor unreservedly. Loyalty and the absence of simulation are so rare in French-language polemics, which are characterized by the use of elision, ellipsis, self-censorship and a strategy that is both artful and indirect. Why did I not succeed? This is just what I shall endeavor to explain.

Among all the adverbial locutions that I have just underlined, whose curious functions may be analyzed at one's leisure, one in particular deserves to become proverbial and I shall indulge myself by citing it once again: ". . . *more than simply a mis*reading . . ."! More than simply a mis-; what might that involve? Where will it lead us? Let us be patient a little while longer.

j

And among all the effects produced, if not intended, I shall for the moment retain only this one, abbreviated for the sake of time, to the hypothesis in [the key of] *mis* (and in more than simply a mis-). This is only one of the effects produced on me.

Listening, with a certain ear, to this percussion in *mis-major*, I have the impression that, despite all appearances to the contrary which I will deal with later on, Sarl has, in fact, very well understood the *Sec*-effect. How else can his passionate and exacerbated struggle to combat arguments that are "obviously false," "major misunderstandings," etc. be explained? How was he capable of replying so seriously to such unserious aberrations? Or even of recognizing an Austin so unrecognizable as to bear *almost* no relation to the original, i.e. an Austin who is never *quite* himself. And how, in view of all this, was he able to find his bearings and himself [*s'y reconnaître*]?

Thus, Sarl did indeed understand. No question here of the essentials being misunderstood. Or rather, if "understanding" is still a notion dominated by the allegedly constative regime of theory or of philosophy, let us not use the word "understood," let us say instead that Sarl was touched. That is, Sarl has not been missed by the set, the ensemble of these misunderstandings, of these misstating missiles. In the family of Latin languages, a speech act, whether written or spoken, is only said to be *pertinent* when it touches: the object to which it seems to refer, but also—why not?—someone, its addressee, upon whom it produces certain effects, let us say of a perlocutionary sort. Thus, in analyzing the violence and the type of evaluative reactions, I had the impression that *Sec* had touched the mark, right in the middle, as it were. If I said that Searle himself had been touched, I would be going out on a limb. For it may very well be not Searle himself, as a whole, or even in part, but in the final analysis a "front," something making its way beneath Searle's more or less indebted or mortgaged signature; something identifying itself so much with Austin that it can only read *Sec* feverishly, unable to support the fact that questions might be posed serenely concerning the limits or the presuppositions of Austin's theory. Or at least unable to tolerate this when it is done by *others*. It is this last feature that I find most interesting: what characterizes a self-proclaimed heir (especially when the father has died too young, at the age of 48!) is the fact that, doubting his own legitimacy, he wishes to be the only one to inherit and even the only one, in a *tête à tête*, to break, now and then, the filial bond of identification, in what is here the height of identification; he alone shall have the right of criticizing or correcting his teacher, defending him before the others at the very moment of murderous identification, of parricide. All this is familiar in philosophy and, mutatis mutandis, has been ever since the *Sophist*; also, ever since the Sophists, and no one will be astonished when I observe that they haunt our present debate, as more than one sign shall indicate. Thus, Sarl would like to be Austin's sole legitimate heir *and* his sole critic: "I should point out that I hold no brief for the details of Austin's theory of speech acts, I have criticized it elsewhere and will not repeat those criticisms here" (p. 204). And forgetting what is demonstrated in *Sec*, namely, that the question of detail is not always a question of detail, Sarl refers several times to articles of J. R. Searle, which, dating from 1975, could not have been taken into account by *Sec* (1971). And yet, knowing me as I do, I would not have escaped a certain sense of guilt here, especially had I been able to anticipate clearly that this trajectory would end by touching Sarl and by impeding the procedure of inheritance and of legitimation. This is why shortly, indeed as soon as possible, I shall incorporate these most recent publications of J. R. Searle into the dossier of this discussion.

How, therefore, will it be possible, from now on, to know just exactly *which* Searle *Sec* has failed to miss? I therefore prefer, out of prudence but also out of courtesy, to endeavor to respond—not reply—to Sarl. Who knows whether J. R. Searle is more dogmatic than Austin in handling with such assurance the obviousness of the true and the false or the wrong? Sarl, however, *is*. *Sec* begins by insisting on those aspects of Austin's analysis that it describes as "patient," "open," in "constant transformation"; and also, by insisting, among other claims to our interest, upon the fact that "Austin was obliged to free the analysis of the performative from the authority of the truth *value*, from the true/false opposition,[4] at least in its classical form, and to substitute for it at times the value of force, of difference of force (*illocutionary* or *perlocutionary force*). (In this line of thought, which is nothing less than Nietzschean, this in particular strikes me as moving in the direction of Nietzsche himself, who often acknowledged a certain affinity for a vein of English thought.)" "5. '. . . two fetishes which I admit to an inclination to play Old Harry with, viz. (1) the true/false fetish, (2) the value/fact fetish.' "

Things are, of course, more complicated. *Sec* takes this supplementary complication into account, in differentiating remarks that seem to have escaped Sarl's attention; one such is the observation, on the next page, which might have served as the sign of a prudent and discriminating reading: "As a result, performative communication becomes once more the communication of an intentional meaning."[7] . . . "7. Which occasionally requires Austin to reintroduce the criterion of truth in his description of performatives. Cf. for example, pp. 50-52 and pp. 89-90."

k

Instead of precipitously, in the name of truth, hurrying on to sentences (in the French—but also English—sense of the word: to the verdicts, the decrees of justice, even to the condemnations) on the wrong or false, or the "obviously false," a theoretician of speech acts who was even moderately consistent with his theory ought to have spent some time patiently considering questions of this type: Does the principal purpose of *Sec* consist in being *true*? In appearing true? In stating the truth?

And what if *Sec* were *doing something else*?

What? All right, some examples: 1. Saying something apparently "false" (the economical and limited hypothesis of Sarl, designed to incorporate the thing), or something dubious, but presenting it in a manner, form, and shape which (full of traps and parasitical in nature) would increase the chances of the debate getting started; and rendering it inevitable that the auto-authorized descendants of "prominent" philosophical traditions could not but reply, would be obliged to reply (a case anticipated by Austin), even if they did not; or, growing angry, would say whatever came to mind, or else very determinate things which would then set the stage for the confrontation they would have always hoped "never quite takes place." Or else, 2. Proposing a text, as is again here the case, a writing and signatures, whose *performance* (structure, event, context, etc.) defines at every moment the oppositions of concepts or of values, the rigor of those oppositional limits that speech act theory endorses by virtue of its very axiomatics; offering the performance of a text which, by raising in passing the question of truth (beyond Austin's intermittent impulses in this direction) does not *simply* succumb to its jurisdiction and remains, at this point, qua textual performance, irreducible to "verdictive" (as Austin might say) sentences of the type: this is true, this is false, "completely mistaken" or "obviously false." "More than simply a misreading," an expression of which I am particularly fond, would be a better description of the operation of *Sec*, on the condition, however—but isn't this always possible? and this is precisely my question—that it is made into a misreading of sorts, or into "more than simply a misreading" with regard to what can be presumed to be the true intention of Sarl. Can one deny what I have just said in 2? How is it possible to miss the point that *Sec*, from one end to the other, is concerned with the question of truth, with the system of values associated with it, repeating *and* altering that system, dividing and displacing it in accordance with the logical force of the *iter*, which "ties repetition to alterity" (*Sec*, p. 7).

One could continue in this vein for quite some time. Here, however, I shall interrupt, decisively, these two series of preliminary [*protocolaires*] hypotheses, *set* and *mis*. For if *Sec* caused a more or less anonymous company of readers, of whom I was not then thinking, to lose their patience, I would not want to become a cause of impatience to those readers of whom I am thinking today, nor to the translator, who is a friend. I shall endeavor, therefore, to address myself now to what is at stake in this debate, and to do this in a manner as normal and serious, as strict, brief, and direct as possible, while reducing the parasitism as much as I can. You can take my word for it.

However, precisely in order to clarify the discussion, I shall have to adopt certain technical procedures and propose several conventions. Naturally, the reader or interlocutor, whom I have neither the means nor the desire to consult on this matter, can always decide not to subscribe and even to interrupt his reading at this point. But in proposing conventions that I deem to be *reasonable*, haven't I already consulted and involved him a bit, inasmuch as I impute a certain degree of reason to him, and even a certain amount of good faith? All this remains forever in doubt.

My first technical convention: concerned to spare Sarl and possible readers the trouble of having to read or reread other texts of mine, I shall make reference only to *Sec*, the sole essay which, according to the implications of the convention, has been read and discussed by Sarl, and the sole, as we now know, to carry, among other signatures, "my own," and that more than once, in an authentic *facsimile*. But naturally, armed with this same convention (Sarl is understood to have read this text), I shall take the liberty of referring to the quasi-totality of this essay, *Sec*, and not, as Sarl has done, only to those passages that are deemed to be "the most important" ("I will concentrate on those [points] that seem to me to [be] the most important and especially on those where I disagree with his conclusion"). As we shall see, these "important" points are hardly separable from a good many others, with which they form a systematic chain of a singular type. On the other hand, as one will have already noticed, I do not "concentrate," in my reading (for instance, of the *Reply*), either exclusively or primarily on those points that appear to be the most "important," "central," "crucial." Rather, I de-concentrate, and it is the secondary, eccentric, lateral, marginal, parasitic, border-line cases which are "important" to me and are a source of many things, such as pleasure, but also insight into the general functioning of a textual system. And were there to be a center to this debate, we would have reached it already, in the form of this difference in styles of reading. But what is involved is more than a difference in style.

Another technical convention: since the readers cannot be expected to remember the two texts verbatim, and yet no resumé will be adequate, I shall quote at length, as I already said, from *Sec* and from the *Reply*, in order, as far as possible, to avoid confusion, distortion, displacement, or biased selection.

But I will have to limit my arguments in number to eighteen. One of the conventions of this debate (and, says *Sec*, not the least determining, in the final analysis) is that it should take place, if it takes place, in a graphic element of a type that is phonetic, and more precisely, alphabetical. This is not without a certain arbitrariness. Its effect: henceforth I will have at my disposal only 18 letters or 18 blows and I will have to make the best of them. But, one will protest, is not this limit utterly contingent, artificial and external? Are we now going to integrate such fringes into the text, and take account of such frames? Are all these parasites to be incorporated into the *economy* of discourse? Must the surface of the paper, the contents of the time at our disposal, etc. all be integrated into our calculations? If so, what about the ink[3] remaining in my typewriter ribbon? And yet: why not? That is the question.

Finally, I give my word of honor that I shall be of good faith in my argument. I promise this in all sincerity and in all seriousness, literally, raising my hand above the typewriter.

I begin.

1

How is it possible to accept the procedure adopted by Sarl, from the paragraph beginning, "His paper [that is, *Sec*] divides naturally into two parts" (!?). With this (!?) I resort to a device that Austin wrongly (?) calls "very jejune"; but, after all, I am writing and I am more or less sure that these mute signs, these "rather crude" artifices, will be understood.[4] And if Sarl's statement is difficult to accept, is it not because in each of its words it is "obviously false"? Even at the level of academic, external signs, *Sec* consists of *three* sections, not two, plus a preamble, an epilogue, a title, and signatures that are difficult to place; and none of all that is either superfluous or entirely fortuitous. Within each section—and each element—the "division," to say the least, can hardly be considered very "natural," and this holds no less for "his paper." Yet if I cannot endorse the statement, it is above all because the comfortable resumé that follows supports the convenient distinction between the "most important" and the rest. Even if we assume *Sec* to be a theoretical text claiming to speak the truth in a serious and systematic form, it would not constitute a juxtaposition of "points," of which some could be singled out at the expense of others. This is not merely a formal or procedural remark concerning the systemic or contextual implications of *Sec*. I shall try, shortly, to show that by ignoring this or that moment of the text he claims to be discussing, Sarl creates for himself a version of *Sec* which is easily domesticated since it is, after all, nothing but Sarl's own autistic representation. Would the reader care to have an initial, general, and massive idea of this? In this case, he can verify without difficulty that among the "points" totally omitted by Sarl are included all those involving

   1. Signature
   2. Event
   3. Context

 I don't know if this was because they were judged to be devoid of importance or whether it was because they were not the object of any disagreement ("I . . . will concentrate on those that seem to me to [be] the most important and especially on those where I disagree with his conclusion."), but in both cases, this monumental omission can hardly be without its consequences. No? Since Sarl does not devote a single word to signature, event, context, I ask the reader interested in this debate to consult *Signature Event Context*, which I do not want to cite or to mention in its entirety, so that he can judge for himself the effects of such serious negligence.

m

 Having proposed a conveniently domesticated résumé of the opening pages of *Sec*, Sarl prepares, under the title *Writing, Permanence, and Iterability*, "to get at what is wrong with these arguments." Imputing to *Sec* the intention of distinguishing between writing and speech, or even of opposing the two, he poses the question: "what is it exactly that distinguishes written from spoken language?" (p. 199). And, by evoking two hypotheses ("Is it iterability . . .?" "Is it absence . . .?") Sarl turns their respective rejection into an objection to *Sec*, or rather, to a certain reading of it. To appreciate fully the strangeness of this operation, it will suffice to reread it. For the moment, it is not yet necessary to reread *Sec* in its entirety. The easily digestible "Reader's Digest" which precedes it will do. This "digest" *itself* recalls that *Sec* generalized certain predicates usually attributed to writing in order to show that they are *also* valid for spoken language, and even beyond it. It is strange that, after having recalled that *Sec* analyzed the characteristics *common* both to writing and speech, the *objection* is made that, from the standpoint of iterability, there is no difference: precisely the thesis of *Sec*, if there is one! And it is no less strange when Sarl asks what it is that distinguishes written from oral language, as though such a distinction were required by *Sec*, and then answers: "Is it iterability, the repeatability of the linguistic elements? Clearly not. As Derrida is aware, any linguistic element written or spoken, indeed any rule-governed element in any system of representation at all must be repeatable . . ." (ibid.). Indeed, it is so "clear" and I am so "aware" of it, that this proposition is one of the indispensable levers in the demonstration of *Sec*. This lever is explicitly posed as such from the very beginning. The demonstration of *Sec* moves in an area where the distinction between writing and speech loses all pertinence and where "every mark, including those which are oral," can be seen as being "a grapheme in general" (*Sec*, p. 10). How Sarl, citing this phrase on the very next page, can turn it into an objection to *Sec*, is a *mis*tery. If the simple argumentation of *Sec* is made into an *objection* to *Sec*, isn't it because, as I said earlier, that *other* hand, the one that signed *Sec*, also dictated the *Reply* behind its back? But we are not yet done with this curious programmation of what, in French, I would call the *objection à-Sec*, and which, in English, might be rendered as *Sec dry up!* or also as the *Dried-out-objection*. However, for reasons of economy and of formalization, I shall refer to this simply as *from/to-Sec*, thus designating a gesture which recurs regularly in the *reply* and consists in taking arguments borrowed *from Sec* [*à Sec*], as though there were nowhere else to turn, and changing them into objections *to Sec* [*à Sec*]. With the other hand. Whence my perplexity at finding myself in this discussion often obliged to argue with a discourse moving *from/to Sec*, seeking to repeat against *Sec* what it has taken from *Sec*, or, in terms of the venerable fantasm of the *copyright*, what "belongs" *to* or stems *from Sec*. Would I have been spared this mistake or this mishap had I stamped each argument in advance with a ©? Concerning iterability, for instance: in reiterating what can be read on each page of *Sec*, re-plying or reapplying it, it is difficult to see how the *Reply* can object to it. Which does not, however, amount to saying that the consequences drawn from this iterability are, to be sure, the same here and there. In brief, since this scene seems destined to reproduce itself incessantly, you shall henceforth understand what I mean to say when I write: "discourse from/to-*Sec*" or "it reapplies" [*ça rapplique*]. The translator has my sympathy, but the difficulty of translation constitutes part of the demonstrandum.

n

And now, absence ("Is it iterability? Is it absence . . .?").

"It reapplies" again, to and towards the "discourse from/to-*Sec*" although this time things are a bit more complicated. In order to treat this second point, Sarl begins *again* with the question disqualified by *Sec,* determining what distinguishes "written from spoken language." "Is it absence," asks the *Reply,* "the absence of the receiver from the sender? Again, clearly not. Writing makes it *possible* to communicate with an absent receiver, *but* it is not *necessary* for the receiver to be absent. Written communication can exist *in the presence* of the receiver, as for example, when I compose a shopping list for myself or pass notes to my companion during a concert or lecture" (ibid.). I have underlined the words "possible," "but," "necessary," "in the presence." The response is easy and clear. *Sec never said* that this absence is *necessary,* but only that it is *possible* (Sarl agrees) and that this possibility must therefore be taken into account: it pertains, *qua possibility,* to the structure of the mark as such, i.e., to the structure precisely of its iterability. And hence must not be excluded from the analysis of this structure. We need only reread *Sec.* We will find the words "possible," "possibility" innumerable times, but not even once the word "necessary." Even Sarl recalls this in the short initial resumé which, as convenient as it is, still cannot help contradicting itself by confusing possibility and necessity. Sarl writes that "the argument [that of *Sec*] is that since writing *can and must be able* to function in the radical absence of the sender, the receiver and the context of production. . . ." Again I have underlined. *Must be able:* to function in the absence of. . . . But this does not mean that it does, *in fact,* necessarily function in the absence of. . . . "Does one really have to point this out?" If I insist here, it is because this is indispensable to the demonstration and even to the minimal intelligibility of *Sec.* I repeat, therefore, since it can never be repeated too often: if one admits that writing (and the mark in general) *must be able* to function in the absence of the sender, the receiver, the context of production, etc., that implies that this power, this *being able,* this *possibility* is *always* inscribed, hence *necessarily* inscribed *as possibility* in the functioning or the functional structure of the mark. Once the mark *is able* to function, once it is possible for it to function, once it is possible for it to function in case of an absence, etc., it follows that this possibility is a *necessary* part of its structure, that the latter must *necessarily be such that* this functioning is possible; and hence, that this must be taken into account in any attempt to analyze or to describe, in terms of necessary laws, such a structure. Even if it is sometimes the case that the mark, in fact, functions *in-the-presence-of*, this does not change the structural law in the slightest, one which above all implies that iterability admitted by Sarl. Such iterability is inseparable from the structural possibility in which it is necessarily inscribed. To object by citing cases where absence *appears in fact* not to be observable is like objecting that a mark is not essentially *iterable* because *here and there* it has not *in fact* been repeated.

But let's go a bit further. Does this kind of *fact* really exist? Where can we find it? How can we recognize it? Here we reach another type of analysis and of necessity. Isn't the (apparent) *fact* of the sender's or receiver's presence complicated, divided, contaminated, parasited by the *possibility of an absence* inasmuch as this possibility is necessarily inscribed in the functioning of the mark? This is the "logic," or rather, the "graphics" to which *Sec* seeks to do justice: As soon as [*aussi sec*] a possibility is essential and necessary, *qua possibility* (and even if it is the possibility of what is named, *negatively,* absence, "infelicity," parasitism, the non-"standard," fictional, citational, ironical, etc.), it can no longer, either de facto or de jure, be bracketed, excluded, shunted aside, even temporarily, on allegedly methodological grounds. Inasmuch as it is essential and structural, this possibility is always at work marking *all the facts,* all the events, even those which appear to disguise it. Just as itera*bility,* which is not iteration, can be recognized even in a mark which *in fact* seems to have occurred only once. I say *seems,* because this one time is in itself divided or multiplied in advance by its structure of repeatability. This obtains *in fact,* at once [*aussi sec*], from its inception on; and it is here that the graphics of iterability undercuts the classical opposition of fact and principle [*le droit*], the factual and the possible (or the virtual), necessity and possibility. In undercutting these classical oppositions, however, it introduces a more powerful "logic." Yet in order to accede to this transformation, one must follow the trajectory that I have just reconstituted and not simply confuse, as Sarl does, the necessary with the possible, or construct an entire line of argument upon two "facts" that *appear* to be exceptions. For if they seem to be exceptional and artificial constructs, the two phenomena introduced by Sarl do not contradict, even as exceptions, the rigorous universality of the law. The "shopping list for myself" would be neither producible nor utilizable, it would not be what it is nor could it even exist, were it not possible for it to function, from the very beginning, in the absence of sender and of receiver: that is, of *determinate, actually present* senders and receivers. And *in fact* the list cannot function unless these conditions are met. *At the very moment* "I" make a shopping list, I know (I use 'knowing' here as a convenient term to designate the relations that I necessarily entertain with the object being constructed) that it will only be a list if it implies my absence, if it already detaches itself from me in order to function beyond my "present" act and if it is utilizable at another time, in the absence of my-being-present-now, even if this absence is the simple "absence of memory" that the list is meant to make up for, shortly, in a moment, but one which is already the following moment, the absence of the now of writing, of the writer maintaining [*du maintenant-écrivant*], grasping with one hand his ballpoint pen. Yet no matter how fine this point may be, it is like the *stigmè* of every mark, already split.[5] The sender of the shopping list is not the same as the receiver, even if they bear the same name and are endowed with the identity of a single ego. Indeed, were this self-identity or self-presence as certain as all that, the very idea of a shopping list would be rather superfluous or at least the product of a curious compulsion. Why would I bother about a shopping list if the presence of sender to receiver were so certain? And why, above all, this example of the reminder, of the memorandum [*pense-bête*]? Why not some other example? It would have been no less pertinent, or no more: even in the extreme case of my writing something in order to be able to read (reread) it *in a moment,* this moment is constituted—i.e. divided—by the very iterability of what produces itself *momentarily.* The sender and the receiver, even if they were the self-same *subject,* each relate to a mark they experience as made to do without them, from the instant of its production or of its reception on; and they experience this not as the mark's negative limit but rather as the positive condition of its possibility. Barring this, the mark would not function and there would be no shopping list, for the list would be impossible. Either I wouldn't need one or it would be unusable as such. This necessitates, obviously, a rigorous and renewed analysis of the value of presence, of presence to self or to others, of difference and of *différance* [differing and deferring—Tr.][6] To affirm, as does Sarl, that the receiver is *present* at the moment when *I write* a shopping list *for myself,* and, moreover, to turn this into an argument against the essential possibility of the receiver's absence from every mark, is to settle for the shortest, most facile analysis. If both sender and receiver were entirely present when the mark was inscribed, and if they were thereby present to themselves—since, by hypothesis here, being present and being present-to-oneself are considered to be equivalent—how could they even be distinguished from one another? How could the message of the shopping list circulate among them? And the same holds force, a fortiori, for the other example, in which sender and receiver are hypothetically considered to be neighbors, it is true, but still as two separate persons occupying different places, or seats. I thus pass from the example of shopping lists to that of my companion in a concert or a lecture. The sender and the receiver certainly seem to be present here, present to each other, present to themselves and to whatever they write or read. But these notes are only legible or writable to the extent that my neighbor can do without my being present in order to read whatever I could write without his being present, and hence, also to the extent that these two possible absences construct the possibility of the message itself, at the very instant of my writing it or of his reading it. Thus, these possible absences, which the note is precisely designed to make up for and which it therefore implies, leave their mark in the mark. They *remark* the mark in advance. *Curiously,* this *re*-mark constitutes *part* of the mark itself. And this remark is inseparable from the structure of iterability: it is and should be capable of being reiterated as though it were the first time, in the absence of the first time, or the second in the absence of the second, in the supplement, mark, or trace of presence-absence. And this holds *for all cases,* whether I am "alone" or in company, whether I pass my time sending myself shopping lists during concerts and lectures, or even if I wink at someone while listening to my favorite music or my favorite ad in a supermarket.

O

Let us pursue our reading of the *Reply*. Thus, Sarl continues to act as though *Sec* sought to oppose "written and spoken language." This point is brought forward with such insistence that I am forced to ask myself whether Sarl did not really believe, in all good faith, that *Sec* sought to oppose "written and spoken language," even though the most cursory reading should have sufficed to demonstrate the contrary.

Attempting, therefore, to show that such an opposition would be erroneous, Sarl is not satisfied with imputing the intention of opposing "written and spoken language" gratuitously to *Sec* (gratuitously, but not disinterestedly). In addition, the following argument is also attributed to *Sec,* no less mistakenly: what supposedly distinguishes writing from speech is the "permanence" of the "text." Then, *Sec* is accused of confounding iterability and permanence. But were the two ever confused? Before responding to this question, I prefer to cite the *Reply:*

> . . . for the purposes of this discussion the most important [*the most important* definitely belongs to Sarl's idiom: there is a constant fear of missing the most important] distinguishing feature is the (relative) permanence of the written text over the spoken word . . . Now the first confusion that Derrida makes, and it is important [again!] for the argument that follows, is that he confuses iterability with the permanence of the text. He thinks the reason that I can read dead authors is because their works are repeatable or iterable. Well, no doubt the fact that different copies are made of their books makes it

a lot easier, but the phenomenon of the survival of the text is not the same as the phenomenon of repeatability: the type-token distinction is logically independent of the fact of the permanence of certain tokens . . . This confusion of permanence with iterability lies at the heart of his argument . . . (p. 200)

Once again, *it-reapplies* in the *discourse from/to-Sec. Sec* furnishes Sarl with an argument that the latter attempts to oppose to it.

Let us recall, to begin with, what is most striking. *At no time, either* in *Sec or* in any of the writings that led to it, was the "permanence" (even relative) of writing, or of anything else for that matter, *either* used *or* even mentioned as an argument. Neither the word nor the concept of permanence. Moreover, both have been *criticized explicitly* elsewhere (but that matters little, here), in the preparatory writings to which I have just alluded. Even without going to the point of actually reading these texts, Sarl might have posed the question of why the word "permanence," which is used and attributed to *Sec, never appears in that essay.* And even if it had appeared there, what matters here is that it would never have been used to oppose writing to speech. Sarl might have considered why it is that *Sec* speaks of "restance" [remainder], and even of *"restance* non-présente" [non-present *remainder*] rather than of "permanence." Had Sarl been sufficiently present to what it was writing or rewriting, the passage in question might have cleared up the misunderstanding: in it, what is discussed, with an insistence that should have prevented all haste and confusion, concerns not permanence, but remainders or remains, *non-present* remains. How, then, can a non-presence be assimilated to permanence, and especially to the substantial presence implied by the temporality of permanence? I shall cite once again, re-citing what was cited by Sarl although without much presence-of-mind to what was being read and being written (had we both been together in Montreal while I was reading *Sec,* I would surely have sent off a note to help Sarl's wandering attention, so that despite this slight tendency to *absent*mindedness, what is "most important" might still not be missed; had *Sec,* now, been a shopping list, we would have to conclude that Sarl had forgotten to buy the necessary items for what in French is called the "plat de résistance"; but doesn't this prove that the *written* list is made to supplement an absence that is always possible, and someone, either Sarl at one moment, or, at another, a part of Sarl—let us say, for instance, D. Searle—can send Sarl back to the list, or even to the supermarket to get what is missing). Thus, I cite Sarl citing *Sec.* Sarl writes: "He writes, 'This structural possibility of being weaned from the referent or from the signified (hence from communication and from its context) seems to me to make every mark, including those which are oral, a grapheme in general: which is to say, as we have seen, the nonpresent remainder [*restance*] of a differential mark cut off from its putative "production" or origin' " (p. 200). I don't know if this phrase is more difficult to read than a shopping list. It does, however, contain numerous signals designed to prevent one from confusing the *remains* of a grapheme in general with the *permanence* or survival of a "written language" in the standard sense. What are these signals? 1. The fact that *restance,* in French a neologism that clearly has the function of replacing a standard and traditional concept, is set in italics. Without even referring to other writings dealing with remains and remainders (I have not forgotten my rule proscribing such references), I would have thought that a neologism in italics would be sufficiently clear to an attentive reader, and especially to a specialist in matters of language, to preclude any rapid retranslation into a standard and trival idiom. 2. Jeffrey Mehlman and Sam Weber, for their part, did well to translate *restance* by *remainder* and not by permanence. I cannot say whether or not *remainder,* by itself, adequately translates *restance,* but it matters little since no single word, out of context, can by itself ever translate another word perfectly. The fact, in any case, that Mehlman and Weber found it necessary to add *restance* in brackets signals a difficulty in translation. That should have sufficed to avoid a careless reading or a trivial interpretation and to indicate the need for a certain labor of thought. Even in French, the neologism, *restance,* is designed to serve as a warning—although one word alone can never suffice—that work will be necessary in order to avoid equivalents such as "permanence" or "substance," which are, by essence, "presences." The confusion is also possible in French and all this supposes that one deconstruct a certain discourse on presence. I cannot elaborate this any further here. Except to note that the graphics of *restance* comprises an indispensable part of any such elaboration. 3. This is why the word *restance* is not only in italics, as a kind of warning light. It is also associated with "*non-present.*" This is, I admit, paradoxical, but *Sec* never promised to be orthodox. This "non-present" adds a spectacular blinking-effect to the warning light. How could a specialist in speech acts have missed it? Would it not have escaped him even had we limited ourselves, out of simplicity, to an *oral* utterance? Blinking is a rhythm essential to the mark whose functioning I would like to analyze. I shall return to it. 4. Finally, if *Sec* had indeed been even remotely interested in the "permanence of the written text over the spoken word" (*Reply,* p. 200), why does the phrase cited by Sarl speak not of the "written text" but of the "grapheme in general"? And why should it include under that heading "oral" marks as well ("seems to me to make every mark, *including those which are oral,* a grapheme in general; which is to say, as we have seen, the non-present *remainder* [*restance*] of a differential mark cut off from its putative 'production' or origin" [p. 10]). How could "permanence" be attributed to an "oral mark"? Once the necessity of passing from writing (in the standard sense) to the grapheme in general, an essential movement of *Sec,* had been neglected, Sarl could only go from one confusion to another.

If *Sec* does not, therefore, write what Sarl can or wants to read there, what does it write? First, among other things, precisely what the *Reply* claims to oppose to it and could have found in it, namely, that "the survival of the text is not the same as the phenomenon of repeatability" (p. 200), although the latter is indeed the condition of the former. The remainder is not that of the signifier any more than it is that of the signified, of the "token" or of the "type," of a form or of a content. Without recalling what has been brought forward elsewhere concerning *remains* [du *reste*] and the *remainder* and limiting myself to the restricted context of this debate, it can be asserted that even in *Sec* the remainder, which has nothing in common with *"scripta manent,"* is bound up with the minimal possibility of the re-mark (see above) and with the structure of iterability. This iterability, as Sarl concedes, is indispensable to the functioning of all language, written or spoken (in the standard sense), and I would add, to that of every mark. Iterability supposes a minimal remainder (as well as a minimum of idealization) in order that the identity of the *selfsame* be repeatable and identifiable *in, through,* and even *in view of* its alteration. For the structure of iteration—and this is another of its decisive traits—implies *both* identity *and* difference. Iteration in its "purest" form—and it is always impure—contains *in itself* the discrepancy of a difference that constitutes it as iteration. The iterability of an element divides its own identity a priori, even without taking into account the fact that this identity can only *determine* or delimit itself through differential relations to other elements and that it hence bears the mark of this difference. It is because this iterability is differential, within each individual "element" as well as between the "elements," because it splits each element while constituting it, because it marks it with an articulatory break, that the remainder, although indispensable, is never that of a full or fulfilling presence: it is a differential structure escaping the logic of presence or the (simple or dialectical) opposition of presence and absence, upon which opposition the idea of permanence depends. This is why the mark qua "non-present remainder" is not the contrary of the mark as effacement. Like the trace it is, the mark is neither present nor absent. This is what is *remarkable* about it, even if it is not remarked. This is why the phrase of *Sec* speaks of "the non-present *remainder* of a differential mark cut off from its putative 'production' or origin." Where does this break [*coupure*] take place? To situate it, it is not necessary (cf. *Sec,* p. 8) to imagine the death of the sender or of the receiver, to put the shopping list in one's pocket, or even to raise the pen above the paper in order to interrupt oneself for a moment. The break intervenes from the moment that there is a mark, at once [*aussi sec*]. And it is not negative, but rather the positive condition of the emergence of the mark. It is iterability itself, that which is remarkable in the mark, passing between the *re-* of the repeated and the *re-* of the repeating, traversing and transforming repetition. Condition or effect—take your pick—of iterability. As I have done elsewhere, I will say that it cuts across [*recoupe*] iterability at once, recovering it as though it were merging with it, cutting the cut or break once again in the remark.

The remainder does not amount [*ne revient pas*] to the repose of permanence, and the "concept" of remainder is not, I confess, a sure thing [*de tout repos*]. I put "concept" between quotation marks because if the concept of "concept" depends upon the logic deconstructed by the graphics of remainder, the remainder is not a concept in the strict sense. To remain, in this sense, is not to rest on one's laurels or to take it easy, as Sarl does, for instance, relaxing with a confident and convenient reading of *Sec*. Especially when, after having found repose in the confusion of remainder and permanence, Sarl concludes with imperturbable assurance: "I conclude that Derrida's argument to show that all elements of language (much less experience) are really graphemes is without any force. *It rests* [My emphasis—J.D.] on a simple confusion of iterability with permanence" (p. 201).

There is no doubt that the "permanence" or the "survival" of the document *(scripta manent),* when and to the degree (always relative) that they take place, imply iterability or remaining in general. But the inverse is not true. Permanence is not a necessary effect of remaining. I will go even further: the structure of the remainder, implying alteration, renders all absolute permanence impossible. Ultimately, remaining and permanence are incompatible. And this is why *Sec* is in fact far removed from implying any kind of permanence to support its argumentation. It clearly distinguishes iterability from permanence. Sarl opposes to it an argumentation that in fact has been borrowed from it. To the extent of this borrowing, at least, Sarl can be said to have understood *Sec* quite well, even if everything is done to create the contrary impression, one which, it must be admitted, often seems very convincing.

p

Is it out of line to recall that *Sec* is a difficult text? I shall attempt later on to indicate certain of the (typical) reasons that render it foreign, in its functioning and in its structure, to the predilections and selections of the theoreticians of speech acts and to the types of acts that can be identified with the categories or categorical oppositions they have fashioned for themselves. For the moment, at this point in the discussion, the difficulty does not simply involve the blinking quasi-concept of "remainder." The latter is the effect not of a conceptual deficiency or theoretical laxity on the part of a particular philosophical discourse, but rather of the iterability to which it is bound and which, it should be realized, allows for no other kind of "concept" (identity *"and"* difference, iteration-alteration, repetition "as" *différance,* etc.). The difficulty also involves what has been called the grapheme in general as well as the strategic reasons that have motivated the choice of this word to designate "something" which is no longer tied to writing in the traditional sense any more than it is to speech or to any other type of mark. But the entire essay explicates this strategy, although Sarl has preferred to ignore it completely. And this, although *Sec* treats the strategy explicitly, in its initial as well as in its concluding pages. I take the liberty, therefore, of referring the reader to these pages. Paying no attention to this strategic movement, Sarl clings stubbornly to the traditional concept of "written language," although what is at stake is precisely the attempt to put this concept into question and to transform it. For Sarl it is this traditional concept that is "genuinely graphematic." Sarl writes, for example: "The principle according to which we can wean a written text from its origin is simply that the text has a permanence that enables it to survive the death of its author, receiver, and context of production. This principle is genuinely 'graphematic.' " (p. 200–201). But from the standpoint of *Sec's* logic and strategy, this particular graphematic instance (which I do not consider to be "genuine," just as I do not seek to establish any kind of authenticity) is nothing more or less than a very determinate form derived from iterability or graphematicity in general. Consequently when, a bit further on, Sarl writes: "But again this possibility of separating the sign from the signified is a feature of any system of representation whatever; and there is nothing especially graphematic about it at all. It is furthermore quite independent of those special features of the 'classical concept' of writing which are supposed to form the basis of the argument," I not only agree fully, but have already argued as much (since the argument was developed in *Sec)*; if, that is, by "especially graphematic" is meant, as is the case, what already has been called "genuinely graphematic": the standard and traditional concept, in its most "classical" form, which *Sec* is precisely proposing to reelaborate by extracting certain predicates that can be extended to every mark. This "classical concept" comprises the "basis" of Sarl's argument, no doubt, but also the *target* of *Sec.* This target, however, is not one object among others. The structure of the area in which we are operating here calls for a strategy that is complex and tortuous, involuted and full of artifice: for example, exploiting the target against itself by discovering it at times to be the "basis" of an operation directed against it; or even discovering "in it" the cryptic reserve of something utterly different.

q

In the same section (p. 201), Sarl then arrives at the problem of intention and of intentionality. This is what is called, once again, "the most important issue" ("I have left the most important issue in this section until last"). Since this occurs, indeed, at the end of the section, there is unfortunately a considerable risk that the premises of Sarl's reading, with all of the confusions that we have just encountered, will bar the way to everything in *Sec* that concerns intention and intentionality. And in fact, Sarl continues to think within a traditional opposition of speech and writing. But what is worse is that Sarl continues to act as if *Sec,* too, were operating within those terms, concluding with blissful tranquility that intentionality "plays exactly the same role in written as in spoken language."

That reapplies, again, the discourse-from/to-*Sec.* I agree, of course, that the role is "the same": *Sec* says it and Sarl, infallibly, reiterates it, but once more in the inverted form of an objection!

But what, after all, is this "role"? On several occasions, passing moreover too quickly from intention to intentionality (but let's skip that), Sarl attributes to *Sec* the following affirmation: intentionality is (supposedly) purely and simply "absent" from writing; writing is supposedly purely and simply cut off, separated, by the effect of a radical interruption ("some break," "radical break"). Having thus translated and simplified *Sec,* Sarl has an easy time objecting that intentionality is not "absent from written communication." For example, still under the heading, "quite plain": "It seems to me quite plain that the argument that the author and intended receiver may be dead and the context unknown or forgotten does not in the least show that intentionality is absent from written communication; on the contrary, intentionality plays exactly the same role in written as in spoken communication." I know this argument well. It, like the entire substratum of Sarl's discourse, is phenomenological in character (cf. Husserl's *Origin of Geometry,* for instance).[7] I have never opposed this position head on, and *Sec* doesn't either. Without returning to what is said in *Sec* about the value of communication (Sarl says, "in written as in spoken *communication"),* I must first recall that *at no time* does *Sec* invoke the *absence,* pure and simple, of intentionality. Nor is there any break, simple or radical, with intentionality. What the text questions is not intention or intentionality but their *telos,* which orients and organizes the movement and the possibility of a fulfillment, realization, and *actualization* in a plenitude that would be *present* to and identical with itself. This is why, as any reader with even the slightest vigilance will have remarked, the words "actual" and "present" are those that bear the brunt of the argumentation each time that it is radicalized. Sarl should have been able to note the insistence and the regularity with which these words accompanied that of "intention." He should have been able to read this, for example, without it being necessary to underline certain words, which I shall do now (as though for a companion, listening to a lecture): "For a writing to be a writing it must continue to 'act' and to be readable even when what is called the author of the writing no longer answers for what he has written, for what he seems to have signed, be it because of a temporary absence, because he is dead or, *more generally, because he has not employed his absolutely actual and present intention or attention, the plenitude of his desire to say what he means,* in order to sustain what seems to be written *'in his name' "* (p. 8). The value of a law, here of an eidetic law, resides not in the indicative and variable examples (an absence that is real or factual, provisional or definitive, such as death for instance), but rather in a condition that may be defined *in general* and that, moreover and once again, is nothing but a consequence of iterability: namely in the fact that intention or attention, directed towards something iterable which in turn determines it as being iterable, will strive or tend in vain to actualize or fulfill itself, for it cannot, by virtue of its very structure, ever achieve this goal. In no case will it be fulfilled, actualized, totally present to its object and to itself. It is divided and deported in advance, by its iterability, towards others, removed [*écartée*] in advance from itself. This re-move makes its movement possible. Which is another way of saying that if this remove is its condition of possibility, it is not an eventuality, something that befalls it here and there, by accident. Intention is a priori (at once) *différante:* differing and deferring, in its inception.

This is what Sarl should have been able to read without its having been necessary to underline certain words, which I am obliged to do once again. Sarl will remark that the words *determinate, actual,* and *present* are, to me, *the most important:* "Why is this identity paradoxically the division or dissociation of itself, which will make of this phonic sign a grapheme? Because this unity of the signifying form only constitutes itself by virtue of its iterability, by the possiblity of its being repeated in the absence not only of its 'referent,' which is self-evident, but

in the absence of a *determinate* signified or of the intention of *actual* signification, as well as of all intention of *present* communication" (p. 10). This is immediately followed by the phrase already commented on, on "the non-present *remainder [restance]* of a differential mark . . ."

(Perhaps it should be said in passing that the *différance,* as we have just seen,
removes from itself what "seems to have been written *'in its* name.' " Namely, the
proper name, which suddenly finds itself removed. It can thus transform itself, at
once, and change itself into a more or less anonymous multiplicty. This is what
happens to the "subject" in the scene of writing. That Searle's seal should become, at once and without waiting for me, Sarl's seal, is therefore anything but
accidental. It is a little like the multitude of stockholders and managers in a company or corporation with limited liability, or in a limited, incorporated system;
or, like that limit which is supposed to distinguish stockholders from managers.
Even here, the signatory is no exception.)

Once again, to be precise: what is at stake here is an analysis that can account
for *structural possibilities.* Once it is *possible* for X to function under certain conditions (for instance, a mark in the absence or partial absence of intention), the
possibility of a certain non-presence or of a certain non-actuality pertains to the
structure of the functioning under consideration, and pertains to it *necessarily.*
But I want to be even more precise on this point since it seems to have troubled
Sarl's reading of *Sec* considerably. The possibility of which I have just been
speaking seems to be understandable in two senses, both of which reinforce the
argument of *Sec.* First of all, there is possibility as what in French is called *éventualité,* eventuality (I shall come back to this word and to its translation): it can
happen that a mark functions without the sender's intention being actualized,
fulfilled, and present, and which *to this extent* must be *presumed.* Even if this
(eventual) possibility only occurred once, and never again, we would still have to
account for that one time and analyze whatever it is in the structural functioning
of the mark that renders such an event possible. The condition will have ob-
tained, and be it only in this unique case, that a fulfilled, actualized, and present
intention was not indispensable. The possibility of a *certain* absence (even a
relative one) must then be conceded and the consequences must be drawn. That
is possibility qua eventuality. It might, however, also be said: *in fact* that doesn't
always happen like that. But at this point, we must pass to possibility qua necessity (see above), and moreover, we must recognize an irreducible contamination
or parasitism between the two possibilities and say: "to one degree or another
that always happens, necessarily, like that": by virtue of the iterability which, in
every case, forms the structure of the mark, which always divides or removes
intention, preventing it from being fully present to itself in the actuality of its aim,
or of its meaning (i.e. what it means-to-say [*vouloir-dire*]). What makes the (eventual) possibility possible is what makes it happen even before it happens as an
actual event (in the standard sense) or what prevents such an event from ever
entirely, fully taking place (in the standard sense). I have already recalled the role
played in all this by another kind of graphics of the event in general. What is here

in question, then, is the value of the kind of event that supports the entire theory of speech acts.

What is valid for intention, always differing, deferring, and without plenitude, is also valid, correlatively, for the object (qua signified or referent) thus aimed at. However, this limit, I repeat (*"without"* plenitude), is also the ("positive") condition of possibility of what is thus limited.

This is why if, on the one hand, I am more or less in agreement with Sarl's statement, ". . . there is no getting away from intentionality, because a *meaningful sentence is just a standing possibility of the corresponding* (intentional) speech act" (p. 202), I would, on the other hand, add, placing undue and artificial emphasis on *-ful,* that for reasons just stated, there cannot be a "sentence" that is fully and actually meaning*ful* and hence (or because) there can be no "corresponding (intentional) speech act" that would be fulfilled, fully present, *active* and *actual.* Thus, the value of the *act* (used so generally and analyzed so little in the theory of speech acts), like that of event, should be submitted to systematic questioning. As in the entire philosophical tradition that supports it, this value implies that of presence which I have proposed to defer to questions of differential [*différantielle*] iterability. But we cannot unfold this analysis here.

What is in question here, for the moment, through the analysis ventured by *Sec* (and elsewhere)—one whose point of departure is in Husserl, but whose consequences work against him—is precisely the plenitude of intentional meaning [*vouloir-dire*], and all of the other values—of consciousness, presence, and originary intuition—which organize phenomenology. But by saying that the graphematic mark (in general) implies the possibility of functioning without the full and actual presence of the intentional act (that of the conscious ego fully present to itself, to what it says, and to the other), *Sec* has not simply effaced or denied intentionality, as Sarl claims. On the contrary, *Sec* insists on the fact that "the category of intention will not disappear, it will have its place . . ." (p. 18). (Let it be said in passing that this differential-deferring [*différantielle*] structure of intentionality alone can enable us to account for the differentiation between "locutionary," "illocutionary," and "perlocutionary" values of the "same" marks or utterances.) With a more active, attentive, and present intention, Sarl would have been able to remark a passage like the one I am now compelled to cite, for reasons of clarity. I trust that the length of this citation will not be held against me, since it contains, with regard to iteration and citation, certain important details that Sarl has omitted and which will be useful a little further on. I cite, therefore, and underline in passing:

> Could a performative utterance succeed if its formulation did not repeat a "coded" or iterable utterance, or in other words, if the formula I pronounce in order to open a meeting, launch a ship or a marriage were not identifiable as *conforming* with an iterable model, if it were not then identifiable *in some way as a "citation"?* [I also underline the quotation marks.] *Not that citationality in this case is of the same sort* as in a theatrical play, a philosophical reference, or the recitation of a poem. That is why there is a relative

specificity, as Austin says, a "relative purity" of performatives. But this relative purity does not emerge *in opposition to* citationality or iterability, but in opposition to other kinds of iteration within a general iterability which constitutes a violation of the allegedly rigorous purity of every event of discourse or every *speech act*. Rather than oppose citation or iteration to the non-iteration of an event, one ought to construct a differential typology of forms of iteration, assuming that such a project is tenable and can result in an exhaustive program, a question I hold in abeyance here. In such a typology, *the category of intention will not disappear; it will have its place,* but from that place it will no longer be able to govern the entire scene and system of utterance [*l'énonciation*]. Above all, at that point, we will be dealing with different kinds of marks or chains of iterable marks and not with an opposition between citational utterances, on the one hand, and singular and original event-utterances, on the other. The first consequence of this will be the following: given that structure of iteration, the intention animating the utterance *will never be through and through present to itself and to its content.* The iteration structuring it a priori introduces into it a *dehiscence* and a cleft [*brisure*] which are essential. . . . Above all, this essential absence of intending the actuality of utterance, this *structural unconsciousness,* if you like, prohibits any saturation of the context. In order for a context to be exhaustively determinable, in the sense required by Austin, conscious intention would at the very least have to be totally present and immediately transparent to itself and to others, since it is a determining center [*foyer*] of context. The concept of—or the search for—the context thus seems to suffer at this point from the same theoretical and "interested" uncertainty as the concept of the "ordinary," from the same metaphysical origins: the ethical and teleological discourse of consciousness. . . . By no means do I draw the conclusion that there is no relative specificity of effects of consciousness, or of effects of speech (as opposed to writing in the traditional sense), that there is no performative effect, no effect of ordinary language, no effect of presence or of discursive event *(speech act).* It is simply that those effects do not exclude what is generally opposed to them, term by term; on the contrary, they presuppose it, in an asymmetrical way, as the general space of their possibility. (*Sec,* pp. 18–19)

Among other words, I have underlined *dehiscence.* As in the realm of botany, from which it draws its metaphorical value, this word marks emphatically that the divided opening, in the growth of a plant, is also what, in a *positive* sense, makes production, reproduction, development possible. Dehiscence (like iterability) limits what it makes possible, while rendering its rigor and purity impossible. What is at work here is something like a law of undecidable contamination, which has interested me for some time.

After the long passage that I have had to cite, *Sec* addresses itself necessarily to the question of signatures. Sarl has totally ignored this question, although it develops, precisely by reading Austin, the consequences of what has just been said. Since Sarl has not made the slightest allusion to this, I shall leave it out of the debate or at least will not treat it directly, leaving it to the reader to reread the pages in question. If he does, he will be in a position to measure the enormity of the exclusion that has taken place: the section on signatures concerns the puta-tive "origin" of oral or written utterances, and thus, the constant and indispensa-ble recourse of all speech act theory.

r

Let us follow, then, the *Reply* as closely as possible. Still occupied with "the most important issue in this section," Sarl thus purports to oppose to *Sec* what could have been had from reading it, namely that "intentionality plays exactly the same role in written as in spoken communication." And he continues: "What differs in the two cases is not the intentions of the speaker but the role of the context of the utterance in the success of the communication" (p. 201).

Here, two remarks. 1. Since the role of context is determinant, and the hori-zon of the "total context" is indispensable to the analysis, the contextual differ-ence here may be fundamental and cannot be shunted aside, even provisionally, in order to analyse intention. Isn't the assertion that the difference involves *only* the context a surprising proposition to make, even from the standpoint of speech act theory? 2. Intention, itself marked by the context, is not foreign to the forma-tion of the "total" context. For Austin it is even an essential element of that forma-tion. And yet, Sarl feels authorized in excluding temporarily the consideration of context. Yet even if it were only temporary and methodological, useful for the clarity of the demonstration, such an exclusion would, it seems to me, be both impossible and illegitimate. To treat context as a factor from which one can ab-stract for the sake of refining one's analysis, is to commit oneself to a description that cannot but miss the very contents and object it claims to isolate, for they are intrinsically determined by context. The method itself, as well as considerations of clarity should have excluded such an abstraction. Context is always, and always has been, at work *within* the place, and not only *around* it.

But let's follow Sarl. For a while, in an initial phase of the argument, context is ostensibly left aside.

1. *Initial phase:* The hypothesis of intention (or of text) without context being considered. To support this hypothesis with a didactic example, Sarl proposes a rich and wondrous fiction. If I ever have the time, I would be tempted to devote one or more works to it. But, interrupting all the fantastic reveries towards which this evocation had begun to draw me, I shall confine myself to a discussion of its logical structure and its demonstrative function. Here it is: ". . . ask yourself what happens when you read the text of a dead author. Suppose you read the sen-tence, 'On the twentieth of September 1793 I set out on a journey from London to Oxford.' Now how do you understand this sentence?" (p. 201)

Having posed this question, Sarl believes it necessary—and possible—to dis-tinguish rigorously between two possibilities.

a. First possibility: "The author said what he meant and you understand what he said." To grant such a possibility, even as a hypothesis, is to grant a myriad of problematic presuppositions. But, for the moment, that is not important; we will return to it later. What does Sarl hope to conclude from this possibility? As always it is better to cite, but I shall permit myself to underline: *"To the extent* that the author said what he meant and you understand what he said you will know that the author intended to make a statement to the effect that on the twentieth of September 1793, he set out on a journey from London to Oxford, and the fact that the *author is dead and all his intentions died with him is irrelevant to this feature of your understanding of his surviving written utterances."*

This last argument, which I have just underlined, should not be opposed to *Sec.* It derives from *Sec:* namely, from the first of its three sections, which places much emphasis on the fact that "death," and in general the non-presence of a vital, actualized, determinate intention, does not prevent the mark from functioning; it also stresses that the *possibility* of this "death" (and of everything implied by this word, in particular the hypothesis formed by Sarl) is inscribed in the functional structure of the mark. This argument even provides indispensable leverage for the demonstration undertaken in *Sec.* It is inseparable from the iterability to which I incessantly return, as constituting the minimal consensus of this discussion. I have used the phrase "functioning of the mark" rather than "understanding" the "written utterance." In the absence of the presumed author this function, which depends upon iterability, operates a fortiori within the hypothesis that I fully understand what the author meant to say, providing he said what he meant. But the function also operates independently of such an hypothesis and without in itself implying either that I *fully* understand what the other says, writes, meant to say or write, or even that he intended to say or write *in full* what remains to be read, or above all that any adequation need obtain between what he consciously intended, what he did, and what I do while "reading." Sarl will retort: such an adequation is for the moment our hypothesis ("to the extent . . ." etc.). Surely. But this ideal hypothesis seems to me untenable. Not so much because of the possibility of a factual accident, which can always (as Sarl will later admit) "corrupt," contaminate parasitically a situation held to be ideal and in some sense essential [*juridique*]. Rather, the very structure of the mark (for example, the minimum of iterability it requires) excludes the hypothesis of idealization, that is, the adequation of a meaning to itself, of a saying to itself, of understanding to a sentence, whether written or oral, or to a mark in general. Once again, iterability makes possible idealization—and thus, a certain identity in repetition that is independent of the multiplicity of factual events—while at the same time limiting the idealization it makes possible: *broaching* and *breaching* it at once [elle l'*entame*]. To put it more simply and more concretely: at the very moment (assuming that this moment itself might be full and self-identical, identifiable—for the problem of idealization and iterability is already posed here, in the structure of temporalization), at the very moment when someone would like to say or to write, "On the twentieth . . . etc.," the very factor that will permit the mark (be it psychic, oral, graphic) to function beyond this moment—namely the possibility of its being repeated *another* time—breaches, divides, expropriates the "ideal" plenitude or self-presence of intention, of meaning (to say) and, a fortiori, of all adequation between meaning and saying. Iterability alters, contaminating parasitically what it identifies and enables to repeat "itself"; it leaves us no choice but to mean (to say) something that is (already, always, also) other than what we mean (to say), to say something other than what we say *and* would have wanted to say, to understand something other than . . . etc. In classical terms, the accident is never an accident. And the *mis* of those misunderstandings to which we have succumbed, or which each of us here accuses the other of having succumbed to, must have its essential condition of possibility in the structure of marks, of remarkable marks or, if Sarl prefers to circumscribe the object, of oral or written utterances. Limiting the very thing it authorizes, transgressing the code or the law it constitutes, the graphics of iterability inscribes alteration irreducibly in repetition (or in identification): a priori, always and already, without delay, *at once, aussi sec:* "Such iterability—(*iter,* again, probably comes from *itara, other* in Sanskrit, and everything that follows can be read as the working out of the logic that ties repetition to alterity) structures the mark of writing itself, no matter what particular type of writing is involved" (*Sec,* p. 7). This etymology, of course, has no value qua proof and were it to be false, the very shift in meaning would confirm the law here indicated: the time and place of the *other time* already at work, altering from the start the start itself, the *first time,* the *at once.* Such are the *vices* that interest me: the other time in (stead of) the first, at once.

This holds for every mark and in particular, since Sarl is only interested in this type, for every speech act, however simple or complex. What sets the times, the *vices,* is a strange law which prescribes that the simpler, poorer, and more univocal an utterance may seem, the more difficult its comprehension, more elusive its meaning, and more indeterminate its context will be. And yet the more complex an utterance becomes, the more the same tendency will prevail. Thus, the example given by Sarl seems to be simple: "On the twentieth . . ." It seems simple, that is, if we leave aside, as I must do here, the enormous problem (broached by *Sec* in the section, "Signatures," ignored by the *Reply,* but also in other works) raised by the fact that the example chosen is an utterance made in the first person. Is this indispensable for the demonstration? Did Sarl consider this trait as pertinent? Or would an utterance in the third person have been as much (or as little) use in this context? The choice of the first person would *seem* to make things easier to the extent to which one might generally be tempted to expect that someone who says *I* and who speaks of himself would best satisfy the idealizing hypothesis of "saying what he means": the intention of the speaker, one might think, is closest to, if not absolutely present in what is said. Yet nothing is less certain: the functioning of the *I,* as is well known, is no less iterable or replaceable than any other word. And in any case, whatever singularity its functioning might possess is not of a kind to guarantee any adequation between saying and meaning. Since I cannot, here, develop this problem any further, I shall leave aside everything in this example relating to "myself saying I." I will make do by remarking the following: the functioning of the mark, a certain iterability, here a certain legibility that is operative beyond the disappearance or demise of the presumed author, the recognition of a certain semantic and syntactic code at work in this phrase—none of all this either constitutes or requires a full understanding of the mean-ing*fulness* of this phrase, in the sense of the complete and original intentionality of its meaning (-to-say), any more than for the phrase, "I forgot my umbrella," abandoned like an island among the unpublished writings of Nietzsche.[8] A thou-sand possibilities will always remain open even if one understands something in this phrase that makes sense (as a citation? the beginning of a novel? a proverb? someone else's secretarial archives? an exercise in learning language? the narra-tion of a dream? an alibi? a cryptic code—conscious or not? the example of a linguist or of a speech act theoretician letting his imagination wander for short distances, etc?), all possibilities that Sarl would no doubt subsume under those contextual elements excluded from phase 1 by hypothesis, or under the "corrup-tions" excluded by possibility 1. Nevertheless, I must repeat that iterability pro-hibits a priori (and in principle) the full and rigorous attainment of the ideal plenitude such exclusions purport to isolate. These hypothetical exclusions can-not be formed. They are illegitimate and impossible inasmuch as they suppose the self-identity of an isolated element which iterability—i.e. an element consti-tutive of the hypothesis—divides at once. And this holds a fortiori for cases of utterances that are more complex than those proposed by the *Reply*.

Since *possibility 1* is only evoked by Sarl as part of what is designated as a "strategy," and since a similar strategic gesture will reproduce itself shortly, I shall reserve until later a general discussion of the law or the rule of this strategy as well as of the problem of strategy in general.

Still within the scope of possibility 1 ("the author said what he meant and you understand what he said"), Sarl admits another supposition. As though by con-cession. I quote:

> But suppose you decide to make a radical break—as one always can—with the strategy of understanding the sentence as an utterance of a man who once lived and had intentions like yourself and just think of it as a sentence of English, weaned from all production or origin, putative or otherwise. Even then there is no getting away from intentionality, because a *meaningful sen-tence is just a standing possibility of the corresponding (intentional) speech act*. To understand it, it is necessary to know that anyone who said it and meant it would be performing that speech act determined by the rules of the languages that give the sentence its meaning in the first place. (pp. 201–2)

The principle of my response to this sub-hypothesis should now be clear and predictable. In order to limit misunderstandings as much as possible, I shall con-fine myself to the following three points:

a. The fact that a "break" with "the strategy of understanding the sentence as an utterance of a man who once . . ." etc., is always possible ("as one always can") and that the mark still does not cease functioning, that a minimum of legibility or intelligibility remains, constitutes the point of departure of *Sec's* argumentation and hence, it can hardly be held up as an objection to it. But it is no less necessary to draw the consequences, as *Sec* does, from this fact, namely that up to a certain point this "break" remains *always possible* without its preventing the mark from functioning. This implies, however, that even in the ideal case considered by the strategy, there must already be a certain element of play, a certain remove, a certain degree of independence with regard to the origin, to production, or to intention in all of its "vital," "simple" "actuality" or "determinateness," etc. For if this were not so, the "break" (with all its consequences, variables, etc.) would be impossible. And if a certain "break" is always possible, that with which it breaks must necessarily bear the mark of this possibility inscribed in its structure. This is the thesis of *Sec.*

b. I repeat that *Sec never* adduced, from the possibility of this "break," the pure and simple absence of all intentionality in the functioning of the mark that remains; rather, what it calls into question is the presence of a fulfilled and actualized intentionality, adequate to itself and to its contents. I cannot see, therefore, to what or to whom such an objection might be addressed since it is one that *Sec,* too, could endorse.

c. As I have already noted, the equivalence between "to understand it," in the sense of grasping its "meaning*fulness,*" and the minimum it is indeed "necessary to know" in order to attain such understanding, seems to me problematical. One of the things *Sec* is driving at is that the minimal making-sense of something (its conformity to the code, grammaticality, etc.) is incommensurate with the adequate understanding of intended meaning. I am aware that the English expression "meaningful" can also be understood in terms of this minimum of making-sense. Perhaps even the entire equivocation of this discussion is situated here. In any case, the incommensurability is irreducible: it "inheres" in intention itself and it is riven [*creusé*] with iterability.

But the equivocation is exacerbated by the fact that the very basis of our consensus is endangered. What is this consensus? What convention will have insured up to now the contract of a minimal agreement? Iterability: here Sarl and I seemed to be in agreement, both concerning iterability itself and concerning the systematic link between iterability and code, or to put it differently, between iterability and a kind of conventionality. The conventional consensus thus concerned ultimately the possibility of conventionality. Our common and minimal code has been the existence and the effects of the code itself. But this basis, as I just said, seems to me to be fragile, limited, and in danger. Why?

The questioning initiated by the logic and the graphics of *Sec* does not stop at the security of the code, nor at its concept. I cannot pursue this problem too far, since that would only add new complications to a discussion that is already too slow, overdetermined, and over-coded in all respects. I shall simply observe that this line of questioning is opened in the first of *Sec's* three parts, and to be exact by the following phrase: "The perhaps paradoxical consequence of my here having recourse to iteration and to code: the disruption, in the last analysis, of the authority of the code as a finite system of rules; at the same time, the radical destruction of any context as the protocol of code" (p. 8). The same direction, that of an iterability that can only be what it is in the *impurity* of its self-identity (repetition altering and alteration identifying), is charted by the following propositions: "As far as the internal semiotic context is concerned, the force of the rupture is no less important: by virtue of its essential iterability, a written syntagma can always be detached from the chain in which it is inserted or given without causing it to lose all possibility of functioning, if not all possibility of 'communicating,' precisely. One can perhaps come to recognize other possibilities in it by inscribing it or *grafting* it onto other chains. No context can entirely enclose it. Nor any code, the code here being both the possibility and impossibility of writing, of its essential iterability (repetition/alterity)" (p. 9). And: ". . . in so doing [i.e. by the iterability *or* the citationality that it permits] it [the sign] can break with every given context, engendering an infinity of new contexts in a manner which is absolutely illimitable. This does not imply that the mark is valid outside of a context, but on the contrary that there are only contexts without any center or absolute anchoring [*ancrage*]" (p. 12).

We are still within the hypothesis of possibility 1. Still very certain that this "rather obvious point" has not been understood, Sarl mulls over the causes of this lack of understanding. The resulting diagnosis is acute and far-reaching: reaching, that is, the obstacles deemed to have prevented this "rather obvious point" from being understood, blinding *Sec* to the evidence.

Let's be serious. Although I have endeavored to demonstrate that this point was so obvious precisely because it had previously been explicitly taken into account and analyzed in *Sec,* I am still ready to examine what those obstacles to understanding *might have been,* had there in fact been misunderstanding or incomprehension. After all, I have promised to be both exceedingly scrupulous and exceedingly serious in my argumentation. These obstacles, then, are supposedly of two kinds: "There are two obstacles to understanding this rather obvious point, one implicit in Derrida, the other explicit."

The diagnosis does not remain at the surface: it delves into the phenomenon in order to seek out the causes lurking behind it, or rather, it penetrates the non-phenomenon in order to search out the obstacles that lie behind and have prevented the natural, normal phenomenon which we have every right to expect, from emerging; moving beyond blindness towards its cause, the diagnosis seeks to uncover the implicit cause hidden behind the explicit one. What is this implicit cause which, behind everything that is already behind, explains this blindness to the "rather obvious"? What is the hindrance here to sight? It is nothing more or less than: an illusion. Which illusion? The illusion that there is something lurking *behind.* Let's see, or rather, cite:

> There are two obstacles to understanding this rather obvious point, one implicit in Derrida, the other explicit. The first is the illusion that somehow illocutionary intentions if they really existed or mattered would have to be something that *lay behind* the utterances, some inner pictures animating the visible signs. But of course in serious literal speech the sentences are

precisely the realizations of the intentions: there need be no *gulf* at all between the illocutionary intention and its expression. The sentences are, so to
speak, fungible intentions. Often, especially in writing, one forms one's intentions (or meanings) in the process of forming the sentences: there need
not be two separate processes. (p. 202)

This first illusion must indeed be unfathomably "implicit." I have looked in
vain for the slightest apparent sign of it in *Sec*. And this perhaps explains why Sarl,
not being able to mention a single example, is forced to take refuge here in the
implicit, i.e., in something that, this time, could only be located precisely "*behind*
the utterances." The illusion thus unmasked *behind* [*derrière*] the text of *Sec*,
namely that someone named Derrida supposedly believes in "something *behind*
the utterances, some inner pictures animating the visible signs," this illusion belongs—and hence the terrifying severity of the accusation—to the repertoire of a
psychology of language (mechanistic, associationist, substantialist, expressionist,
representationalist, pre-Saussurian, prephenomenological, etc.), more exactly to
a pre-critical psychologism; one can only wonder by means of what perverse or
baroque regression *Sec* might have succumbed to such psychologism, especially
since such doctrine has long since disappeared from the curriculum, and the
works which stand "behind" *Sec* not only presuppose its critique but graphically
accentuate it. However, I recognize that this argument alone is not sufficient.
What should suffice, by comparison, is the *explicit* criticism, from the initial pages
of *Sec* on, of the concepts of "representation," "communication," and "expression" (p. 5 ff.). All such concepts appeal to a notion of intention as something
separable, intrinsic, and "behind" the "expression." What should also suffice is
the suspicion concerning the *sign* and even concerning the opposition signifier/
signified: this suspicion, legible in every line, bears on the entire system that
supports this opposition, and consequently, among others, on that of an intention hidden behind the "visible sign" (the signifier). Hence, the substitution of
"mark" for "sign," of intentional effect for intention, etc.

Nevertheless: to assert, against this purported "illusion," that "the sentences
are precisely the realizations of the intentions" is to employ a language that
seems to me to stem from that good old representationalist and expressionist
psychology (Sarl speaks, moreover, continually of "representations," and always
designates language as a set of "expressions"), for which the distinctions between "intention" and "realization," "intention" and "expression" are still intact.
They are intact both as purely conceptual (non-real) oppositions in the ideal case
to which we shall return in a moment ("in serious literal speech"), in which
utterances "are precisely the realizations of intentions, and as simply real oppositions in the other cases, or at least in almost all other cases." Just such a psychology (disarmingly enough today, I must confess) seems to me to permeate this
short, rather improvised description of the process of writing: "Often [?], especially [?] in writing, one forms one's intentions (or meanings) in the process of
forming the sentences. . . ." Even if it were not simplistic, empiricist, and vague,

this kind of descriptive psychology could not teach us anything about the object in which we are interested precisely because it is a psychology whereas that object is not essentially psychological. Unless, that is, Sarl considers it to be psychological, or deems the theory of those objects designated as speech acts to be a psychology, an interior domain of psychic life. In this case, however, the illusion that Sarl denounces would be explicitly Sarl's own. This would not be the first such case, nor the last.

We are not quite done with this "first" "illusion," which is "implicit." Will my snail's pace ever be forgiven? If I am abusing everyone's patience (including my own), it is in the hope of leaving as little as possible—above all, of those illusions—implicit. That was my "promise." To be sure, in the examination of this objection, I have saved the most important point for last: "serious literal speech." Everything, of course, begins here: "But of course in serious literal speech the sentences are precisely the realizations of the intentions: there need be no *gulf* at all between the illocutionary intention and its expression."

Let us anticipate a bit the discussion that will develop about the second section of the *Reply,* that which concerns Austin and what is called "serious" discourse. Sarl has just opposed the case of "serious literal speech" to *Sec,* speech in which intention is presumed to be "realized." *Sec,* however, proposes, even if Sarl fails to make the slightest allusion to it, an *explicit* deconstructive critique of the oppositions "serious/non-serious," "literal/non-literal" and of the entire system of related oppositions. One need only consult, for instance, what is said there concerning "the suspicious status of the 'non-serious' "(p. 23) and everything that forms its context. Involved are not merely the extreme difficulties which, *in fact,* can arise in the attempt to isolate the ideal purity of what is "serious" and "literal." Such difficulties are familiar enough to John R. Searle. The embarrassed, even endless precautions that he feels constrained to take, in *Speech Acts* for instance, bear sufficient witness to this fact. Rather, what is at stake above all is the structural impossibility and illegitimacy of such an "idealization," even one which is methodological and provisional. The word "idealization" here is a citation from *Speech Acts.* In imposing the convention upon my readers, I have agreed not to cite anything but *Sec* among the writings which carry, among other things, "my" own signatures, but I never said that I would not cite John R. Searle, co-signatory, director, and, within the limits of his liability responsible [*responsable limité*] for the *Reply.* In a gesture that appears thoroughly classical in its rigor and logic, dictated by those exigencies to which philosophy, from Plato to Rousseau, from Kant to Husserl, has always sought to respond, Searle acknowledges the necessity of an "idealization of the concept analyzed" at the very moment when he undertakes to define the "structure of illocutionary acts."[9] In face of "the looseness of our concepts," which could "lead us into a rejection of the very enterprise of philosophical analysis," he reacts much as, in appearance at least, the great philosophers of the tradition have always done (Austin being in this respect a partial exception). He considers this "looseness" as something extrinsic, essentially accidental, and reducible. And he writes (I underline):

. . . rather the conclusion to be drawn is that certain forms of analysis, especially analysis into necessary and sufficient conditions, are likely to involve
(in varying degrees) *idealization of the concept analyzed*. In the present
case, our analysis will be directed at the *center* of the concept of promising. *I
am ignoring marginal, fringe, and partially defective promises*. . . . Furthermore, in the analysis I confine my discussion to *full blown explicit promises
and ignore promises made by elliptical turns of phrase, hints, metaphors, etc.*
. . . In short, I am going to deal only with a *simple and idealized* case. This
method, one of constructing idealized models, is *analogous* to the sort of
theory construction that goes on in *most* sciences, e.g., the construction of
economic models, or accounts of the solar system which treat planets as
points. *Without abstraction and idealization* there is no systematization. . . . I
want to give a list of conditions for the performance of a certain illocutionary
act, which do not themselves mention the performance of any illocutionary
acts. . . . (pp. 55–56)

And, a little further on, in a subsection entitled:

1. *Normal input and output conditions obtain.*
    I use the terms "input" and "output" to cover the large and indefinite
range of conditions under which any kind of *serious and literal*[1] linguistic
communication is possible. . . . Together they [the two terms] include such
things as that the speaker and hearer both know how to speak the language;
both are conscious of what they are doing; they have no physical impediments to communication, such as deafness, aphasia, or laryngitis; *and they
are not acting in a play or telling jokes,* etc. It should be noted that this
condition excludes *both* impediments to communication such as deafness
and also *parasitic* forms of communication such as *telling jokes or acting in a
play.*
    1. I contrast "serious" utterances with play acting, teaching a language, re-
citing poems, practicing pronunciation, etc., and *I contrast "literal" with metaphorical, sarcastic, etc.* (p. 57)

This long quotation will not have been excessive if it has clarified the logic of
the *Reply,* and above all of the phrase: "But of course in serious literal speech the
sentences are precisely the realizations of the intentions." And if, at the same
time, it has clarified my reading of it. In this passage I find confirmation not only
of the fact that the criterion of intention (responsible, deliberate, self-conscious)
is a necessary recourse in order that the "serious" and the "literal" be defined—
something which is self-evident and which Searle would probably not deny—but
also and above all of the fact that this intention must indeed, according to his own
arguments, be situated "behind" the phenomenal utterance (in the sense of the
"visible" or "audible" signs, and of the phono-linguistic manifestation as a
whole): no criterion that is simply *inherent* in the manifest utterance is capable of
distinguishing an utterance when it is serious from the same utterance when it is
not. Solely intention can decide this and it is not identical with "realization."
Nothing can distinguish a serious or sincere promise from the same "promise"

that is nonserious or insincere except for the intention which informs and animates it. And the same holds for the other oppositions. But I have already broached this above and if we shall meet it again, this is not what interests me most at the moment. What does is the "center" of this sweeping theoretical perspective. As we have just seen, the isolation of "serious literal speech" presupposes an entire system of theoretical-methodological idealizations and exclusions. I shall not object to such an undertaking, the classical and profoundly philosophical necessity of which I do not ignore, either by referring to the factual difficulties it poses, to the labyrinths of empiricity or to the interminability of the analysis. For the empirical difficulties involved in isolating this ideal residue do not, in fact, exclude the possibility of a juridicial-theoretical process [*le procès juridico-théorique*] leading to an essential definition. And if one wishes to know what conditions are necessary for a promise, for instance, to be a promise, it ultimately matters little whether or not *in fact* a promise has ever existed, or whether one has ever been actually discovered which would fully and rigorously satisfy the requisite conditions. In any case, inasmuch as classically fact has been opposed to essence (or to principle), matters would become more complicated if the object named "speech act" (as well as the very enterprise of a theory of speech acts, in Austin's version) were to render such oppositions invalid. Nor will I object to the fact that certain concepts, which intervene under the names of "non-strict," or "metaphorical," "sarcastic," etc., are treated as though they were self-evident. Instead, I shall go directly to the "center" (since, as Searle has once again made perfectly clear, it is always the "center" that holds his interest), to the center of the question of essence or principle [*de droit*]. And I will confine myself for the moment to two arguments.

Firstly, it is in the name of *analogy,* underlined in my citation, that Searle justifies the idealizing method within the theory of *speech acts* when he speaks of the structure of illocutionary acts. He authorizes this procedure by drawing an analogy with the construction of models in "most" sciences. Let us pass over the fact that this fundamental theoretical preamble [*protocole*], which defines and delimits the entire enterprise, that this metalanguage on the different theoretical languages already involves a lax (or non-strict, if you prefer) recourse to a resemblance, indeed to a non-literal figure. Let us also pass over the enormous problem of the construction of "models" in the sciences, in *different* sciences at different moments of their history. To speak simply of "most" sciences is in this regard to resort to woolly approximations that are most surprising, especially in this particular place. But all this would hold us up too long. Let us consider solely a limit *of principle* that obtains in this analogy: namely, that by contrast with *all* the other sciences, the theory of speech acts has as its object—lest we forget—speech acts said to be ordinary in languages said to be natural. This fact, far from facilitating the process of abstraction and of idealization, which in turn is always a process of objectification, on the contrary limits it. The language of theory always leaves a residue that is neither formalizable nor idealizable in terms of that theory of language. Theoretical utterances are speech acts. Whether this fact is regarded as a privilege or as a limit of speech act theory, it ruins the analogical value (in the strict sense) between speech act theory and other theories. Not only is analogy between essentially heterogeneous theories not strictly legitimate, but the very utterance which poses, proposes, supposes, alleges such an analogy ultimately *refers* to an analogical or metaphorical utterance even if it is not in itself metaphorical. In Searle's terms, it is based *ultimately* on the metaphorical, the sarcastic, on the non-literal. And this is rather disturbing for an utterance that purports *to found the entire methodology* (abstraction, idealization, systematization, etc.) of the theory of speech acts.

This argument of principle concerns a structural *limit*. (In passing I note with astonishment that Searle chooses to ignore "marginal, fringe" cases. For these always constitute the most certain and most decisive indices wherever essential conditions are to be grasped. On this point at least, Searle does not follow the tradition, but in view of the fact that he does not call the overall logic of the traditional procedure into question, I view this merely as a slight inconsistency of an empiricist type). This argument concerning the structural limit is of the same kind as the set-argument a while back. Here, now, is an argument of another kind.

Secondly: the iterability of the mark does not leave any of the philosophical oppositions which govern the idealizing abstraction intact (for instance, serious/non-serious, literal/metaphorical or sarcastic, ordinary/parasitical, strict/non-strict, etc.). Iterability blurs a priori the dividing-line that passes between these opposed terms, "corrupting" it if you like, contaminating it parasitically, qua limit. What is re-markable about the mark includes the margin within the mark. The line delineating the margin can therefore never be determined rigorously, it is never pure and simple. The mark is re-markable in that it "is" also its margin. (This structure is analyzed in *Sec* and in its context; for instance—but not only—in the essays collected under the title, *Marges* [Margins], and which operate "marginally" from their very opening [*Tympan, La double séance, Glas,* etc.]. Even if it only threatens with a perpetually possible parasitism; this menace is inscribed a priori in the limit. It divides the dividing-line and its unity at once. Moreover, why (for whom) should this possibility appear as a menace, as a purely "negative" risk, as an "infelicity"? Once it is iterable, to be sure, a mark marked with a supposedly "positive" value ("serious," "literal," etc.) can be mimed, cited, transformed into an "exercise" or into "literature," even into a "lie"—that is, it can be made to carry its other, its "negative" double. But iterability is also, by the same token, the condition of the values said to be "positive." The simple fact is that this condition of possibility is structurally divided or "differing-deferring" [*différ-ante*].

But in this case, one will say, in view of the irreducibility and generality of this structure of iterability ("iterability looms large in both of these arguments," Sarl observes with apparent regret: but so it is with structures that are universal and necessary), will it not be susceptible of idealization, abstraction, simplification, purification? Does it not authorize an *overall* systematization [systématisation d'*ensemble*] which in turn will be vulnerable to the preceding objection? I would say that this is not the case: the unique character of this structure of iterability, or rather of this chain, since iterability can be supplemented by a variety of terms (such as *différance,* grapheme, trace, etc.), lies in the fact that, comprising identity *and* difference, repetition *and* alteration, etc., it renders the *project* of idealization possible without lending *"itself"* to any pure, simple, and idealizable conceptualization. No process [*procès*] or project of idealization is possible without iterability, and yet iterability "itself" cannot be idealized. For it comports an internal and impure limit that prevents it from being identified, synthesized, or re-appropriated, just as it excludes the reappropriation of that whose iteration it nonetheless broaches and breaches [*entame*].

But under such circumstances, one will reply, no scientific or philosophical theory of speech acts in the rigorous, serious, and pure sense would be possible. That is, indeed, the question. Or rather, it is what I am suggesting, at least as long as we continue to invoke the traditional model of theory as our reference. And it is because of this that I agree with Sarl that the "confrontation" here is not between two "prominent philosophical traditions" but between *the* tradition and its other, an other that is not even "its" other any longer. But this does not imply that all "theorization" is impossible. It merely de-limits a theorization that would seek to incorporate its object totally but can accomplish this only to a limited degree. This object, for example, would have to include the hierarchy of oppositional values. For it can hardly be denied that these value-oppositions constitute hierarchies, that they are posed and repeated as such by the very theory which claims to analyze, in all neutrality, their mere possibility. I am well aware of the fact that the speech acts theoretician does not, on moral grounds, advise us to prefer the serious to the nonserious, for instance, or the normal to the parasitic. Not, that is, in the sense of non-theoretical, ordinary language. But even prior to the hypothesis of such neutrality, the opposition serious/nonserious (sarcastic, etc.—but there are also other species of the nonserious), literal/metaphorical, ironic etc., cannot become the object of an analysis in the classical sense of the term: strict, rigorous, "serious," without one of the two terms, the serious or the literal, or even the strict, proceeding to determine the *value* of the theoretical discourse itself. This discourse thus finds itself an integral part—part and parcel, but also *partial*—of the object it claims to be analyzing. It can no longer be impartial or neutral, having been determined by the hierarchy even before the latter could be determined by it. A theoretical discourse of this (classical, traditional) type must indeed tend, in accordance with its intrinsic ethics and teleology, to produce speech acts that are in principle serious, literal, strict etc. The only way that speech act theory might escape this traditional definition would be for it to assert (theoretically and practically) the right of its own speech acts not to be serious, etc., or rather not *simply* serious, strict, literal. Has it done this up to now? Might it have escaped me? In all seriousness, I cannot exclude this possibility. But am I serious here?

Thus, it does not suffice merely to say that such oppositions are inherited, pre-critical philosophemes, dogmatically employed; or that the hierarchical trait governing the relation of one value to another has, from its inception, been blurred, lacking purity and rigor from the start. We must add this: the necessity, assumed by classical theory, of submitting itself to the very normativity and hierarchy that it purports to analyze, deprives such theory of precisely what it claims for itself: seriousness, scientificity, truth, philosophical value, etc. Because the model speech act of current speech act theory claims to be serious, it is normed by a part of its object and is therefore not impartial. It is not scientific and cannot be taken seriously. Which is what constitutes the drama of this family of theoreticians: the more they seek to produce serious utterances, the less they can be taken seriously. It is up to them whether they will take advantage of this opportunity to transform infelicity into delight [*jouissance*]. For example, by proclaiming: everything that we have said-written-done up to now wasn't really serious or strict; it was all a joke: sarcastic, even a bit ironic, parasitical, metaphorical, citational, cryptic, fictional, literary, insincere, etc. What force they would gain by doing this!! But will they take the risk? Will we have to take it for them? Why not?

Hasn't *Sec* indeed already done it? At the very moment of invoking "serious literal speech" to support the objection being advanced, Sarl might have foreseen that none of these values could be considered as self-evident in such a discussion. He might have foreseen this had he considered *Sec* as constituting part of the context of the discussion of *Sec*. He might have foreseen it had he read what is said there concerning the "suspicious status of the 'non-serious'" (already cited), but also point 1 of the introduction: ". . . the value of the notion of *literal meaning* [*sens propre*] appears more problematical than ever." It is not, of course, necessary to know or to adopt the conclusions of other writings on this subject, but it is necessary to take into account the fact that in this context, in *Sec,* the notion of "literality" or of the "serious" is posed as being problematical. Since this problematic character of the serious constitutes part of *Sec's* premises, can one legitimately, "seriously," oppose to it, qua dogma, what it seeks to call into question?

Let us return to our point of departure. It is, we see, no accident if Sarl has so laboriously sought out the "implicit"—having found nothing explicit to support the strange allegation that *Sec* was referring to "something *behind* the utterances," to "some inner pictures animating the visible signs." To reject the belief in "intentions" or "inner pictures" *behind* the utterances, however, does not amount to endorsing the belief in any simple adequation of the utterance to itself, or, in terms that are strictly those of Sarl, in an adequation between "the intention and its expression" in an ideal utterance which would be the "realization" of the intention. Even were I to accept this expressionist or representationalist description of language; even were I to consider the utterance as the "realization" of an "intention," I would at the very least have to recall that the dehiscence already discussed does not intervene, primarily, between an "intention" and an "expression," but already, from the start, as an effect of iterability within each of these putative instances. And although I am convinced that this problem is even more complex than described, I shall limit myself to what has been said in order not to stray too far from the *Reply* and its code.

This leads me to the second "illusion" diagnosed by Sarl, the "explicit" one this time. According to *Sec*—so Sarl—"intentions must all be conscious" (p. 202). Confronted with this assertion I must confess that I had to rub my eyes. Was I dreaming? Had I misread? Mistranslated? Was the text suddenly becoming sarcastic? Or even, as I had just wished, ironic? Was it all a joke? Was the patented theoretician—or theoreticians—of speech acts calling us to task for forgetting the existence of the unconscious? What a fake-out, leaving me flat-footed in the camp of those insufficiently aware of the unsconscious! I always love to watch a good fake-out, even if it's at my expense. But my delight, unfortunately, is short-lived. I cannot imagine how Sam Weber is going to translate "fake-out." For his benefit let me specify that, ever since my adolescence, I have understood the word above all as a soccer term, denoting an active ruse designed to surprise one's opponent by catching him off balance. Littré, however, lists the following, which can be used as necessary: "CONTRE-PIED 1. Hunting term. The trail followed by the prey and which the dogs, led astray, take instead of the new trail upon which the animal continues. To follow the *contre-pied* is to follow tracks in the wrong direction. 2. Fig. The contrary of something. 'People have taken precisely the *contre-pied* of the will.' La Fontaine."

To claim that for *Sec* all intentions are conscious is to read *à contre-pied,* fake(d) out, in the sense of Littré. For not only does *Sec* say that all intentions are *not* conscious: it says that *no* intention can *ever* be fully conscious, or actually present to itself. Nor is this so different from Austin, who in "Three Ways of Spilling Ink" asserted, "the only general rule is that the illumination [shed by intention] is always *limited,* and that in several ways."

More systematically, *Sec's* enterprise is in principle designed to demonstrate a type of "structural unconscious" (p. 18) which seems alien, if not incompatible with speech act theory given its current axiomatics. The latter seem constructed in order to keep the hypothesis of such an Unconscious at a safe distance, as though it were a giant Parasite. I am speaking here, briefly, summarily, but in a direct and unequivocal manner of the Unconscious—of what is still designated by this name in psychoanalysis—and of its relation to graphematics in general and to speech in particular. I am not speaking of unconsciousness in the sense that Sarl seems to envisage, as a kind of lateral, virtual potential of consciousness. What is at stake in the debate initiated by *Sec* situates itself in this area as well, and it involves ethical and political consequences to which we shall doubtless have occasion to return. Each time that the question of the "ethical and teleological discourse of consciousness" (ibid.) arises, it is in an effort to uncover and to break the security-lock which, from *within the system*—inside of the prevailing model of speech acts that governs the current theory in its most coherent and even most productive operation—condemns the unconscious as one bars access to a forbidden place. By placing under lock and key, or by sealing off; here, by prohibiting that the Unconscious—what may still be called the Unconscious—*be taken seriously;* be taken seriously, that is, *in (as) a manner of speaking,* up to and including its capacity for making jokes. The Unconscious not only as the great Parasite of every ideal model of a speech act (simple, serious, literal, strict, etc.), but the Unconscious as that parasite which subverts and dis-plays [*déjoue*], parasitically, even the concept of parasite itself as it is used in the theoretical strategy envisaged by Austin or by Searle. This is what *Sec* was aiming at. If the question of a bond between intention and consciousness is indeed raised there, it is solely insofar as Austin deems that bond indispensable in order to maintain precisely what *Sec* criticizes. Who will be persuaded that Austin took *this Unconscious* into account in his analysis of speech acts? And who will be persuaded that Searle is here doing what Austin failed to? Confining myself to the analysis of the ideal structure of illocutionary acts and to the passage from *Speech Acts* that has already been cited, I wish only to recall that the conditions of a "strict and literal" speech act, here a promise, included the following: the exclusion of all "parasites," and the necessity that speaker and hearer be "conscious of what they are doing." And in the *Reply* itself this condition is reiterated at the very moment that Sarl, without convincing anyone, claims to be taking a certain unconsciousness into account. In fact what is thereby evoked is only a potential, limited consciousness that has not yet become thematically self-conscious; and above all Sarl reminds us that we must not "separate" (but had anyone done this?) "conscious states" on the one hand, from operations of writing and of speaking on the other. I underline: "This illusion [the implicit one] is related to the second, which is that intentions must all be conscious. But in fact rather few of one's intentions are ever brought to consciousness as intentions. *Speaking and writing are indeed conscious* intentional activities, but the intentional aspect of illocutionary acts does not imply that there is a separate set of conscious states apart from simply writing and speaking" (p. 202). It could not be more clearly stated that writing and speaking are considered to be conscious activities through and through and structurally. As for the "structural unconscious" proposed by *Sec,* it was at least supposed *to situate* the possibility of articulating a general graphematics based not on an axiomatics confined to the "psychology" or the "phenomenology" of consciousness, but on what for instance and for the instant can be called the Unconscious. This Unconscious is absolutely excluded by the axiomatics (which is also an axiology) of current speech act theory, in particular as formulated by Searle. To give only one example: suppose that I seriously promise to criticize implacably each of Sarl's theses. If I consult *Speech Acts* (ch. 3, p. 58), I discover that such a promise has no meaning. It is a *threat or warning,* and there is a "crucial distinction between promises on the one hand and threats on the other." Wherein does the crucial, and hence insurmountable distinction consist? In the fact "that a promise is a pledge to do something for you, not to you; but a threat is a pledge to do something to you, not for you. A promise is defective if the thing promised is something the promisee does not want done; and it is further defective if the promisor does not believe the promisee wants it done, since a non-defective promise must be intended as a promise and not as a threat or warning.

. . . The promisee wishes (needs, desires, etc.) that something be done, and the promisor *is aware* of this wish (need, desire, etc.)" (my emphasis). And after an examination of apparent counter-examples, defined as "derivative from genuine promises," sometimes qua "emphatic denial," Searle then concludes: ". . . if a purported promise is to be non-defective, the thing promised must be something the hearer wants done, or considers to be in his interest, or would prefer being done to not being done, etc; and the speaker *must be aware of or believe or know*, etc., that this is the case" (my emphasis). This description ultimately excludes every criterion other than the distinct, determining, and determinable consciousness of the intentions, desires, or needs involved. The rigorous distinction between promise and warning or threat, for instance, is established only by this expedient. Yet what would happen if in promising to be critical I should then provide everything that Sarl's Unconscious desires, for reasons which remain to be analyzed, and that it does its best to provoke? Would my "promise," in such a case, be a promise, a warning or even a threat? Searle might respond that it would constitute a threat to Sarl's consciousness, and a promise for the unconscious. There would thus be two speech acts in a single utterance. How is this possible? And what if Sarl *desired* to be threatened? And what if everything that is given to please or in response to a desire, as well as everything that one promises to give, were structurally ambivalent? What if the gift were always poisoned (gift/ *Gift*) in a manner so as to prevent any *simple* logic (desire/non-desire, for example) from being able to decide, i.e. to distinguish between the two or to determine their meaning univocally? And if, now, I were unable *to know* (to "be aware of or believe or know," as *Speech Acts* puts it) what it is that Sarl as speaker consciously or unconsciously desires, would I not be incapable as speaker either of promising or of threatening to criticize? What is the unity or identity of the speaker? Is he responsible for speech acts dictated by his unconscious? Mine, for instance, might well wish to please Sarl by gratifying the wish to be criticized; or it might want to cause Sarl unhappiness by refusing to be critical; or to please Sarl by being uncritical and cause pain by being critical; or to promise Sarl a threat or to threaten with a promise; also to offer myself as a target for criticism by taking pleasure in saying things that are "obviously false," inviting Sarl to delight in my weakness or to enjoy the exhibition from above, etc. All that simply to suggest, briefly, that it is sufficient merely to introduce, into the manger of speech acts, a few wolves of the type "indecidability" (of the *pharmakon,* of the *gift,* of the supplement, of the hymen) or of the type "unconscious" (an unconscious pleasure may be experienced as pain, according to *Beyond the Pleasure Principle),* of the type "primary masochism," etc., for the shepherd to lose track of this flock: one is no longer certain where to find the identity of the "speaker" or the "hearer" (visibly identified with the conscious ego), where to find the identity of an intention (desire or non-desire, love or hate, pleasure or suffering) or of an effect (pleasure or non-pleasure, advantage or disadvantage, etc.). This is only another reason why, at the "origin" of every speech act, there can only be Societies which are (more or less) anonymous, with limited responsibility or liability—Sarl—a multitude of instances, if not of "subjects," of meanings highly vulnerable to parasitism—all phenomena that the "conscious ego" of the speaker and the hearer (the ultimate instances of speech act theory) is incapable of incorporating as such and which, to tell the truth, it does everything to exclude. Without ever fully succeeding, since incorporation, in "psychoanalytical" terms, requires that the defending body of the subject make place "inside" for that which it excludes. And yet, how can the theory of speech acts in its current state account for this kind of incorporation, which nevertheless registers essential effects on all language? Especially in view of the highly simplistic and univocal manner in which the theory deals with distinction and exclusion! At the end of the passage quoted a moment ago on the conditions of *genuine* promises, we read the following: "I think a more elegant and exact formulation of this condition would probably require the introduction of technical terminology of the welfare economics sort." Perhaps. But economics—even "welfare" economics— is not one domain among others or a domain whose laws have already been recognized. An economics taking account of effects of iterability, inasmuch as they are inseparable from the economy of (what must still be called) the Unconscious as well as from a graphematics of undecidables, an economics calling into question the entire traditional philosophy of the *oikos*—of the *propre:* the "own," "ownership," "property"—as well as the laws that have governed it would not only be very different from "welfare economics": it would also be far removed from furnishing speech acts theory with "more elegant" formulations or a "technical terminology." Rather, it would provoke its general transformation.

Sarl will probably assert that I have examined all sorts of contextual variables or possible corruptions of the promise. None of all that, Sarl will then say, contradicts the following proposition: if a promise (genuine, serious, univocal, strict) were to take place (even if there never was such a thing), it would have to involve a speaker who is conscious with regard to a hearer who is equally conscious and desirous of what is promised to him. Such a proposition, Sarl might then conclude, in the very poverty of its logical armature, is unassailable; it constitutes part of the semantic-axiomatic analysis of the concept of promise. Let us grant this. It would then, however, also have to be granted that this entire machinery of idealization firstly implies ("logically," Sarl would say) and concerns speakers and hearers only inasmuch as they are "conscious egos," and secondly presupposes the univocity of ethical-teleological values in language. To this extent, within the very *limited* and apparently well-founded scope of such phenomena, would not the coherence of this proposition be unassailable? It would seem to fit into the great tradition of Kant and of Husserl. Its only "defect," however, is that these "phenomena" are not phenomena: they never appear as such. The same holds for the effect, "conscious ego," which, however limited it may be, can never be isolated ideally in its pure identity; the reasons for this I have already discussed above: they involve that iterability which ruins (even ideally) the very identity it renders possible. (I refer here to the end of the second section of *Sec,* dealing with the "ethical and teleological discourse of consciousness" and with

76

speech acts qua "effects.") All this amounts to the following: the hypothesis of possibility 1, with which we are still concerned ("the author says what he means"), cannot even be formulated ideally. Except, that is, under the heading of "fiction," about which I could not say whether or not it would be serious, or external to the field of other types of fiction (in particular, to that of literature), but which would certainly lead to the following question: in what way, or to what extent does traditional philosophical discourse, and that of speech act theory in particular, derive from fiction? Is it capable of assuming full responsibility for such fictional discourse, or of positing itself as such, and if so, how? etc. But I do not believe that this latter concept of fiction would be very compatible with Searle's thematics of fiction.

Let us now proceed to possibility 2, still situated within the *initial phase*.

S

Second Possibility. What hitherto has been excluded, as though it were an accident: "corruption," a word that does not imply, as Sarl will emphasize a bit farther on with regard to "parasitical," "non-serious," "empty," etc., *any* pejorative connotation, or even any value judgment, be it ethical or axiological in general. Let us grant, therefore (*concesso non dato*, for such an admission is not easy, given a word such as "corruption"), that the qualification of "corrupt" does not imply any evaluation of this type, and let us read the following: "To the extent that the author says what he means the text is the expression of his intentions. It is always possible that he may not have said what he meant or that the text may have become corrupt in some way; but exactly parallel considerations apply to spoken discourse. The situation as regards intentionality is exactly the same for the written word as it is for the spoken . . ."(p. 202).

I shall not return to this "parallel" or identity ("exactly parallel," "exactly the same"). Once more, "it reapplies" as an argument from/to-*Sec*. It is the nerve of the demonstration in *Sec* and it takes nerve to raise it as an objection to *Sec*. As for the inadequation between meaning and saying, as well as the alleged "corruption" of the text, once they have been acknowledged to be "always possible," their exclusion, whether on provisional-methodological, or on theoretical grounds, constitutes the very object of the critique proposed by *Sec*. A corruption that is "always possible" cannot be a mere extrinsic accident supervening on a structure that is original and pure, one that can be purged of what thus happens to it. The purportedly "ideal" structure must necessarily be such that this corruption will be "always possible." This *possibility* constitutes part of the *necessary* traits of the purportedly ideal structure. The ("ideal") description of this structure should thus include, and not exclude, this possibility, whereby "include" here does not simply mean "to incorporate" it (in the psychoanalytical sense, i.e., retaining the object within itself but as something excluded, as a foreign body which is impossible to assimilate and must be rejected: this is what happens with Austin and Searle when they speak of all the "negative" effects: corruption, infelicities, parasites, etc.). What must be included in the description, i.e., in *what* is described, but also in the practical discourse, in the *writing that describes*, is not merely the factual reality of corruption and of alteration [*de l'écart*], but corrupt*ability* (to which it would be better henceforth not to give this name, which implies generally a pathological dysfunction, a degeneration or an ethical-political defect) and dissocia*bility*, traits tied to itera*bility*, which *Sec* proposes to account for. That can only be done if the "-bility" (and not the lability) is recognized from the *inception* on [dès l'*entame*] as broached and breached [*entamée*] in its "origin" by itera*bility*.

2. *Second Phase.* Just as only a few lines are devoted to what Sarl feels justified in excluding under the rubric of corruption and of alteration, so only seven or eight lines are consecrated to contextual variations ("When we come to the question of context . . ." p. 202) after they have been excluded from the long examination of possibilities 1 and 2. Shall we say that such a lack of interest in the effects of context marks a corruption or degeneration of the Austinian heritage, or an alteration of Austin's intentions, of what he meant to say? No, because what Austin said and did was sufficiently ambiguous, in its iterability, to authorize such an exclusion *as well*. If one were fond of this word, and of the evaluation it carries with it, one would have to say that corruptability, too, is part of the heritage and of its legitimation.

Thus, when Sarl arrives at context, it is to say things that would be simply trivial were they not above all dubious. One might even, in fact, depending on the context, assert precisely the contrary of what is stated in the lines that I will begin by citing, underlining certain of the words: "When we come to the question of *context*, as Derrida is aware, the situation really is quite different for writing than it is for speech. In speech one can invoke all sorts of *features of the context* which are not possible to use in writing intended for absent receivers, without explicitly *representing these features in the text*. That is why verbatim *transcripts* of conversations are so hard to interpret. In conversation a great deal can be *communicated* without being made explicit in the sentence uttered" (pp. 202–3).

Considering that I have already essentially addressed this question, I shall simply add several remarks dealing specifically with this paragraph.

1. How can a theoretician of speech acts treat a contextual criterion as though it were of secondary importance, or at least as a criterion that can be excluded or deferred from consideration without impairing the latter? *Either* the contextual difference changes everything, because it determines what it determines *from within*: in this case, it can hardly be bracketed, even provisionally. *Or* it leaves certain aspects intact, and this signifies that these aspects can always separate themselves from the allegedly "original" context in order to export or to graft themselves elsewhere while continuing to function in one way or another, thus confirming the "graphematic" thesis of *Sec*. In order that this either/or not be an alternative or an insurmountable logical contradiction, the value of context must be reelaborated by means of a new logic, of a graphematics of iterability. Such a

reelaboration, however, does not appear to me to be possible in accordance with the theoretical axiomatics of Austin and of Searle. It is this reelaboration that *Sec* endeavors to initiate. In passages such as the following, which I re-cite: "Every sign, linguistic or non-linguistic, spoken or written (in the current sense of this opposition), in a small or large unit, can . . . break with every given context, engendering an infinity of new contexts in a manner which is absolutely illimitable. This does not imply that the mark is valid outside of a context, but on the contrary that there are only contexts without any center or absolute anchoring [*ancrage*]." (pp. 185–86). I shall take advantage of this citation to acknowledge that the word "engendering" is not sufficiently rigorous. It might, in an insufficiently explicit context, falsify or "corrupt" (!) the dominant argument of *Sec*. It would have been better and more precise to have said "engendering *and* inscribing itself," or being inscribed *in*, new contexts. For a context never creates itself *ex nihilo*; no mark can create or engender a context on its own, much less dominate it. This limit, this finitude is the condition under which contextual transformation remains an always open possibility.

2. Sarl adheres to a narrow definition of writing as the *transcription* or *representation* of speech. He thereby adheres to a certain interpretation of phonetic writing, indeed to the alphabetic model, to the *a b c*'s of logo-phonocentrism. Hence, his *discriminating* example: "verbatim transcripts of conversations. . . ." This model of writing is precisely called into question in *Sec* (and elsewhere).

3. Sarl adheres to a definition of language as *communication*, in the sense of the communication of a *content* ("a great deal can be communicated . . ."). This definition is precisely called into question in *Sec* (and elsewhere).

4. Sarl adheres to a definition of the text as the contents of an oral utterance, whether it is directly "present" or merely transcribed (". . . representing these features in the text"). This definition of the text is precisely called into question in *Sec* (and elsewhere).

t

That the import of context can never be dissociated from the analysis of a text, and that despite or because of this a context is always transformative-transformable, exportative-exportable—all this is exemplified in the following paragraph of the *Reply*, one that will permit me to cite once again, without the slightest modesty: "Derrida has a distressing penchant for saying things that are obviously false." In the example and demonstration given to support this assertion, Sarl *cuts, avoids, omits*: cutting one of the examples of *Sec* out of its dominant or most determining context; avoiding to cite more than three words; omitting the most "important" word, Sarl then hastens to apply the scheme prefabricated in *Speech Acts* around the distinction—itself rather laborious and problematical—of *mention* and *use*. This procedure may not correspond to a conscious, deliberate intention, or even to any intention at all. Austin would surely ask: "Intentionally?" "Deliberately?" "On purpose?" But the fact remains and it can be analyzed. As might be expected, I choose to cite at length. Because of my oath to act in good faith and with all seriousness, to be sure, but also, as some will doubtless suspect, to endow the promised criticism with a stronger pertinence. I shall begin, once again, with the *Reply*.

> Derrida has a distressing [why distressing? for whom?] penchant for saying things that are obviously false. I will discuss several instances in the next section but one deserves special mention at this point. He says the meaning-less example of ungrammatical French, "le vert est ou," means (*signifie*) one thing anyhow, it means an example of ungrammaticality. But this is a simple confusion. The sequence "le vert est ou" does not MEAN an example of un-grammaticality, it does not mean anything, rather it IS an example of ungram-maticality. The relation of meaning is not to be confused with instantiation. This mistake is important because it is part of his generally mistaken account of the nature of quotation, and his failure to understand the distinction be-tween use and mention. The sequence "le vert est ou" can indeed be *men-tioned* as an example of ungrammaticality, but to mention it is not the same as to *use* it. In this example it is not used to mean anything; indeed it is not used at all. (p. 203)

I now cite the passage from *Sec* which is thus incriminated after having been precipitously abstracted and furiously truncated:

> Thus, it is solely in a context determined by a will to know, by an epistemic intention, by a conscious relation to the object as cognitive object within a horizon of truth, solely in this oriented contextual field is "the green is ei-ther" unacceptable. But as "the green is either" or "abracadabra" do not con-stitute their context by themselves, nothing prevents them from functioning in another context as signifying marks (or indices, as Husserl would say). Not only in contingent cases such as a translation from German into French, which would endow "the green is either" with grammaticality, since "either" (*oder*) becomes for the ear "where" [*où*] (a spatial mark). "Where has the green gone (of the lawn: the green is where)," "Where is the glass gone in which I wanted to give you something to drink?" [*Où est passé le verre dans lequel je voulais vous donner à boire?*] But even "the green is either" itself still signifies an *example of agrammaticality*. And this is the possibility on which I want to insist: the possibility of disengagement and citational graft which belongs to the structure of every mark, spoken or written, and which constitutes every mark in writing before and outside of every horizon of semio-linguistic communication; in writing, which is to say in the possibility of its functioning being cut off, at a certain point, from its "original" desire-to-say-what-one-means [*vouloir-dire*] and from its participation in a saturable and constraining context. (p. 12)

The "confrontation" of the two citations ought to be clear enough. As clear as the operation undertaken by Sarl. And yet, I shall insist. In what way is the "confu-sion" "mentioned" by Sarl most of all the one into which Sarl cannot avoid rush-ing? What are the first signs of this?

To begin with, instead of quoting even a single sentence of the paragraph without interruption, the citation has been cut precisely before the one little word that suffices to ruin the point Sarl is trying to make. Where in *Sec* we can read, and I underline, "But even 'the green is either' *still* signifies *an example of agrammaticality,"* [. . . signifie *encore exemple d'agrammaticalité*], Sarl cuts out the *encore*, which I have just underlined and which transforms the utterance entirely. *"Signifie encore"* still signifies that yet another, supplementary meaning can be added, grafted onto the first, even onto a non-meaning. It is this possibility of the graft that is manifestly and principally in question throughout this paragraph. The "encore" that Sarl blissfully forgets also marks the fact that the supplementary graft has been added to another mark which itself, of course, does not "originally" [*primitivement*] signify an "example of agrammaticality," but which also does not constitute an authentic, elementary, initial, normal state of the mark existing *before* the graft.

To avoid a confusion in which distinct interests play their part—a confusion that I was naive enough to believe would have been excluded by a context as clear and as insistent as this one—I should perhaps have taken a supplementary precaution for Sarl's sake. I should have followed an indication given by Searle in *Speech Acts*, precisely in the chapter on *Use and Mention*.[9] I should perhaps have multiplied the quotation marks and written: "the green is either" indeed signifies nothing (to the extent, at least, to which signification or meaning is bound to discursive grammaticality, something that is by no means obligatory), but the citation of the (mentioning) phrase ". . . "the green is either" . . ." can also, as a citational reference, signify *in addition (encore)*: "this is an example of agrammaticality," this example of agrammaticality " " "the green is either" " " proving unmistakably, by virtue of its functioning, that a graft is always possible; just as every phrase endowed with grammaticality that is cited in a certain context, for example in a grammmar book, can *also* signify (*encore*): I am an example of grammar. Yet even had I done all this, would I have thus prevented (and why, after all, should one even try?) a phrase from being cut, or a graft from being torn out of context? Would I have appeased Sarl's anger at the confusion of "use" and "mention," treated as a radical evil, which I agree it may very well be, although I don't have the time here to elaborate why (beyond noting that if, in fact, good and evil are involved, it is because use and mention are always susceptible of being confused). Thus, even if I had been able to calm Sarl down, I would certainly have had no luck with Searle, who, in the same chapter of *Speech Acts*, mounts a crusade against that "philosophy of language" which leads to the interminable multiplication of quotation marks upon quotation marks. He finds this point of view "absurd" and he adds (but why?) that "it is not harmlessly so," having "infected other areas of the philosophy of language."[10] What is there in a theory that can be harmful and infectious? I can only advise all those interested in such matters of public health and welfare, and in particular in distinctions such as "use" and "mention" or any of the others, no less fraught with concern and passion, to read the entire chapter attentively. The recourse, there, to what is called "normal use" (are these quotation marks necessary or superfluous?) in order to distinguish between what "has its normal use" and what "does not have its normal use" (p. 74) is as stubborn and insistent as the criterion between normal and not-normal is essentially elusive. To say, for instance, that an expression which has become an object of discourse or a citation "is not being used normally" (p. 75), is to make an assertion that requires justifications not to be found in the demonstration of Searle. And if, as he says, "we already have perfectly adequate use-mention conventions" (p. 76), it is hard to see how such harmful and infectious absurdities might arise, harmful and dangerous in the sense that masturbation or writing seemed so to Rousseau (I want to suggest that this analogy is not entirely artificial, or at least no more so than quotation marks around quotation marks, or masturbation "itself").

If conventions are, in fact, never entirely adequate; if the opposition of "normal" and "abnormal" will always be lacking in rigor and purity; if language can always "normally" become its own "abnormal" object, does this not derive from the structural iterability of the mark? The graft, by definition, and herein no different from the parasite, is never *simply* alien to and separable from the body to which it has been transplanted or which it already haunts [*hante*]. This graft, which is discussed in the paragraph butchered by Sarl, also defines (for instance) the relation between "use" and "mention." This possibility must be taken into account. Its mode is defined as the obsession [*la hantise*] of the graft.

I shall not dwell on this for fear of further trying the reader's patience. I will restrict myself to a single example, in order to test the distinction between "use" and "mention," and will pose a single question. *"Iter,"* in the subtitle of *Sec,* and hence everywhere else, is *also* [*encore*] a citation. The word appears for the "first time" in the title of the section devoted to Austin, which we shall discuss in a moment. I recall this title: *"Parasites. Iter, Of Writing: That It Perhaps Does Not Exist."* I cannot here give an exhaustive commentary on this subtitle. Whether Sarl (or any other reader) may have recognized it or not—and this double possibility already poses all kinds of problems—there is also a citation there, more or less cryptic ("perhaps" cryptic), more or less parodic, ironic, altered, lateral and literal, but at the same time very serious (as serious as the question concerning the proof of the existence of God): a citation of the fifth of Descartes' *Metaphysical Meditations.* But is it a citation in the strict sense? There are no quotation marks. And yet, if the word "iter" is itself here an iteration without quotation marks, it is difficult, given the context—that of a text addressed to a distinguished gathering of specialists of "Philosophy in the French Language" (the Congress in Montreal)—not to speak here of a citation. But for the moment this is of little matter, for the question lies elsewhere. I cite the title of Descartes: *De essentiâ rerum materialum; et iterum de Deo, quod existat,* which is translated in French as: *De l'essence des choses matérielles; et derechef de Dieu, qu'il existe* [*On the Essence of Material Things; And Likewise of God, That He Exists*]. The latter part of the title, beginning with *iterum,* is, as is well known, a subsequent addition of Descartes, who thus returned to his original title, repeating and changing it in this way, augmenting and completing it with a supplementary *iterum*. I cannot here take up again the classical debate and pursue the question—this time referring to our discussion of the structure of iterability—of why Descartes deemed it necessary to demonstrate the existence of God for a second time, after the proof had already seemed established according to the order of reasons in the third *Meditation*. Had I room for it here, I would endeavor to shift the question out of the necessary and rigorous debate held some twenty years ago and involving certain great Descartes scholars (Guéroult, Gouhier, Brunschwig), and draw it toward the regions in which we have been navigating. What of *use* and *mention* in the case (unique or not?) of the Divine name? What, in such a case, of reference and of citation? What shall we think of the possibility or even of the necessity of repeating the same demonstration several times, or rather of multiplying the demonstrations in view of the same conclusion, concerning the same object? And this precisely where the object concerned (God) is held to be beyond all doubt and the ultimate guarantee (being unique, irreplaceable, beyond all substitution, both *absolutely repeatable* and *unrepeatable)* of all certitude, all proof, all truth? What is repetition—or the iteration of "iterum"—in this exemplary case, if this exemplariness is both that of the unique and that of the repeatable? What does its possibility or its necessity imply, in particular concerning the event of language and, in the narrow sense or not, that of writing? In substituting "of writing" for "of God," *Sec* has not merely replaced one word by another, one meaning or finite being by another which would be its equivalent (or not): *Sec* names writing in this place where the iterability of the proof (of God's existence) *produces writing,* drawing the name of God (of the infinite Being) into a graphematic drift [*dérive*] that excludes (for instance) any decision as to whether God is more than the name of God, whether the "name of God" refers to God or to the name of God, whether it signifies "normally" or "cites," etc., God being here, *qua* writing, what at the same time renders possible and impossible, probable and improbable oppositions such as that of the "normal" and the citational or the parasitical, the serious and the non-serious, the strict and the non-strict or less strict (it all amounting, as I have tried to show elsewhere, to a *différance* of *stricture*). But let's leave all that. The "perhaps" of the "that it perhaps does not exist" does not oppose the status of writing to that of God, who, Himself, should certainly exist. It draws the consequences from what has just been said about God himself and about existence in general, in its relation to the name and to the reference. In leaving the existence of writing undecidable, the "perhaps" marks the fact that the "possibility" of graphematics places writing (and the rest) outside the authority of ontological discourse, outside the alternative of existence and non-existence, which in turn always supposes a simple discourse capable of deciding between presence and/or absence. The rest of the trace, its remains [*restance*] are neither present nor absent. They escape the jurisdiction of all ontotheological discourse even if they render the latter at times possible.

As for the function of the word "parasites" (in the plural), as in the other title, "Signatures," it designates *both* (thus already functioning parasitically) parasites in general (phenomena of language treated in this section of *Sec* and in the works of Austin) *and* what immediately follows in the title, namely an example, an event of parasitism, that of one title by another (which hence is no longer quite a title), the parasitism of the famous title borrowed from [*prêté à*] *René Descartes,* a title that had already parasited itself, as we just saw. In view of this parasitism, effected *in* and *by* a discourse on parasitism, are we not justified in considering the entire chapter, the entire discussion of Austin, as only an exercise in parody designed to cause serious philosophical discourse to skid towards literary play? Unless, that is, this seriousness were already the para-site of such play, a situation which could have the most serious consequences for the serious. But—one may enjoin—if he has discussed Austin solely in order to play games with Descartes' titles, it's not serious and there is no theoretical issue worthy of discussion: he is evading the discussion. This might be true: I detest discussions, their subtleties and ratiocinations. But I still have to ask myself how it can be explained that such a frivolous game, doing its best to avoid all discussion, could have involved and fascinated other "philosophers" (from the very first day on), responsible theoreticians aware of being very serious and assuming their discourse? How could such thinkers have been moved to argue so seriously, even nervously, against a kind of game which they were the first, if not the only ones, to take so seriously, while at the same time being unable to take into account (but *that* can't be serious) the structure of utterances such as titles and subtitles, unable to recognize the parasitism that they are so intent on flushing out wherever it may be? Who, or what, is responsible?

But let's leave all that. What is a title anyway? Is it a normal speech act? Can one imagine a sequence without a title, etc.? Such sophisticated considerations could occupy us for some time. But here is the promised question: Does *"Parasites. Iter, Of Writing: That It Perhaps Does Not Exist"* involve *use* or *mention?* This question can no longer be confined to this sequence. It concerns everything that surrounds the sequence, and that it, in turn, involves, frames, determines, contaminates. And if one responds that this is a case where we have both at once (*use* and *mention*), intermingled or interwoven, I can only reiterate: where is the dividing-line between the two? Can it be rigorously located? I shall wait patiently for an answer. And if this title is judged (but on what grounds?) to be too complex, perverse, or singular; if it is considered not entitled to be a title because it is both the object and the definition of the text that follows it, producer and product, seminal and fertilized, then I shall settle for an answer to the same question, bearing this time on a title that is apparently simpler, for instance *Speech Acts.* Or *Limited Inc,* which aside from its use-value in the legal-commercial code that marks the common bond linking England and the United States (Oxford and Berkeley), also *mentions* in translation a seal related to the French code (s.a.r.l.);[11] *condenses* allusions to the internal regulation through which the capitalist system seeks to limit concentration and decision-making power in order to protect itself against its own "crisis"; *entails* everything said by psychoanalysis about incorporation, about the *limit* between incorporation and non-incorporation, incorporation and introjection in the work of mourning (and in work generally), a limit in which I have been much interested during these last years, with the result that texts such as *Glas* and *Fors* (two untranslatable titles) become, in principle, inseparable from our debate and indispensable for a minimal reading of the title *Limited Inc.* And hence, of all the rest: et cetera.

u

"Derrida's Austin" is the title of the second section of the *Reply.* The way in which Sarl's "Derrida's Austin" presents itself is familiar enough by now: "I believe he [Derrida] has misunderstood Austin in several crucial ways and the internal weaknesses in his argument are closely tied to these misunderstandings. In this section therefore I will very briefly summarize his critique and then simply list the major misunderstandings and mistakes" (p. 203).

Although it is overloaded, because or despite of its reduced dimensions, Sarl's "Derrida's Austin" races ahead. This is always a risky business on roads that aren't straight, but I won't belabor this word of warning. If the summary is "very brief," whose fault is it? Concerning this very brief summary I shall have only two things to say, neither of which bear on its brevity.

1. Before proposing a more gradual and more patient analysis, I recall, for the sake of better determining a context that Sarl has done everything to obliterate, that the relation of *Sec* to Austin is far from being simple or simply critical as Sarl would like to suggest. I have already pointed out that at the beginning of section III four reasons are mentioned to explain why Austin's undertaking can be regarded as being new, necessary, and fecund, both in itself and in the developments that it has provoked. The arguments of *Sec* were meant less to criticize individual analyses of Austin than to show in what respects the "general doctrine" he says he "is not going into" could not be a simple *extension,* a development that might be postponed for strategic or methodological reasons, but that on the contrary it would have to entail a reelaboration of the axiomatics or of the premises themselves. Sarl's accusation notwithstanding, *Sec* indicates with all clarity that the exclusions practiced by Austin *present themselves as* procedures of strategic or methodological suspension, even though, as I shall endeavor to show later, such a strategy is fraught with metaphysical presupposition. But concerning the strategic or methodological *intention* there is no misunderstanding in *Sec.* In this regard Sarl's charge does not bear the slightest examination, such as, for instance, the citation of this passage (one among others):

> Now it is highly significant that Austin rejects and defers that "general theory" on at least two occasions, specifically in the Second Lecture. I leave aside the first exclusion: "I am not going into the general doctrine here: in many such cases we may even say the act was 'void' (or voidable for duress or undue influence) and so forth. Now I suppose some very general high-level doctrine might embrace both what we have called infelicities *and* these other 'unhappy' features of the doing of actions—in our case actions containing a

performative utterance—in a single doctrine: but we are not including this kind of unhappiness—we must just remember, though, that features of this sort can *and do constantly obtrude* into any case we are discussing. Features of this sort would normally come under the heading of 'extenuating circumstances' or of 'factors reducing or abrogating the agent's responsibility', and so on" (p. 21, my emphasis). The second case of this exclusion concerns our subject more directly. *(Sec,* p. 16)

How could anything be clearer as to what is here "highly significant," namely: a. the purportedly methodological character of an exclusion (referring to a "general doctrine" of action or acts while failing to submit this value of the *act* in general to those fundamental deconstructive questions necessitated, in my view, by the graphematics of iterability. Austin argues as though he knew what an act is). b. the difficulty (here only suggested, but rendered explicit by the entire context) in following Austin when he undertakes to exclude provisionally "these other 'unhappy' features in the doing of actions" which not only "can" always occur, but which, as he too must admit, "*do constantly obtrude* into any particular case we are discussing." I have discussed this matter above and I shall return to it.

2. It is in dealing with the "second exclusion," still within that "very brief" initial summary of *Sec,* that Sarl gravely *falsifies* matters. I note here that I seem to have become infected by Sarl's style: this is the first time, I believe, that I have ever accused anyone of deception, or of being deceived. Since the entire discussion rests upon this massive falsification, it should suffice to re-cite *Sec* to make short shrift of the problem. First, I shall cite the *Reply:* "More to the point [! I would specify that the exclamation-point were mine, were there not, among other difficulties involved in signing for an exclamation-point, that requiring me to mention here, cryptically (*sous crypte*), another text apparently "signed" by me on the exclamation-point ("!"), for instance in Mallarmé, which should serve as an extenuating circumstance reducing or abrogating my responsibility; and Sarl will henceforth scarcely be able to deny Austin's recourse, in the above citation, to responsible intentionality and to ethical-juridical value-judgments!], according to Derrida, Austin excludes the possibility that performative utterances (and a priori every other utterance) can be quoted. Derrida makes this extraordinary charge on the grounds that Austin has excluded fictional discourse. . . ." (p. 203).

More to the point! Naturally, I defy anyone to find anything in *Sec* that would sustain this "extraordinary charge," which Sarl charges me with charging Austin. But not only does *Sec* never do anything of the sort: it *begins,* on the contrary, by recalling that Austin evokes the possibility of a performative being cited (and a fortiori of other utterances as well), and that he is hence aware, in a certain way, of this as a constant possibility. This is indisputable—it is the *abc's* of our reading—and the only question at stake concerns the manner in which Austin takes this into account and the treatment he reserves for it. In this respect, *Sec* distinguishes clearly between *possibility* and *eventuality;* the possibility or fact that performatives can always be cited ("can be quoted," as Sarl puts it; and *Sec* never said that Austin excluded the fact "that performative utterances *can be quoted*") is not the same as the *eventuality,* that is the fact that such possible events—citations, "unhappinesses"—do indeed happen, occur, something which Austin, no less indisputably, excludes from his analysis, at the very least *de facto* and for the moment ("we are deliberately at present excluding"). Evidently it is regrettable that the distinction made in *Sec* between *possibility* and *eventuality* was not rendered in the English translation. This might have constituted an extenuating circumstance for Sarl, whose reading refers primarily to the translation, were it not for the fact that the entire paragraph plainly dissipates the difficulty. How, within an interval of two lines, could one possibly assert both that Austin excludes this possibility and that he insists upon defining it as the ever-present possibility of parasitism or abnormality? In any event, Sarl's charge against *Sec*—that is, against its supposed charge against Austin—is so grave that one would be justified in expecting a somewhat closer attention to detail and to the strict literality of the text. In order to elucidate graphically the "falsification" involved in the *Reply,* I will have to cite again from *Sec,* at length and adding emphasis:

> The second case of this exclusion concerns our subject more directly. It involves [*il s'agit de*] precisely the *possibility* for every performative utterance (and a priori every other utterance) to be quoted [the text says *il s'agit de,* literally: "what is involved or concerned"—and not, "what is excluded"—is the possibility . . .; moreover how, given the hypothesis of such an exclusion, could Austin be suspected of excluding the possibility of "every other utterance" being quoted?!] Now Austin excludes this *eventuality* [*éventualité,* initially translated as "possibility"] (and the general theory which would account for it) with a kind of lateral insistence, all the more significant in its offhandedness [*latéralisant*]. He insists on the fact that this possibility remains *abnormal, parasitic,* that it constitutes a kind of extenuation or agonized succumbing of language that we should strenuously distance ourselves from and resolutely ignore. And the concept of the "ordinary," thus of "ordinary language," to which he has recourse is clearly marked by this exclusion. As a result, the concept becomes all the more problematical, and before demonstrating as much, it would no doubt be best for me simply to read a paragraph from the Second Lecture: "(ii) Secondly, as *utterances* our performances are *also* heir to certain other kinds of ill, which infect *all* utterances. And these likewise, though again they might be brought into a more general account, we are deliberately at present excluding. I mean, for example, the following: a performative utterance will, for example, be *in a peculiar way* hollow or void if said by an actor on the stage, or if introduced in a poem, or spoken in soliloquy. This applies in a similar manner to any and every utterance—a seachange in special circumstances. Language in such circumstances is in special ways—intelligibly—used not *seriously* [my emphasis, J.D.] but in many ways *parasitic* upon its normal use—ways which fall under the doctrine of the *etiolations* of language. All this we are *excluding* from consideration. Our performative utterances, felicitous or not, are to be understood as issued in

ordinary circumstances" (pp. 21–22). Austin thus excludes, along with what he calls a "sea-change," the "non-serious," "parasitism," "etiolation," "the non-ordinary" (along with the whole general theory which, if it succeeded in accounting for them, would no longer be governed by those oppositions), *all of which he nevertheless recognizes as the possibility available to every act of utterance.* It is as just such a "parasite" that writing has always been treated by the philosophical tradition, and the connection in this case is by no means coincidental. (p. 16)

This is surely very clear: nowhere does *Sec* say or even suggest that Austin excludes the fact "that performative utterances can be quoted." How could *Sec* have possibly asserted as much while at the same time citing at length passages from Austin in which this very possibility is not only admitted, but described as being *ever-present?* What is no less clear, however, is that once this possibility ("can be quoted") has been recognized everywhere and by everyone, Austin nevertheless excludes from his considerations "at present"—we have just verified this literally—the *fact* or *facts* that transform this ever-present possibility into an event, making the possible come to pass: precisely what *Sec* designates as eventuality. Austin thus proposes a theoretical fiction that excludes this eventuality in order to purify his analysis.

I have just recalled what *can always* happen when Sarl writes "I will very briefly summarize his critique and then simply list. . . ." This summary is so summary, so "void" and "false" that I would be tempted to repeat, with the very words of the *Reply;* "The problem is rather that Derrida's Austin is unrecognizable. He bears almost no relation to the original." This is true. But what is unrecognizable, bearing no relation to the original, is not simply Austin, but indeed "Derrida's Austin." I fully subscribe to what Sarl says: reading it there, "Derrida's Austin *is* unrecognizable."

It will therefore not come as too great a shock to find that the five criticisms directed at "Derrida's Austin" are, from their very inception, trapped in the most resistant autism. I could have made do with having quoted, but I don't want to abuse this advantage. I shall cite Sarl again, copiously, and I shall make every effort not to leave the slightest detail obscure.

.V

First objection. We read in the *Reply:*

> 1. Derrida has completely mistaken the status of Austin's exclusion of parasitic forms of discourse from his preliminary investigations of speech acts. Austin's idea is simply this: If we want to know what it is to make a promise or make a statement we had better not *start* our investigation with promises made by actors on stage in the course of a play or statements made in a novel by novelists about characters in the novel, because in a fairly obvious way such utterances are not standard cases of promises and statements. We do not, for example, hold the actor responsible today for the promise he made

on stage last night in the way we normally hold people responsible for their promises, and we do not demand of the author how he knows that his characters have such and such traits in a way that we normally expect the maker of a statement to be able to justify his claims. Austin describes this feature by saying that such utterances are "hollow" or "void" and "nonserious." Furthermore, in a perfectly straightforward sense such utterances are "parasitical" on the standard cases: there could not, for example, be promises made by actors in a play if there were not the possibility of promises made in real life. The existence of the pretended form of the speech act is logically dependent on the possibility of the nonpretended speech act in the same way that any pretended form of behavior is dependent on nonpretended forms of behavior, and in that sense the pretended forms are *parasitical* on the nonpretended forms. (pp. 204–5)

Here is my response to this objection. *Sec never* suggested that the "investigation" "start" with promises made by actors on stage. (Moreover, I want to stress that according to the logic of this hypothesis, it would not be the actor who should be held responsible but rather the speaker committed by the promise *in the scene,* that is, the character. And indeed, he is held responsible in the play and in the *ideal*—i.e. in a certain way *fictional*—analysis of a promise, the choice between the two being a matter of indifference here. But let's leave that for the moment.) Thus, although *Sec* never suggested beginning with theatrical or literary fiction, I do believe that *one neither can nor should begin by excluding* the possibility of these eventualities: first of all, because this *possibility* is part of the structure called "standard." What would a so-called "standard" promise or a statement be if it could not be repeated or reproduced? If, for example (an *example* of iteration in general), it could not be mimed, reproduced on the stage or, *another* example (my emphasis, a *different* example), in a citation? This *possibility* is part of the so-called "standard case."It is an essential, internal, and permanent part, and to exclude what Austin himself admitted is a *constant* possibility from one's description is to describe something other than the so-called standard case.

Translated into the code of Austin or Searle, *Sec's* question is, in a word, the following: if what they call the "standard," "fulfilled," "normal," "serious," "literal," etc. is *always capable* of being affected by the non-standard, the "void," the "abnormal," the "nonserious," the "parasitical" etc., what does that tell us about the former? Parasitism does not need the theater or literature to appear. Tied to iterability, this possibility obtains constantly as we can verify at every moment, including this one. A promise that could not be reiterated (was not reiterable) a moment afterwards would not be a promise, and therein resides the possibility of parasitism, even in what Sarl calls "real life," that "real life" about which Sarl is so certain, so inimitably (almost, not quite) confident of knowing what it is, where it begins and where it ends; as though the meaning of these words ("real life") could immediately be a subject of unanimity, without the slightest risk of parasitism; as though literature, theater, deceit, infidelity, hypocrisy, infelicity, parasitism, and the simulation of real life were not part of real life!

It should also be remembered that the parasite is by definition never simply *external,* never simply something that can be excluded from or kept outside of the body "proper," shut out from the "familial" table or house. Parasitism takes place when the parasite (called thus by the owner, jealously defending his own, his *oikos)* comes to live *off the life* of the body in which it resides—and when, reciprocally, the host incorporates the parasite to an extent, willy nilly offering it hospitality: providing it with a place. The parasite then "takes place." And at bottom, whatever violently "takes place" or occupies a site is always *something* of a parasite. *Never quite* taking place is thus part of its performance, of its success as an event, of its taking-place.

The "standard" case of promises or of statements would never occur as such, with its "normal" effects, were it not, from its very inception on, parasited, harboring and haunted by the possibility of being repeated in *all kinds of ways,* of which the theater, poetry, or soliloquy are only examples, albeit examples that are more revelatory or congenial for the demonstration. From this iterability— recognized in principle by Austin and Sarl—*Sec* seeks to draw the consequences: the first and most general of which being that one neither can nor ought to exclude, even "strategically," the very roots of what one purports to analyze. For these roots are two-fold: you cannot root-out the "parasite" without rooting-out the "standard" [*le "propre"*] at the same time. What is at work here is a *different* logic of mimesis. Nor can the "pretended forms" of promise, on the stage or in a novel for instance, be "pretended" except to the extent that the so-called "standard cases" are reproduced, mimed, simulated, parasited, etc. *as* being in themselves reproducible, already *parasiticable,* as already impure. *Sec:* "For, ultimately, isn't it true that what Austin excludes as anomaly, exception, 'non-serious,' *citation* (on stage, in a poem, or a soliloquy) is the determined modification of a general citationality—or rather, a general iterability—without which there would not even be a 'successful' performative? So that—a paradoxical but unavoidable conclusion—a successful performative is necessarily an 'impure' performative, to adopt the word advanced later on by Austin when he acknowledges that there is no 'pure' performative" (p. 17).

It will not have escaped notice that the notion of "logical dependence" or of "logical priority" plays a decisive role in Sarl's argumentation no less than in Searle's *Speech Acts.* We are constantly told: to respect the order of logical dependency we must begin with the "standard," the "serious," the "normal," etc., and we must *begin by excluding* the "non-standard," the "non-serious," the "abnormal," the parasitical. Temporary and strategical, such an exclusion thus supposedly submits its *ordo inveniendi* to a *logical* and onto-logical order. In the passage quoted Sarl writes: "The existence of the pretended form of the speech act is *logically dependent* on the possibility of the nonpretended speech act in the same way that any pretended form of behavior is *dependent* on nonpretended forms of behavior, and in that sense the pretended forms are *parasitical* on the nonpretended forms" (my emphasis). This argument of "logical dependence" constructs the axiomatics and the methodology of speech act theory as well as of the book that bears this title. It underlies the first of the five criticisms addressed to *Sec* on the subject of Austin. It is because of the confidence placed in this kind of "logical dependence" that Sarl feels able to make the distinction between "research strategy" or "temporary exclusion" on the one hand and "metaphysical exclusion" on the other. Before multiplying counterobjections of various types, I shall cite and underline yet another paragraph from the *Reply:*

> Austin's exclusion of these parasitic forms from consideration in his prelimi-
> nary discussion is a matter of research strategy; he is, in his words, excluding
> them "at present"; but it is not a metaphysical exclusion: he is not casting
> them into a ditch or perdition, to use Derrida's words. Derrida seems to think
> that Austin's exclusion is a matter of great moment, a source of deep meta-
> physical difficulties, and that the analysis of parasitic discourse might create
> some insuperable difficulties for the theory of speech acts. But the history of
> the subject has proved otherwise. Once one has a general theory of speech
> acts—a theory which Austin did not live long enough to develop himself—it
> is one of the relatively simpler problems to analyze the status of parasitic
> discourse, that is, to meet the challenge contained in Derrida's question,
> "what is the status of this parasitism?" Writings subsequent to Austin's have
> answered this question. But the terms in which this question can be intelligi-
> bly posed and answered already presuppose a general theory of speech acts.
> Austin correctly saw that it was necessary to hold in abeyance one set of ques-
> tions, about parasitic discourse, until one has answered a logically prior set of
> questions about "serious" discourse. But the temporary exclusion of these
> questions within the development of the theory of speech acts, proved to be
> just that—temporary. (p. 205)

I am *not* in agreement with *any* of these assertions. For the following reasons:

a. The determination of "positive" values ("standard," serious, normal, literal, non-parasitic, etc.) is dogmatic. It does not even derive from common sense, but merely from a restrictive interpretation of common sense which is implicit and never submitted to discussion. More disturbingly: nothing allows one to say that the relation of the positive values to those which are opposed to them ("non-standard," nonserious, abnormal, parasitical, etc.), or that of the "nonpretended forms" to the "pretended forms," should be described as one of *logical dependence.* And even if this were the case, nothing proves that it would entail *this* relation of *irreversible* anteriority or of *simple* consequence. If a form of speech act that was "serious," or in general "nonpretended," did not, in its initial possibility and its very structure, include the power of giving rise to a "pretended form," it would simply not arise itself, it would be impossible. It would either not be what it is, or not have the value of a speech act.

And *vice-versa,* for I do not mean simply to *invert* the order of logical dependence. A standard act depends as much upon the possibility of being repeated, and thus potentially [*éventuellement*] of being mimed, feigned, cited, played, simulated, parasited, etc., as the latter possibility depends upon the possibility said to be opposed to it. And both of them "depend" upon the structure of iterability which, once again, undermines the simplicity of the oppositions and alternative distinctions. It blurs the simplicity of the line dividing inside from outside, undermines the order of succession or of dependence among the terms, *prohibits* (prevents and renders illegitimate) the procedure of exclusion. Such is the *law* of iterability. Which does not amount to saying that this law has the simplicity of a logical or transcendental principle. One cannot even speak of it being fundamental or radical in the traditional philosophical sense. This is why I spoke of "two-fold roots" a while ago: two-fold roots cannot play the role of philosophical radicality. All problems arise from this non-simplicity which makes possible *and* limits at one and the same time.

b. If, as Sarl claims, the question here were simply one of "logical dependence," of logical priority ("logically prior"), it would be impossible to comprehend all the value-judgments (valorization/devalorization) that obtrude so massively in Austin no less than in Searle. For in the last analysis, seriously, who ever said that a dependent (logically dependent) element, a secondary element, a *logical* or even chronological consequence, could be qualified, without any further ado or justification, as "parasitical," "abnormal," "infelicitous," "void," etc.? How is it possible to ignore that this axiology, in all of its systematic and dogmatic insistence, determines an object, the analysis of which is in essence not "logical," objective, or impartial? The axiology involved in this analysis is not intrinsically determined by considerations that are merely logical. What logician, what theoretician in general, would have dared to say: B depends logically on A, therefore B is parasitic, nonserious, abnormal, etc.? One can assert of anything whatsoever that it is "logically dependent" without immediately qualifying it (as though the judgment were analytical, or even tautological) with all those attributes, the lowest common denominator of which is evidently a pejorative value-judgment. All of them mark a *decline* [*déchéance*] or a *pathology,* an ethical-ontological deterioration [*dégradation*]: i.e., more or less than a mere logical derivation. This axiological "more or less" cannot be denied. Or at least not without constituting, as far as Searle is concerned, the object of what is known [psychoanalytically] as a denial [*dénégation*].

c. The effect of this denial: the purported recourse to logical considerations is only one of "the pretended forms" of this discourse, i.e., of speech act theory. That the determining instance is not logical in character, that another kind of decision (non- or alogical) is at work here, can be discerned in another feature. Which? The analysis must now go further (higher or lower, whichever one prefers). Logic, the logical, the *logos* of logic cannot be the decisive instance here: rather, it constitutes the object of the debate, the phenomenon that must first be explained before it can be accepted as the deciding instance. The matter we are discussing here concerns the value, possibility, and system of what is called logic in general. The law and the effects with which we have been dealing, those of iterability for example, govern the possibility of every logical proposition, whether considered as a speech act or not. No constituted logic nor any rule of a logical order can, therefore, provide a decision or impose its norms upon these prelogical possibilities of logic. Such possibilities are not "logically" primary or secondary with regard to other possibilities, nor logically primary or secondary with regard to logic itself. They are (topologically?) alien to it, but not as its principle, condition of possibility, or "radical" foundation; for the structure of iterability divides and guts such radicality. It opens up the *topos* of this singular topology to the un-founded, removing language, and the rest, from its philosophical jurisdiction.

d. I therefore cannot accept the distinction between *strategical* decision and *metaphysical* presupposition. Every strategical operation, or more classically, every methodological aspect of discourse, involves a decision, one which can be more or less explicit, concerning metaphysics. And in the case with which we are dealing, this is quite spectacularly so. For it to be spectacular, however, it is not indispensable that a philosopher manifest his anxiety before "a matter of great moment" or before "a source of deep metaphysical difficulties." Such pathos is indeed alien to Austin (at least in appearance) and I find him considerably more serene and less nervous than his heirs. But the question of metaphysics lies elsewhere. The more confident, implicit, buried the metaphysical decision is, the more its order, and calm, reigns over methodological technicity.

Metaphysics in its most traditional form reigns over the Austinian heritage: over his legacy and over those who have taken charge of it as his heirs apparent. Two indications bear witness to this: 1. The hierarchical axiology, the ethical-ontological distinctions which do not merely set up value-oppositions clustered around an ideal and unfindable limit, but moreover *subordinate* these values to each other (normal/abnormal, standard/parasite, fulfilled/void, serious/nonserious, literal/nonliteral, briefly: positive/negative and ideal/non-ideal); and in this, whether Sarl likes it or not, there is metaphysical pathos (infelicity, nonserious, etc. . . .). 2. The enterprise of returning "strategically," ideally, to an origin or to a "priority" held to be simple, intact, normal, pure, standard, self-identical, in order *then* to think in terms of derivation, complication, deterioration, accident, etc. All metaphysicians, from Plato to Rousseau, Descartes to Husserl, have proceeded in this way, conceiving good to be before evil, the positive before the negative, the pure before the impure, the simple before the complex, the essential before the accidental, the imitated before the imitation, etc. And this is not just *one* metaphysical gesture among others, it is *the* metaphysical exigency, that which has been the most constant, most profound and most potent. In *Sec* (as in its entire context) this force is not ignored but rather put into question, traced back to that which deploys it while at the same time limiting it. Although this "exigency" [*"requête"*] is here essentially "idealistic" I do not criticize it as such, but rather ask myself what this idealism is, what its force and its necessity are, and where its intrinsic limit is to be found. Nor is this idealism the exclusive property of those systems commonly designated as "idealistic." It can be found at times in philosophies that proclaim themselves to be anti-idealistic, in "materialisms." Or in discourses that declare themselves alien to philosophy. All discourse involves this effect of idealism in a certain manner. This particular one, for example, in a different manner.

e. Hence, the exclusion under discussion could not be "temporary." To avoid it, a different strategy would have been required. This is precisely what *Sec* sought to point out. The exclusion could not be temporary and in fact, contrary to what Sarl asserts, it has not been. Neither in Austin, nor to my knowledge in the self-proclaimed heirs of his problematic. This holds in particular for Searle, whose *Speech Acts* seem to me to reproduce Austin's strategy of idealizing exclusions, or even, I would say, to systematize and to rigidify it (with the ensuing losses and gains), using essentially the same conceptual instruments, hierarchical oppositions, and axiology. As to the "general theory," Sarl would like Austin both to have had one (which would put him beyond the pale of empiricism) and also, having died too young, not to have really had (or "developed") one, so that the copyright of the "general theory" in the proper, literal sense, as an adult and fully developed speech act, could be the rightful property only of the more or less anonymous company of his sons, here represented by the footnoted reference to John R. Searle. This is why—as we shall see in an instant—the paragraph beginning with "Once one has a general theory of speech acts . . ." constitutes a true wonder, a masterpiece of metaphysical-oedipal rhetoric. Imagine the scene: Austin's will is about to be unsealed. Although the envelope has not yet been entirely opened, the lawyer of one of the sons begins to speak: "Once one has a general theory of speech acts. . . ." Once? We still don't know if Austin had one or was going to have one. This "once," from a rhetorical point of view and floating as it does between the logical and the chronological, organizes the suspense among all the presumptive heirs. Did Austin have it? In which case the heritage would be more certain? Did he not quite have it, in which case it would still have to be developed? If so, by whom, with what justification, in what direction? Sarl has said "Once one has. . ." Ah! That "one": it is the moment of anonymity, oscillating between Austin and Searle, who, at the end of this paragraph, is going to take things in hand, or rather, in a footnote. I re-cite and underline: *"Once one has a general theory of speech acts*—a theory which Austin did not live long enough *to develop himself*—it is one of the relatively simpler problems to analyze the status of parasitic discourse, that is, to meet the challenge contained in Derrida's question, 'What is the status of this parasitism?' Writings subsequent to Austin's have answered this question.[4]" And his footnote to this "subsequence": "4. For a detailed answer to the question, see J. R. Searle, 'The Logical Status of Fictional Discourse,' *New Literary History* 5 (1975)."

I sincerely regret that "Austin did not live long enough," and my regret is as sincere as anyone else's is, for there are surely many of us who mourn his loss. It is unfortunate, even infelicitous. But through my tears I still smile at the argument of a "development" (a word sufficiently ambiguous to mean both produce, formulate, *as well as* continue, so as to reach those "detailed answers") that a

94

longer life might have led to a successful conclusion. Searle might thus be considered to have "developed" the theory: to have produced it, elaborated, and formulated it, *and* at the same time to have merely extended it in detail, guided it to adulthood by unfolding its potential.

Like Sarl I also believe that Austin had, in an implicit state, a general theory. It was presupposed (Sarl says "presuppose" in the following line) and it cannot be the effect of an extension or accumulation of results or analyses of details. But this general theory did not permit him—and has never permitted anyone—to integrate what it started out by excluding, even strategically, in the name of those metaphysical concepts, values, and axioms upon which this theory was constructed qua general theory.

And after Austin? What happens *once* ("Once one has . . ."), using the general theory, detailed answers have supposedly been given to the questions left in suspense by the will?

After Austin? I don't know if the signatory of *Sec* should have apologized, in 1971, for having not yet read or anticipated the article of Searle which, in 1975, is supposed to have "answered the question." For my part, I have just read it. With considerable interest and attention. With the desire to reread it and to discuss it elsewhere in detail. But I have yet to find the slighest answer, in principle or in detail, to the questions that concern us here. Notably involving the "status" of parasitism. This notion is still operational in the recent article (see especially p. 326), where it is used to explain the "break" with or "suspension" of the "vertical rules" that govern the "normal operation" of illocutionary acts and the world, by means of horizontal conventions (of an extralinguistic, nonsemantic character) which render "fiction" possible. But concerning the structure and the possibility of parasitism itself, or the value judgment normal/abnormal, nothing further is said. All the distinctions proposed (the two meanings of *to pretend,* the interaction of the so-called vertical rules with the horizontal conventions, the difference between "work of fiction" and "fictional discourse"), however interesting they may be, seem to me to reproduce the logical apparatus that I am calling into question here: they re-pose the same questions instead of, as Sarl claims, providing an answer, whether in principle or in detail. Leaving the discussion of each of these distinctions, and even of each of these examples, until a later date, I will have to make do here with an indication. But it will be general and sweeping. Here it is. I was surprised to see this article cited as a "detailed answer" to the questions (and above all to the decisive question of parasitism) that Austin, allegedly for lack of time, left unresolved: either unresolved in detail or insufficiently "developed." In 1977 Sarl recalls that Searle's article "answered this question." But in 1975 Searle didn't seem to think this at all. His conclusion was clear: "The preceding analysis leaves one crucial [again!] question unanswered: why bother? That is, why do we attach such importance and effort to texts which contain largely pretended speech acts?" If this excellent question indeed imposes itself and remains unresolved, it is because all the previous distinctions are not rigorous, either in fact or in principle. Had they been so, there would have been no

contamination possible between our (serious) interest for the one and our dis-
interest for the other. The problem, in a word, is that the logic of parasitism is not
a logic of distinction or of opposition, and that Searle constantly seeks to analyze
parasitism *in* a logic that it has rendered possible and impossible at once. A parasite is neither the same as nor different from that which it parasites. The possibility of fiction cannot be derived.

I said that the Searle of 1975, by contrast with the Sarl of 1977, did not claim to
have furnished an answer either to the "crucial" question or to that of the "general theory" which would have resolved it. Instead, there is, first of all, a disap-
pointing reference to the mystery of "imagination" in "human life," as though the
mention of this "faculty" would be of the slightest help. Here it is: "The preceding analysis leaves one crucial question unanswered: why bother? That is, why do
we attach such importance and efforts to texts which contain largely pretended
speech acts? The reader who has followed my argument this far will not be surprised to hear that I do not think there is any simple or even single answer to that
question. Part of the answer would have to do with the crucial [again!] role, usually underestimated, that imagination plays in human life, and the equally crucial [!]
role that shared products of the imagination play in human social life." A big
help. And concerning the "imagination" (why should this name, which traditionally covers an entire field of problems of interest to us here, be refused?) there is
not even an allusion to the extraordinary richness of a traditional philosophical
discourse that would never have deigned to accept the little that is offered us
here. But the conclusion of the article is close at hand. And nine lines further
down, we discover indeed that the general theory of how "pretended illocu-
tions" can "convey" such "serious illocutionary intentions," that this "general
theory" (which itself comprises only a part of the overall general theory) does
not yet exist. And if one believes, as I do, that this particular part—on parasitism—is parasitic on the whole, certain consequences become inescapable. Here
are the final words of this "detailed answer to the question": "Literary critics have
explained on an ad hoc and particularistic basis how the author conveys a serious
speech act through the performance of the pretended speech acts which constitute the work of fiction, but there is as yet no general theory of the mechanisms
by which such serious illocutionary intentions are conveyed by pretended illocu-
tions." The End.

W

Sarl's *second objection* is practically redundant with regard to the first. It consists in recalling that Austin's concept of "parasitism" involves a relation of "logical dependence": "It does not imply any moral judgment and certainly not that
the parasite is somehow immorally sponging off the host." I have already answered this objection in principle. I will simply add that it is not necessary to
point to a flesh-and-blood example, or to write moralizing pamphlets demanding the exclusion of wicked parasites (those of language or of the *polis,* the effects

of the unconscious, the *pharmakoi,* people on welfare, nonconformists or spics) in order to speak an ethical-political language or—and, in the case of Austin at least, this is all that I wished to indicate—to reproduce in a discourse said to be theoretical the founding categories of all ethical-political statements. I am convinced that speech act theory is fundamentally and in its most fecund, most rigorous, and most interesting aspects (need I recall that it interests me considerably?) a theory of right or law, of convention, of political ethics or of politics as ethics. It describes (in the best Kantian tradition, as Austin acknowledges at one point) the pure conditions of an ethical-political discourse insofar as this discourse involves the relation of intentionality to conventionality or to rules. What I wanted to emphasize above, however, in this regard was simply the following: this "theory" is compelled to reproduce, to reduplicate in itself the law of its object or its object as law; it must submit to the norm it purports to analyze. Hence, both its fundamental, intrinsic moralism and its irreducible empiricism. And Hegel knew how to demonstrate how compatible both are with a certain kind of formalism.

As for the second part of this second objection ("it is simply a mistake to say that Austin thought parasitic discourse was not part of ordinary language," p. 206), I remind you that *Sec* never said anything of the sort. Merely this: according to Austin, the parasite *is part* of so-called ordinary language, and it is part of it *as* parasite. That's all. I also recalled, just a little while ago, that the parasite *is part,* in its way (neither the same nor other), of what it parasites and is not simply external or alien to it. But if Austin recognized this "being-part-of," it didn't prevent him from proposing to "exclude" (see above) this part. That's all. "All this [i.e., *'parasitic'* as opposed to *'normal'* use'—my emphasis] we are *excluding* from consideration." Isn't that clear enough? Did or did not Austin propose to exclude, under the rubric of parasitism, something which *is part* of ordinary language but which, he claimed, is not *normally* a part of *normal* ordinary language? This is why *Sec* never argued that for Austin the parasite is not part of ordinary language but rather, that "the concept of the 'ordinary,' thus of 'ordinary language' to which he has recourse is clearly marked by this exclusion." *"Marked by* this exclusion"—can this be denied?

X

We now come to the *third objection.* It is aimed at what is so admirably entitled *"more than simply a misreading of Austin."* This objection repeats—or makes slightly more explicit—the preceding ones. The response has already been given twice: in *Sec* and here. But I am certainly ready to try patiently to adapt these responses to the precise literality of this third objection. I shall cite it, responding to it point by point. I am referring to the first three paragraphs of point 3 of the *Reply* (pp. 206–7). The fourth paragraph begins with "On a sympathetic reading of Derrida's text we can construe. . . ." Although it hardly satisfies me, this remorse is an interesting signal. It deserves to be treated separately. Here, now, are my responses:

a. It was *never* said or suggested in *Sec* that "Austin somehow denied the very possibility that expressions can be quoted." It was said rather that by the exclusion of which we have just spoken, he deprived himself of the means that would have enabled him to take into account both the *possibility* of citation within that allegedly normal structure, and certain other things as well. He deprives himself of the means with which to account for a possibility inscribed in the use he himself calls "normal."

b. It was *never* said or suggested in *Sec* that the "phenomenon of citationality" is "the same as the phenomenon of parasitic discourse." It was never said in *Sec* that the novelist, poet and actor are "in general *quoting*," although they can also do that. What *Sec* was driving at, without confusing citationality with parasitism (or fiction, literature, or theater), was the possibility they have in common: the iterability which renders possible *both* the "normal" rule or convention *and* its transgression, transformation, simulation, or imitation. From this, *Sec* drew consequences different from those drawn by Austin; above all, the illegitimate and unfeasible character of the exclusions proposed either on strategic grounds or on methodological (idealizing) ones. I will add here (and is this only a matter of detail?) that parasitism (in the strict sense, if one can still speak of this) is always susceptible to the parasitism of citation, just as citationality can always be parasited by the parasite. The parasite parasites the limits that guarantee the purity of rules and of intentions, and this is not devoid of import for law, politics, economics, ethics, etc.

I have already stated my reservations concerning the ultimate rigor of the distinction between *use* and *mention*. But even to the extent that such a distinction is accepted as being trivially evident, as the initial manifestation of a rigidified effect, even at this level there is still no confusion ever in *Sec* of citation (in the sense considered strict by Sarl: that which is indicated by quotation marks) with that other effect of iterability, the "parasite" excluded by Austin. Nor was citationality ever confused with iterability in general, but simply traced back to it, as in the case of a more spectacular or more pedagogical example or illustration. *Sec* even warned of the confusion Sarl charges it with having committed. The proof? Here it is. Of course it's a quotation, taken from the very statement cited and hence presumably read by Sarl, but which evidently requires rereading. The "or rather" in this passage marks, as might be expected, a distinction, as does the series enumerating the different types of excluded phenomena: "For, ultimately, isn't it true that what Austin excludes as anomaly, exception, 'non-serious' *citation* (on stage, in a poem, or a soliloquy) is the determined modification of a general citationality—*or rather, a general iterability*—without which there would not even be a 'successful' performative?" (p. 17) (This time I have underlined what might not have performed "successfully" or sufficiently so for certain readers.)

By virtue—here as always—of a certain interest, Sarl has paid insufficient attention to the *very* letter of the *very* phrase that was cited; Sarl was inattentive to what this citation said about what should not be confused with citation. But if this is so, how can one expect Sarl to have paid attention to all the other statements he didn't cite? To all those utterances (perhaps he'll begin looking for them now) where the *or* which articulates the relation between citation and iteration (citation "or" iteration), between citationality and iterability (citationality "or" iterability), evidently signifies *neither* equivalence, dissociation, nor opposition? This "or" marks another relationship. The "confusion" that Sarl denounces precipitously in *Sec* ("Derrida in this argument confuses no less than three separate and distinct phenomena: iterability, citationality, and parasitism"), this "confusion" is precisely that of which *Sec* warns: explicitly, insistently, *literally.* For example, and I underline here:

> We should first be clear on what constitutes the status of "occurrence" or the eventhood of an event that entails in its allegedly present and singular emergence the intervention of an utterance [*énoncé*] that in itself can be only repetitive or citational in its structure, *or rather, since those two words may lead to confusion: iterable.* (pp. 17–18)

Is this clear enough? No? Then let us continue:

> I return then to a point that strikes me as fundamental and that now concerns the status of events in general, of events of speech or by speech, of the strange logic they entail and that often passes unseen.
> Could a performative utterance succeed if its formulation did not repeat a "coded" or iterable utterance, or in other words, if the formula I pronounce in order to open a meeting, launch a ship or a marriage were not identifiable as *conforming* with an iterable model, if it were not then identifiable *in some way as a "citation"?* (p. 18)

Is this clear enough, with quotation-marks around " "citation" " and "in some way"? No? Then let us continue:

> *Not that citationality in this case is of the same sort* as in a theatrical play, a philosophical reference, or the recitation of a poem. That is why there is a relative specificty, as Austin says, a "relative purity" of performatives. But this relative purity does not emerge *in opposition to* citationality *or* iterability, but in opposition to *other kinds of iteration* within a general iterability which constitutes a violation of the allegedly rigorous purity of every event of discourse or every *speech act.* Rather than oppose citation or iteration to the non-iteration of an event, one ought to construct a differential typology of forms of iteration, assuming that such a project is tenable and can result in an exhaustive program, a question I hold in abeyance here. (p. 18)

Is this finally clear? The reasons for my reservation at the end will perhaps be more evident now: once iterability has established the possibility of parasitism, of a certain fictionality altering at once—*Sec* too [*aussi sec*]—the system of (il- or perlocutionary) intentions and the systems of ("vertical") rules or of ("horizontal") conventions, inasmuch as they are included within the scope of iterability; once this parasitism or fictionality can always add *another* parasitic or fictional structure to whatever has preceded it—what I elsewhere designate as a "supple-mentary code" [*"supplément de code"*]—everything becomes possible against the language-police; for example "literatures" or "revolutions" that as yet have no model. Everything is possible except for an exhaustive typology that would claim to limit the powers of graft or of fiction by and within an analytical logic of distinction, opposition, and classification in genus and species. The theoretician of speech acts will have to get used to the idea that, knowingly or not, willingly or not, both his treatment of things and the things themselves are marked in ad-vance by the possibility of fiction, either as the iterability of acts or as the system of conventionality. He will therefore never be able to *de-limit* the object-fiction or the object-parasite except by another counter-fiction.

Sec has not, therefore, confused iterability, citationality, or parasitism. If all the same it did not simply set them in opposition to one another in an alternative distinction; if it, on the contrary, associated them without confusing them, name-ly, by means of an *or, or rather,* it is because the logic of iterability demands such an opposition. Iterability cannot be simply the genus, of which citation or other phenomena (the parasite in the "strict" sense, for instance) would be the species. Fiction (parasite) can always re-work [*re-traverser*], remark *every* other type of iteration. But iterability is, however, not a transcendental condition of possibility making citation and other phenomena (parasites, for example) into conditioned effects: it is neither an essence nor a substance to be distinguished from phenom-ena, attributes, or accidents. This kind of (classical) logic is fractured in its code by iterability. Parasitic contamination, once again, broaches and breaches all these relations. If *Sec* had confused citation with iteration, how would it be possi-ble to explain that each of these words would have to be regularly qualified or supplemented by the other (precisely to guard against such confusion)? We have seen how the *or*, and *or rather* function between the two terms. Here, now, is the device of the parenthesis: "The graphematic root of citationality (iterability) is what creates this embarrassment and makes it impossible, as Austin says, 'to lay down even a list of all possible criteria' " (*Sec,* note 10). The parentheses do not mark synonyms or an identification but rather the *possibility* referred to by cita-tionality, which here, a traditional philosopher might say, serves as the guiding thread of the analysis. No citation without iteration. Who could doubt that citation implies iteration? Placed in parentheses, "iterability" can define citationality *in its possibility,* and its "graphematic root" as well.

I have just evoked the figure of the traditional philosopher. This figure is still necessary, if only to remind Sarl that the word "modification," in the phrase cit-ed, refers to *mode* and not merely, as it often implies (parasitically enough) in an all too ordinary language, to *transformation. Sec* uses/mentions the code of tradi-tional philosophy (among others); one of its conventions which, like all others, cannot be fully and rigorously justified, supposes the knowledge of certain *a b c*s of classical philosophy, so that when it uses or mentions the word "modifica-tion," it is also to signify modal determination: the contraction of a substance or an attribute into a mode or a modality. "Modification" is therefore not opposed to exemplification ("instantiation"), as Sarl seems to think in objecting: "Like all utterances, parasitic forms of utterances are instances of, *though not modifications of,* iterability, for—to repeat—without iterability there is no language at all" (p. 206, my emphasis). Sarl here misconstrues the classical sense of the word "modification." But this being said—to repeat—without iterability there is no language at all, nor many other things either. But the latter is precisely the argument of *Sec,* from beginning to end; and I repeat it here. Once again: it-reapplies.

The mechanism of the "it-reapplies," which consists in not wanting to read in *Sec* the arguments one tries to use against it, is kept in motion by a sort of fascinated allergy which all of a sudden, presumably due to exhaustion, turns (recognizing itself?) into a movement of sympathy hitherto strictly forbidden. It is the final paragraph of the third objection, which, as I said, I shall treat separately. It recalls that precisely this general iterability cannot be made into an objection to Austin. As if anyone had ever done this! I cite this paragraph of "sympathy." The latter, as you will see, is rather limited:

> On a sympathetic reading of Derrida's text we can construe him as pointing out, quite correctly, that the possibility of parasitic discourse is internal to the notion of language, and that performatives can succeed only if the utterances are iterable, repetitions of conventional—or as he calls them, "coded"—forms. But neither of these points is in any way an objection to Austin. Indeed, Austin's insistence on the conventional character of the performative utterance in particular and the illocutionary act in general commits him precisely to the view that performatives must be iterable, in the sense that any conventional act involves the notion of the repetition of the same. (p. 207)

(I have again quoted a paragraph *in extenso.* Adding up all the quotes, I believe that I will have cited the *Reply* from beginning to end, or almost. Did I have the right(s)? I have, so to speak, incorporated (with or without quotation-marks) it into this "Limited Inc," without even being certain, at the moment of writing this—while Sam Weber is translating and the Johns Hopkins Press is harrying the two of us—who exactly will be entitled to its copyright ©, or who is going to share it with whom, both the "original" and/or the so-called translation. I might add that the writing of the so-called "original," in return, has continually been transformed by the translation: a case of parasitic feedback, including this very parenthesis. I cannot even say if the lawyer representing the Company holding the copyright of the *Reply* is going to bring suit against the Company of "Limited Inc" for having reproduced and incorporated (I didn't say destroyed) all or almost all of the *Reply.* Perhaps then at least I may get to explain to the court all the implications (psychoanalytic, political, juridical, censorial [*policières*], economic, etc.) of this debate, something that I have not been able to do here, the incorporation of the *Reply* having taken up too much time and space.)

In view of the fact that the paragraph of sympathy is one of the briefest, I can only ask: had something of this sort, i.e., a sympathetic reading of *Sec,* been able to take place and to last, wouldn't it have endowed the *Reply* with a kind of absolute brevity?

But as feeble and intermittent as it may be, this sympathy does not suffice. Look at this paragraph of "sympathetic reading": it still contains the charge that *Sec* accuses Austin of forgetting iterability. Nonsense. *Sec* endeavors to account otherwise for this iterability and to draw rigorous consequences from this account, something that Austin, for reasons already discussed, did not do in a systematic manner.

This iterability (about which there seems to be general agreement) is immediately associated, in the same paragraph, with conventionality and "the repetition of the same." But despite all the sympathy between us, I cannot follow Sarl here: neither concerning the "repetition of the same" (I have already said why the other and alteration work parasitically within the very inner core of the iter qua repetition of the identical), nor concerning conventionality. I do not believe that iterability is necessarily tied to convention, and even less, that it is limited by it. Iterability is precisely that which—once its consequences have been unfolded—can no longer be dominated by the opposition nature/convention. It dislocates, subverts, and constantly displaces the dividing-line between the two terms. It has an essential rapport with the force (theoretical and practical, "effective," "historical," "psychic," "political," etc.) deconstructing these oppositional limits. This is indeed a very important ("crucial"!) motif for our discussion, although I cannot go into it any farther here. I have done so elsewhere, and very often.

y

I will now cite Sarl's fourth objection, underlining several words here and there to be taken up in my response.

> 4. Derrida *assimilates* the sense in which writing can be said to be *parasitic* on spoken language with the sense in which fiction, etc., are parasitic on nonfiction or standard discourse. But these are quite different. In the case of the distinction between fiction and nonfiction, the relation is one of *logical dependency*. One could not have the concept of fiction without the concept of serious discourse. But the dependency of writing on spoken language is a *contingent fact* about the history of human languages and not logical truth about the nature of language. Indeed, in mathematical and logical symbolism, the relation of dependence *goes the other way*. The spoken, oral version of the symbols is simply an orally communicable way of representing the primary written forms. (p. 207)

Responses. a. It is imprudent to assimilate too quickly, more quickly than one can, what is not easily assimilable. Otherwise, what is liable to result is what certain psychoanalysts call incorporation without introjection: a sort of indigestion more or less desired by the unconscious and provoked by the other or alien body which cannot yet be assimilated.

Sec never, nowhere, "assimilated" what Sarl would like it to have assimilated so that it in turn could then be assimilated by Sarl to something else. It never assimilated the parasitism of writing in regard to speech to that of fiction in regard to "standard" discourse. Had Sarl taken the trouble, as I have been doing, to cite the incriminated phrase, the confusion could have been easily avoided: "It is *as just such* [*Aussi comme un*] a 'parasite' that writing has always been treated by the philsophical tradition, and the connection in this case is by no means coincidental" (p. 190). If the translation here is ambiguous, the French is not: *"Aussi comme un* 'parasite'. . ."* that is, *"as another such* parasite . . ."! It is not a question of assimilating these parasites to each other but of remarking that *also* [*aussi*], in the case of writing, one speaks of a parasite *as well* [*encore*], and that it is neither fortuitous nor insignificant that this is done in all these cases. The symptom has interested me for a long time. The parasitic structure is what I have tried to analyze everywhere, under the names of writing, mark, step [*marche*], margin, *différance*, graft, undecidable, supplement, *pharmakon*, hymen, *parergon*, etc. Just as the phrase of *Sec* that we have just read is itself a kind of citation, in a hidden, fictitious, or parasitic way, I am *also* quoting *Sec* (thus conforming to the rule that I adopted or imposed upon myself by force: not to cite any other text signed by me) in citing this: "It is in the course of this second demonstration that the literally Saussurian formulas reappear within the question of the relationships between speech and writing; the order of writing is the order . . . of the *'parasitic'* (*Of Grammatology* [Baltimore: Johns Hopkins Univ. Press, 1976], p. 54). This citation, sub-cited by *Sec*, includes a citation from Jakobson and Halle, who write in *Phonology and Phonetics:* "There is no such thing in human society as the supplantation of the speech code by its visual replicas, but only a supplementation of this code by parasitic auxiliaries."[12] As though an auxiliary could not supplant! As though a parasite should not supplant! As though "supplanting" were a simple operation, the object of a simple cognition! As though "to add" something like a "parasite" constituted a simple addition! As though an addition were ever simple! As though that to which a parasite is "added" could possibly remain as it is, unaltered! As though an addition or repetition did not alter! Finally, still developing the sub-citation of *Sec*, the following—and I will have then finished with this point—which *directly* concerns our debate:

> The purity of the within can henceforth only be restored by *accusing* exteriority of being a supplement, something inessential and yet detrimental to that essence, an excess that *should not have been* added to the unadulterated plenitude of the within. The restoration of inner purity must therefore reconstitute, *recite*—and this is myth itself, the *mythology*, for example, of a *logos* recounting its origin and returning to the eve of a pharmacographical assault—that to which the *pharmakon* should not have been added, thereby intruding and becoming a *literal parasite:* a letter invading the interior of a living organism, *nourishing* itself there and disturbing the pure audibility of a voice. Such are the relations between the supplement of writing and the *logos-zoôn*. To heal the latter of the *pharmakon* and to banish the parasite,

the outside must be put back in its place. The outside must be kept out. This is the gesture inaugurating "logic" itself, that good "sense" in accord with the self-identity of *that which is:* the entity is what it is, the outside is out and the inside in. Writing should thus become once more what it should never have ceased being: accessory, accidental, excessive.[13]

b. I have already said why relations of a logical order have seemed to me devoid of all pertinence. When Sarl writes: "One could not have the concept of fiction without the concept of serious discourse," one could with equal legitimacy reverse the order of dependence. This order is not a one-way street [*à sens unique*] (how can the serious be defined or postulated without reference to the nonserious, even if the latter is held to be simply external to it?) and everything that claims to base itself upon such a conception disqualifies itself immediately. This is the case of speech act theory and all its "strategic" exclusions: they must always invoke the authority of this one-way movement.

c. This does not, however, imply that the asserted "dependence" of writing in regard to spoken language is "a contingent fact about the history of human language." This dependence is not, of course, "a logical truth about the nature of human language." I agree, and I have sought elsewhere to draw all sorts of consequences from this. But to reduce it to a "contingent fact" seems to me very simplistic. Structural and historical laws have constructed this "dependence" everywhere where it has manifested itself, with everything it has produced, above all in the way of symptoms and of lures. The length and nature of the analyses that I have endeavored to devote to this question cannot be summarized here. It's not a serious problem, but it is unfortunate, infelicitous, inasmuch as these analyses form part of the implicit context of *Sec,* and hence of its conventional premises, its rules. To this extent at least the speech acts of *Sec* remain unintelligible, illegible and in any case inoperative for anyone who is not also interested in the questions that gave rise to such analyses. This is also an extenuating circumstance for anyone who does not understand them. In saying "infelicitous" and "extenuating circumstance" I am, of course, citing *Sec* citing Austin (pp. 15–16).

d. As for the argument according to which the dependency-relation of writing to speech is different "in mathematical and logical symbolism," I can hardly take it as an objection since it can be retraced to *Sec* even more quickly than usual. It is one of the essential arguments in the deconstruction of phono-logocentrism. And it can even be found in the forefront. Ten years ago it opened the first chapter of the book cited a few pages back, and it dealt with the question of parasitism. Neither Sarl nor anyone else can, of course, be expected to know something which, although outside of *Sec,* still forms part of its context. But whoever accepts the convention that consists in saying that one is going to read and criticize *Sec* is required to read what, within its limited corpus, points towards this context: for example, the *three conclusions* concerning "the exposure [*mise en cause*] of this effect that I have called elsewhere logocentrism." These three conclusions open with the formula, "To conclude this *very dry* [sec] discussion:" (pp. 20–21)

And, for the second time, I am going to conclude a bit abruptly, since I see that all I have left is the letter

Z

Nor, finally, can I accept as an argument against *Sec* what Sarl claims to oppose to it in the fifth and last *objection*: "Indeed, I shall conclude this discussion by arguing for precisely the converse thesis: The iterability of linguistic forms facilitates and is a necessary condition of the particular forms of intentionality that are characteristic of speech acts" (pp. 207-8). This "necessary condition" is one of *Sec*'s most insistent themes. How can one seriously claim to raise this as an objection to it, much less assert it to be "the converse thesis," when in fact one is saying the very same thing? Naturally, in the effort to reach this point, Sarl must act as though *Sec* had postulated the pure and simple disappearance of intention in speech acts. I have already recalled that this is not the case. What is limited by iterability is not intentionality in general, but its character of being conscious or present to itself (actualized, fulfilled, and adequate), the simplicity of its features, its *undividedness*. To cite once again: "In such a typology, *the category of intention will not disappear*; it will have its place, but from that place it will no longer be able to govern the entire scene and system of utterance [*l'énonciation*]. Above all, at that point, we will be dealing with different kinds of marks or chains of iterable marks and not with an opposition between citational utterances, on the one hand, and singular and original event-utterances, on the other. The first consequence of this will be the following: given that structure of iteration, the intention animating the utterance will never be through and through present to itself and to its content. *The iteration structuring it a priori* introduces into it a dehiscence and a cleft [*brisure*] which are essential" (p. 18, my emphasis). How, after this, can one seriously assert that, for *Sec*, iterability is "in conflict with the intentionality of linguistic acts" (p. 208)?

The *fifth objection* thus develops one of *Sec*'s arguments while at the same time pretending to pose it as an objection—all this by means of a feint or pose which could either be a sort of infelicitous ruse (the first sense of *to pretend*) or a successful fiction (or at least for the duration of a good show, in the second sense of *to pretend*). (I shall leave this question open and not claim the copyright, in the name of the signatories of *Sec*, to the arguments borrowed from it and reproduced, almost literally and with regularity by Sarl, while pretending to pose them as objections. I will not claim the copyright because ultimately [*en dernière instance*] there is always a police and a tribunal ready to intervene each time that a rule [constitutive or regulative, vertical or not] is invoked in a case involving signatures, events, or contexts. This is what I meant to say. If the police is always waiting in the wings, it is because conventions are by essence violable and precarious, *in themselves* and by the fictionality that constitutes them, even before there has been any overt transgression, in the "first sense" of *to pretend*. Here, parenthetically, I shall give Searle some advice, if he permits, while awaiting a later date to renew this debate more patiently and to use another *a b c*. In his article in *New Literary History,* Searle gives us the following explanation of the two meanings of to *pretend*: "If I pretend to be Nixon in order to fool the Secret Service into letting me into the White House, I am pretending in the first sense; if I pretend to be Nixon as part of a game of charades, it is pretending in the second sense. Now in the fictional use of words, it is pretending in the second sense which is in question" [pp. 324-25]. All this is true, and yet I am not entirely satisfied, as I shall explain elsewhere. In what sense and to what extent is the example itself ["If I . . ."] a fiction? For the moment, here is my advice: it applies to the day when the person who says *I* [Searle] will no longer, as in 1975, be in *New Literary History*, Virginia, but instead will be dreaming of being taken [I don't say mistaking himself] for Jimmy Carter and demanding to be finally admitted to the White House. Upon encountering certain difficulties, as one can anticipate, he will, if he takes my advice, tell the Secret Service: it was all a fiction, I was pretending in the second sense; I was pretending [in the second sense] to pretend [in the first sense]. They, of course, will ask for proof, for witnesses, not being satisfied with declarations of intention; they will ask which of the "horizontal conventions" were involved in this game. My advice to Searle, at this point, is to say that he is playing all by himself, that he alone forms a company, just like certain chess players who play by themselves or with fictitious opponents; or he can also say that he was experimenting with a fiction ["to pretend" in the second sense] in view of writing a novel or a philosophical demonstration for *Glyph*. Let's not worry about details. If he insists upon entering the White House with such declarations, he will be arrested. If he continues to insist, the official psychiatrist will not be long in coming. What will he say to this expert? I leave that to the imagination; and although my advice stops here, my foresight doesn't: at one moment or another he will notice that between the notion of responsibility manipulated by the psychiatric expert [the representative of law and of political-linguistic conventions, in the service of the State and of its police] and the exclusion of parasitism, there is something like a relation. My last bit of advice, then, is for Searle to try to move the psychiatric expertise in the direction of the questions posed by *Sec*. That will also leave us enough time to take up this discussion again. Apropos: in what sense did Nixon pretend to be Nixon, President of the United States up to a certain date? Who will ever know this, in all rigor? He himself?

I shall therefore not claim a copyright because this entire matter of the police must be reconsidered, and not merely in a theoretical manner, if one does not want the police to be omnipotent; and also because the copyright is the object of *Sec*, its issue [*chose*] and its business, its cause [*Sache, Ursache*] and its trial, process, proceeding [*procès*], albeit one that is impossible to appropriate. I close the parenthesis.)

It is clear that, despite all its borrowing from *Sec*, I am far from subscribing to all the statements made in the *Reply*. For instance, each time it is a question of "communication" (almost all the time), of "mastery" and of identity (". . . the speaker and hearers are masters of the sets of rules we call the rules of language, and these rules are recursive," p. 208). Iterability is at once the condition and the limit of mastery: it broaches and breaches it. And this cannot be devoid of consequences for the concepts of "application," of "rules," of "performance," etc.

I promised (very) sincerely to be serious. Have I kept my promise? Have I taken Sarl seriously? I do not know if I was supposed to. Should I have? Were they themselves serious in their speech acts? Shall I say that I am afraid they were? Would that mean that I do not take their seriousness very seriously?

What am I saying? What am I doing when I say that?

I ask myself if we will ever be quits with this confrontation.

Will it have taken place, this time?

Quite?

NOTES

1. What is a title, according to the general theory of speech acts? And for example, from this point of view, the title *Speech Acts*? And *Signature Event Context*, these three nouns juxtaposed without either copula or apparent attribution? And what I am deciding here and from this instant on to designate with the conventional sign (but conventional to what point?), *Sec*? And is it only due to brevity? The translator can, if he likes, say *Dry*. He has already done so (in the text) and will find his authorization (a supplementary one, since he has every right) in the fact that the presumed author of *Sec* deliberately programmed the thing. Three pages before the end of *Sec* you can read this: "In order to function, that is, to be readable, a signature must have a repeatable, iterable, imitable form; it must be able to be detached from the present and singular intention of its production. It is its sameness which, by corrupting its identity and its singularity, divides its seal [*sceau*]. I have already indicated above the principle of this analysis.

"To conclude this very *dry* discussion [*Pour conclure ce propos très sec*] . . ."

Sec is set there—in a manner which, you may take my word for it, was hardly fortuitous—in italics. Three points follow, which lead to the apparent simulacrum of "my" signatures, of my seal in bits and pieces, divided, multiplied. All that isn't very serious, Sarl will perhaps say. Serious? Not serious? That is the question: why does that absorb and irritate Sarl to such a degree? And were Sarl to object that in each one of these examples (titles, names, abbreviations, etc.) there are several *functions* at the same time, cohabiting parasitically with each other, how is that possible? And all that within the appearance of one and the same body, one and the same utterance? And how could this lack of seriousness have been taken so seriously?

The "very dry discussion" conducting *continuously* to the multiple signature of *Sec, Sec* will henceforth designate the whole of *Sec* plus (including) its multiple, presumed, divided, and associated signatories. Which signals—to arrive at a temporary conclusion concerning the question of titles, under the title of "perhaps more serious than one thinks,"—that *Signature Event Context* might also lend credence to the parasite of a "true" dependent proposition: "signature event that one texts" [*signature événement qu'on texte*]. Concerning the calculated necessity of this neological usage of the verb *to text* [*texter*], cf. "*Having the Ear of Philosophy*," [*Avoir l'oreille de la philosophie*], Conversation with Lucette Finas, reprinted in *Écarts, Quatre essais à propos de Jacques Derrida* (Paris, 1973). In particular, one can read there the following: "That which for the discursive consciousness is impossible to anticipate [*l'inanticipable*] calls for a new logic of the repressed [*re-foulé*]. Concerning the effects of timbre (*tympanon*) and of signature, *Qual Quelle* situates a "paradoxical logic of the event": this should account for the irreplaceable, which only produces itself in losing itself *aussi sec* [a French idiom meaning immediately, on the spot, without delay—*at once*], textually, in the process of iteration: signature, event that one texts [*signature, événement qu'on texte*]. The *sur-number* [*surnombre*] *of La dissémination* already marked this pluralization that fractures the event, even of the unique, while at the same time causing it *to occur* [*arriver*]. The system of presence, of the origin, of archeology, or of production must be deconstructed so that the event can occur, and not simply be thought or uttered. One could even say that the event (is what) deconstructs. Blanchot: 'Does that happen'—'No, that doesn't happen.'—'Something, nevertheless, is coming."

Does that ever quite take place?

2. The film, "The Front," starring Woody Allen, was shown in France under the title, "Le Prête-nom." (Translator's note)

3. A propos, the dossier of this debate should include Austin's article, "Three Ways of Spilling Ink" (in his *Philosophical Papers* [London: Oxford University Press, 1976], pp. 272-87). In it Austin analyzes the differences between "intentionally," "deliberately," "on purpose (purposely)." I refer to it here in a kind of *oratio obliqua*. After a paragraph explaining why it "would be wholly untrue . . . to suggest that 'unintentionally' is the word that 'wears the trousers,' " Austin underlines the word *limited* in the passage that follows (where "my idea of what I'm doing" is compared to "a miner's lamp on our forehead"): "The only general rule is that the illumination is always *limited*, and that in several ways. It will never extend indefinitely far ahead . . . Moreover, it does not illuminate *all* of my surroundings. Whatever I am doing is being done and to be done amidst a background of *circumstances* (including of course activities by other agents). . . . Furthermore, the doing of it will involve *incidentally* all kinds of minutiae of, at the least, bodily movements, and often many other things besides" (p. 284). I am indebted to Sam Weber for bringing this text, which is highly illuminating in more ways than one, to my attention.

4. For a more detailed discussion of the divided *stigmè*, in regard to philosophical conceptions of temporality (in Aristotle, Hegel and Heidegger), see: J. Derrida, *"Ousia* and *Grammé*: A Note to a Footnote in *Being and Time*," translated by Edward S. Casey, in F.J. Smith (ed.), *Phenomenology in Perspective* (The Hague: Martinus Nijhoff, 1970), pp. 54-93. The French text may be found in: J. Derrida, *Marges de la philosophie* (Paris: Editions de Minuit, 1972). (Translator's note) (The English translation has subsequently been published as *Margins of Philosophy*, trans. Alan Bass [Chicago: University of Chicago Press, 1982]. G.G.)

5. J. L. Austin, *How to Do Things with Words* (London: Oxford University Press, 1976), p. 74.

6. See "La différance," in *Marges*, op. cit. An English translation of this essay (by David B. Allison) is included in: J. Derrida, *Speech and Phenomena* (Evanston: Northwestern University Press, 1973). (Translator's note)

7. Derrida has translated and introduced this text, an English translation of which (by John Leavey) was published by Nicholas Hays Ltd. in 1977. See Edmund Husserl, *L'origine de la géométrie*, tr. Jacques Derrida (Paris: Presses Universitaires de France, 1962). (Translator's note)

8. Nietzsche's phrase is discussed at the conclusion of Derrida's essay on Nietzsche, "Eperons. Les styles de Nietzsche." The French text, as well as translations in English, Italian, and German, may be found in: J. Derrida, *Eperons/Sproni/Spurs/Sporen* (Venice: Corbe e Fiore Editori, 1976). (Translator's note) (A French-English version has subsequently been published as *Spurs: Nietzsche's Styles/Eperons: Les Styles de Nietzsche*, trans. Barbara Harlow [Chicago: University of Chicago Press, 1978]. G.G.)

9. John R. Searle, *Speech Acts: An Essay in the Philosophy of Language* (London: Cambridge University Press, 1970), pp. 73–76.

10. Ibid., p. 74.

11. *Société à responsabilité limitée* and not, as the French often misinterpret it, *société anonyme à responsabilité limitée*, which would yield, once again, one *a* more or less. As though one would translate S.a.r.l. by Speech Acts *à responsabilité limitée* [i.e. with limited liability]. My friends know that

I have composed an entire book with *ça* (the sign of the Saussurian signifier, of Hegel's Absolute Knowing, in French: *savoir absolu*, of Freud's Id [the Ça], the feminine possessive pronoun [sa]). I did not, however, think at the time of the s.a. of speech acts, nor of the problems (formalizable?) of their relation to the signifier, absolute knowing, the Unconscious or even: to the feminine possessive pronoun. If that didn't interest me, perhaps I wouldn't have had enough desire to respond. All of this [*ça*] in order to pose the question: *ça,* is it *used* or *mentioned?*

12. Roman Jakobson, Morris Halle, "Phonology and Phonetics," in Jakobson/Halle, *Fundamentals of Language* (The Hague: Mouton, 1956), p. 117.

13. J. Derrida, *La dissémination* (Paris: Editions du Seuil, 1972), p. 147. (This book has subsequently been translated as *Dissemination*, trans. Barbara Johnson [Chicago: University of Chicago Press, 1981]; the passage here is on p. 128 of the Johnson translation. G.G.)

Afterword
Toward An Ethic of Discussion

Dear Gerald Graff,

Allow me to answer you in the form of a letter. I would like to try this for several reasons.

A. *On the one hand*, it will permit me to express my gratitude to you, directly and publicly. I thank you for having taken the initiative in regard to this book and for having addressed these questions or these objections to me.[1] I find them important and capable of advancing the discussion. They are formulated in an uncompromising manner, but also—something rare enough to be worth mentioning—with prudence and courtesy. Above all, you have given another chance to a debate which, at the opening of "Limited Inc . . . ," I described as "improbable." I asked then, of this debate: Has it taken place? What is its place if it takes place? Will it take place, will it have taken place one day? At what time, in what time, according to what mode, under what conditions? (pp. 29–30) These questions remain posed. But has not your gesture already begun to displace them?

Am I right to insist, even before beginning, on the debate itself, its possibility, its necessity, its style, its "ethics," its "politics"? You know, of course—many readers were doubtless struck by this—that what went on more than ten years ago around *Sec* and "Limited Inc . . ." concerned above all our experience of violence and of our relation to the law—everywhere, to be sure, but most directly in the way we discuss "among ourselves," in the academic world. Of this violence, I tried at the time to *say* something. I also tried, at the same time, to *do* something. I will return to this in my answers.

I want to refer here to a sort of friendly contract between us: it is clearly understood that this republication and our exchange should serve above all as an invitation to *others*, in the course of a discussion that is both open and yet to come. I have accepted your invitation with this hope in mind and not at all with the aim of providing a finishing touch or having the last word. What matters most to me today in these texts is perhaps not so much their theoretical or philosophical "contents." For these "contents" have been elaborated elsewhere more systematically, explicitly, and demonstratively. This is true of my two essays (which

111

refer to many other texts, of mine and of others) and it is doubtless also true of Searle's *Reply*.

Beyond these theoretical or philosophical contents, what counts for me more today are all the symptoms that this polemical "scene" can still make legible. These symptoms amount to an invitation to decipher the rules, the conventions, the uses which dominate the academic space and the intellectual institutions in which we debate, with others but also with ourselves. With or without success, with a success that is always changing, these laws "contain" and thus also betray all sorts of violence.

On what side was the worst violence in this controversy to be found, in 1977? What are the roots—or the nonroots—of this violence? And of right? Of morality? Of politics? Why are such large questions inscribed in an exchange of arguments that is ostensibly so limited, even academic and "micrological," concerning the structure of speech acts, of intentionality, of citation, of metaphor, of writing and of the signature, of philosophy and of literature, and other similar matters? More broadly, why and in what respects are such questions of right, of morality and of politics, incapable of being contained within the academic compound which serves us here as an experimental micromodel? They take us well beyond the university and the intellectual field. They even render something else apparent: the delimitation of this field, were it to be interpreted naively in terms of a discussion held to be theoretical, disinterested, liberal, nonviolent, apolitical, would be the artifice of an untenable denial, the practical effect of scanty analysis and voracious interest. The violence, political or otherwise, at work in academic discussions or in intellectual discussions generally, must be acknowledged. In saying this I am not advocating that such violence be unleashed or simply accepted. I am above all asking that we try to recognize and analyze it as best we can in its various forms: obvious or disguised, institutional or individual, literal or metaphoric, candid or hypocritical, in good or guilty conscience. And if, as I believe, violence remains in fact (almost) ineradicable, its analysis and the most refined, ingenious account of its conditions will be the least violent gestures, perhaps even nonviolent, and in any case those which contribute most to transforming the legal-ethical-political rules: *in* the university and *outside* the university.

"In" and "outside": this is not unrelated to the significant fact that the controversy here revolves around the interpretation (theoretical and practical) of "marginality" and of "parasitism."

B. *On the other hand*, by addressing myself to you in the form of a letter, I will reduce just a little (but only a little) the essential predicament [*trouble*] of all speech and of all writing, that of *context* and of *destination*. The questions or potential objections that you formulate are, I think I understand, in part your own. But to what point and, above all, until what point in time? My feeling is that you yourself hesitate and formulate these questions in a movement that is open, perhaps even as part of an evolution in progress, as though your own theoretical-political perspectives or your strategic choices were in the process of changing. For these questions and objections are also those of other readers, of whom you feel obliged to make yourself the interpreter. You represent them in their absence, but also in order to permit me to respond to them and thus allow the largest possible community to speak out. The anonymous society, the corporation [*la société anonyme*] of these readers, such as you interpret it, includes above all those who are not exactly consumed by the desire to understand me or in any case to approve of me ("some American critics of your work," "those who attack deconstruction," "the popular criticisms of your work," "American commentators," "some of your commentators"). Who are these readers or these commentators? How many are they? How are they to be situated? Why define them in this way or that? We will return to these questions. I allude to the "pragmatic" aspect of the situation because its traits already bear upon the fundamentals of the debate engaged by "Limited Inc . . ." and which we *reiterate*, which we repeat while transforming it in a new context (absence or relative indetermination of emitting subjects or addressees, writing, signature, interpretation, citation without citation, etc.).

In addressing my answers to *you*, in the first place and as directly as possible, in entrusting myself to the contextual limits determined by *your questions*, I shall reduce just a little the violence and the ambiguity. For that is what we want, isn't it, to reduce them, if possible. Is it certain that we can, on one side or the other, ever eliminate them? Is it even certain that we should try, *at all costs*? I knew, while writing my response to Searle, that it was not devoid of aggressivity. I have just reread myself: with a certain uneasiness, but also with the desire to be fair. I perceive even today in this violence of mine the very clear—and I hope distinctly formulated—concern to distinguish and submit to analysis the brutality with which, beneath an often quite manifest exterior, Searle had read me, or rather avoided reading me and trying to understand. And why, perhaps, he was not *able* to read me, why this inability was exemplary and symptomatic. And for him lasting, doubtless irreversible, as I have since learned through the press. In a more general way, I wanted to show how certain practices of academic politeness or impoliteness could result in a form of brutality that I disapprove of and would like to disarm, in my fashion. To put it even more generally, and perhaps more essentially, I would have wished to make legible the (philosophical, ethical, political) axiomatics hidden beneath the code of academic discussion. The values of propriety and of property, of the proper name, of copyright (the rights of the author), are only one example or guiding thread. It turns out that these axiomatics are presupposed by speech act theory, in Searle's version at least. In the best of cases, they are not only presupposed there but interpreted, and in my eyes, inadequately. This is what *obliges* us (I am speaking here of *duty*) to treat it both theoretically and practically, including our ways of speaking, writing, conducting ourselves when participating in academic discussions. *Politeness and politics*— might well have been the subtitle of "Limited Inc . . ."

C. *Finally*, I address myself to you in the form of a letter and in as "straightforward" a way as possible because, as I have always been aware, the text of "Limited Inc . . ." must have seemed not only violent (even if it was in response to a form

113

of aggression that, in its blindness, I persist in deeming to be far worse) but also difficult to read. I shall return shortly to certain causes of these difficulties, which relate to the manner in which the *concept* itself (nothing less!) is thought or treated there. But even now, I would like to say a word about the writing of the rhetoric of the text, in its principal modality. In so doing I shall also explain why things will be different as far as this letter is concerned. "Limited Inc . . ." makes uncomfortable reading because its text is written in at least two registers at once, for it answers to at least two imperatives. On the one hand, I try to submit myself to the most demanding norms of classical philosophical discussion. I try in fact to respond point by point, in the most honest and rational way possible, to Searle's arguments, the text of which is cited almost in its entirety. On the other hand, in so doing I multiply statements, discursive gestures, forms of writing, the structure of which reinforces my demonstration in something like a practical manner: that is, by providing instances of "speech acts" which by themselves render impracticable and theoretically insufficient the conceptual oppositions upon which speech act theory in general, and Searle's version of it in particular, relies (serious/nonserious; literal/metaphoric or ironic; normal forms/parasitical forms; use/mention; intentional/nonintentional; etc.). This *dual writing* seemed to me to be consistent with the propositions I wanted simultaneously to demonstrate on the theoretical level and to exemplify in the *practice* of speech *acts*. Of speech acts concerning which I did not want it forgotten that they are *written*, and that this opens up possibilities and problems which are not negligible. *Moreover*, it was as though I was telling Searle, *in addition*: Try to interpret this text too with your categories—and to you, as well as the reader, I say: enjoy!

At the time, this wish was quite sincere. Today, however, the context having changed, I have decided to avoid writing here in this dual mode. Or at least to try, since it is not always possible, by definition. In addressing myself to you in the most direct manner possible, I return to a very classical, "straightforward" form of discussion. But before beginning with your first question, I will also ask those readers of this "open letter" who already have read the pieces of this small corpus more than ten years ago, not to rely upon their memory and not to rush straight to what seems new to them, that is, to this afterword, to your questions and to my answers. I ask them first to *reread* attentively the preceding texts. Not only because I consider them very difficult, overdetermined, and extremely intricate, but also because your questions and my answers will thereby gain in clarity without being obliged to develop or rehearse excessively.

Question.

Some American critics of your work (Searle among them) accuse you of setting up a kind of "all or nothing" choice between pure realization or self-presence and complete freeplay or undecidability. They argue that you posit a state of "ideal purity" ("Limited Inc . . . ," p. 67) as the goal of language or of interpretation, and then, when this goal predictably proves illusory, you conclude that language and interpretation are in some profound way problematized. But are these the only alternatives? Could one not object to attributing the goal of "ideal purity" to language to begin with? In his review of Jonathan Culler's On Deconstruction: Theory and Criticism after Structuralism *(in the* New York Review of Books, *27 Oct. 1983), Searle associates you with the assumption, "oddly enough derived from logical positivism," that "unless a distinction can be made rigorous and precise it isn't really a distinction at all."*

To put this point another way, in an interesting sentence in Of Grammatology, *you say, "We are dispossessed of the longed-for presence in the gesture of language by which we attempt to seize it" (p. 141). But if one refrained from ascribing to language a "longed-for" metaphysical presence, would language then need to be seen as dispossessed of something? In other words, is there not a danger here of keeping certain linguistic superstitions alive in order to legitimate the project of calling them into question?*

To apply this argument to Sec *and "Limited Inc . . .," are not concepts like intention made to seem vulnerable there by being identified with metaphysical claims that they need not entail? For example, in "Limited Inc . . ." you say that what* Sec *"questions is not intention or intentionality but their* telos, *which orients and organizes the movement and the possibility of a fulfillment, realization, and* actualization *in a plenitude that would be* present *to and identical with itself" (p. 56). But to what extent do Searle and Austin (or the more "secularized" tradition of language philosophers since Wittgenstein) invest intention with the longing for metaphysical plenitude? Could they not object that intention doesn't necessarily imply pure plenitude, that they are treating it merely as a pragmatic concept?*

Another example would be your statement on p. 56 that in no case will intention be "totally present to its object and to itself." One imagines the retort: perhaps not, but then who said intention is totally self-present in that way?

Answer.

You are entirely right to ask: "Could one not object to attributing the goal of 'ideal purity' to language [and interpretation] to begin with?" Yes, precisely, and it is by this very objection that I in fact began. This is what my discourse on parasitism and impurity, ambiguity, etc., signifies. It is the point of my questions on the opposition between the "normal (standard)" and the "nonstandard," the "serious" and the "nonserious," and all sorts of other oppositions designed to save at least the concept of an "ideal purity." I will come back to this, but for the moment let us continue.

First of all, I never proposed "a kind of 'all or nothing' choice between pure realization of self-presence and complete freeplay or undecidability." I never believed in this and I never spoke of "complete freeplay or undecidability." I am certain that the "American critics of [my] work" can find nothing in my texts which corresponds to that. And for good reason. There can be no "completeness" where freeplay is concerned. Greatly overestimated in my texts in the United States, this notion of "freeplay" is an inadequate translation of the lexical network connected to the word *jeu*, which I used in my first texts, but sparingly and in a highly defined manner. Above all, no completeness is possible for undecidability. This, I have often stated, is to be understood in a variety of senses.

For the sake of schematizing, at least three meanings can be distinguished:

1. One of them determines in a manner that is still too *anti*dialectical, hence too dialectical, that which resists binarity or even triplicity (see in particular *Dissemination*).

2. The other defines, still *within the order of the calculable*, the *limits* of decidability, of calculability or of formalizable completeness.

3. The third remains *heterogeneous* both to the dialectic and to the calculable. In accordance with what is only ostensibly a paradox, *this particular* undecidable opens the field of decision or of decidability. It calls for decision in the order of ethical-political responsibility. It is even its necessary condition. A decision can only come into being in a space that exceeds the calculable program that would destroy all responsibility by transforming it into a programmable effect of determinate causes. There can be no moral or political responsibility without this trial and this passage by way of the undecidable. Even if a decision seems to take only a second and not to be preceded by any deliberation, it is structured by this *experience and experiment of the undecidable*. If I insist on this point from now on, it is, I repeat, because this discussion is, will be, and ought to be at bottom an ethical-political one. I sense too that this is the dimension that preoccupies you the most.

In none of these three meanings is any completeness possible for undecidability. The effect of the latter is precisely to render all totalization, fulfillment, plenitude impossible. The pathos of an indecision or an undecidability that would be opposed, as in your question, to the symmetrical pathos of "pure self-presence" was never mine, even if some insisted on reading their own in(to) it.

I have certainly not sought to keep "certain linguistic superstitions alive in order to legitimate the project of calling them into question." For several reasons. What you designate by these words, and what indeed I try to "deconstruct," seems to me, insofar as it is desire or need, to be indestructible, or, I would even venture to say, "immortal," and moreover, for the same reasons, mortal, or, rather, deadly, in the sense of death-bearing [*mortifère*]. Is not the "pure realization of self-presence" itself also death? Indestructible desire or need, then, but of what, precisely?

Of something I shall define in an instant and which cannot be reduced to the order of the linguistic. Of something that is neither a "superstition" nor merely vestigial [*survivance*], but sometimes also the condition of the most vital, most active, most contemporary science. Of something that, in the metaphysical axiomatics I question, is confounded with the demands of rational logic and of philosophy as a rigorous science. Every concept that lays claim to any rigor whatsoever implies the alternative of "all or nothing." Even if in "reality" or in "experience" everyone believes he knows that there is never "all or nothing," a concept determines itself only according to "all or nothing." Even the concept of

116

"difference of degree," the concept of relativity is, qua concept, determined according to the logic of all or nothing, of yes or no: differences of degree *or* nondifference of degree. It is impossible or illegitimate to form a *philosophical concept* outside this logic of all or nothing. But one can (and it is what I try to do elsewhere) think or deconstruct the concept of concept otherwise, think a *différance* which would be neither of nature nor of degree, and of which I say—as of other analogous motifs, iterability for example, about which there will be much to rediscuss—that they are not entirely words or concepts. But it is true, when a concept is to be treated as a concept I believe that one has to accept the logic of all or nothing. I always try to do this and I believe that it always has to be done, at any rate, in a theoretical-philosophical discussion of concepts or of things conceptualizable. Whenever one feels obliged to stop doing this (as happens to me when I speak of *différance*, of mark, of supplement, of iterability and of all they entail),[2] it *is better* to make explicit in the most conceptual, rigorous, formalizing, and pedagogical manner possible the reasons one has for doing so, for thus changing the rules and the context of discourse. This is better for thought and for the relation to the other, the two of which I do not separate here: neither from each other nor from the "experience" of *différance*.

To take up once again several examples central to this debate, the discourse that seems problematic to me—and Searle's is only one example of it—neither can nor should avoid saying: it's serious *or* nonserious, ironical *or* nonironical, present *or* nonpresent, metaphorical *or* nonmetaphorical, intentional *or* nonintentional, parasitic *or* nonparasitic, citational *or* noncitational, promissive *or* nonpromissive, etc. To this oppositional logic, which is necessarily, legitimately, a logic of "all or nothing" and without which the distinction and the limits of a concept would have no chance, I oppose nothing, least of all a logic of *approximation* [*à peu près*], a simple empiricism of difference in degree; rather I add a supplementary complication that calls for other concepts, for other thoughts beyond the concept and another form of "general theory," or rather another discourse, another "logic" that accounts for the impossibility of concluding such a "general theory."

This other discourse doubtless takes into account the conditions of this classical and binary logic, but it no longer depends entirely upon it. If the proponents of binary opposition think that the "ideal purity" to which they are obliged to appeal reveals itself to be "illusory," as you say, then they are obliged to account for this fact. They must transform concepts, construct a different "logic," a different "general theory," perhaps even a discourse that, more powerful than this logic, will be able to account for it and reinscribe its possibility. This is what I try to do. I try to show not only that the ideal purity of the distinctions proposed (by Searle, for example) is inaccessible, but also that its practice would necessitate excluding certain essential traits of what it claims to explain or describe—and yet cannot integrate into the "general theory." To be sure, all conceptual production appeals to idealization. Even the "concept" of iterability, which plays an organizing role in "Limited Inc . . .," supposes such idealization. But it has a strange status. Like that of "différance" and several others, it is an aconceptual concept or another kind of concept, heterogeneous to the philosophical concept of the concept, a "concept" that marks both the possibility and the limit of all idealization and hence of all conceptualization.

You asked, then: "Could one not object to attributing the goal of 'ideal purity' to language to begin with?" First, a few clarifications.

As I just said, this objection could above all be addressed to Searle, and I have done so. I am obliged to cite Searle once again to make this clear: "... certain forms of analysis, especially analysis into necessary and sufficient conditions, are likely to involve (in varying degrees) idealization of the concept analyzed. In the present case, our analysis will be directed at the center of the concept of promising. I am ignoring marginal, fringe, and partially defective promises. Furthermore, in the analysis I confine my discussion to full blown explicit promises and ignore promises made by elliptical turns of phrase, hints, metaphors, etc. In short, I am going to deal only with a simple and idealized case.... Without abstraction and idealization there is no systematization."

Note that, having cited these phrases of Searle in their context, I did not criticize them directly or head-on (see pp. 68ff.), as you might have done, following the logic of the objection you address to me. On the contrary, I acknowledge a certain necessity, even a certain legitimacy of the classical exigency defined by Searle, to which I did not oppose "empirical difficulties" (p. 69).

My objections were different.

1. They aimed on the one hand at the "analogy" invoked by Searle to justify his "idealization," that is, the analogy between a theory of language and all other scientific theory. There can be no rigorous analogy between a scientific theory, no matter which, and a theory of language, for several reasons, which I formulate (pp. 69–70). I do not exclude the possibility of this leading to extreme consequences, but in my eyes this is neither obscurantist nor antiscientific; on the contrary, it is not certain that what we call language or speech acts can ever be exhaustively determined by an entirely objective science or theory. It is more "scientific" to take this limit, if it is one, into account and to treat it as a point of departure for rethinking this or that received concept of "science" and of "objectivity."

2. But on the other hand, even from the point of view of classical theory and of its necessary idealization in the construction of conceptual models, I objected to the series of exclusions practiced by Searle (see the passages cited, p. 68). Inasmuch as it does not integrate the *possibility* of borderline cases, the *essential* possibility of those cases called "marginal," of accidents, anomalies, contaminations, parasitism, inasmuch as it does not account for how, *in* the ideal concept of a structure said to be "normal," "standard," etc. (for example, that of the promise), such a divergence is *possible*, it may be said that the formation of a general theory or of an ideal concept remains insufficient, weak, or empirical. In such a case, the idealization practiced itself remains defective; it has not taken into

account certain essential predicates. It fails to render an account of that whose ideal concept it is seeking to construct.

3. These two types of objection ensconced themselves, as it were, within the axiomatics of idealization in order to reveal the incoherence or the inconsistency (for instance, that of Searle) by which they can, upon occasion, be afflicted. But in going further, it must be shown why, for what reasons (which are structural, and not empirical or accidental) such idealization finds its limit. This limit is neither external nor internal; it is not simply negative since it renders possible the very idealization that it at the same time limits. Such is the strange alogical logic of what I call "iterability." I hasten to add, for I am not certain that I said it clearly in "Limited Inc . . . ," that the concept of iterability itself, like all the concepts that form or deform themselves in its wake,[3] is an ideal concept, to be sure, but also the concept that marks the essential and ideal limit of all pure idealization, the ideal concept of the limit of all idealization, and not the concept of nonideality (since it is also the concept of the possibility of ideality). Let us not forget that "iterability" does not signify simply, as Searle seems to think, repeatability of the same, but rather alterability of this same idealized in the singularity of the event, for instance, in this or that speech act. It entails the necessity of thinking *at once* both the rule and the event, concept and singularity. There is thus a reapplication (without transparent self-reflection and without pure self-identity) of the *principle* of iterability to a *concept* of iterability that is never pure. There is no idealization without (identificatory) iterability; but for the same reason, for reasons of (altering) iterability, there is no idealization that keeps itself pure, safe from all contamination. The concept of iterability is this singular concept that renders possible the silhouette of ideality, and hence of the concept, and hence of all distinction, of all conceptual opposition. But it is also the concept that, *at the same time*, with the same stroke marks the limit of idealization and of conceptualization: "concept" or quasiconcept of concept in its conceptualizable relation to the nonconcept (cf. p. 71). These things are difficult, I admit; their formulation can be disconcerting. But would there be so many problems and misunderstandings without this complexity and without these paradoxes? One shouldn't complicate things for the pleasure of complicating, but one should also never simplify or pretend to be sure of such simplicity where there is none. If things were simple, word would have gotten around, as you say in English. There you have one of my mottos, one quite appropriate for what I take to be the spirit of the type of "enlightenment" granted our time. Those who wish to simplify at all costs and who raise a hue and cry about obscurity because they do not recognize the unclarity of their good old *Aufklärung* are in my eyes dangerous dogmatists and tedious obscurantists. No less dangerous (for instance, in politics) are those who wish to purify at all costs.

It would no doubt be of little use for me to take up again here the demonstration of page 68 and following. I did however feel it necessary, in response to your objection, to recall the true place of the discussion in which I was engaged. I will try to be brief.

1. The " 'all or nothing' choice" was not "set up" by me. It is implied in every distinction or every opposition of concepts, which is to say, of idealities. For example, and here it is Searle who says this, a speech act ought to be serious or not, literal or not, intentional or not: "Either . . . or," "yes or no," "all or nothing." What indeed would become of speech act theory without this "all or nothing choice"? It would immediately disintegrate. There are those who think that this is precisely what is in fact happening or is bound to happen if this logic, which undoubtedly must be maintained, is not at last put to work differently, in a more discriminating way, with a greater power of formalization, integrating what it thought obliged to exclude.

2. It was not I who posed "a state of ideal purity" as the goal of all language. When I employ the words "ideal purity" (p. 67), it is not in direct or exclusive relation to language *itself* and in general, even if something of the sort existed and might be made the object of metalinguistic concepts of linguistics. Rather, more precisely, more narrowly, it is to address the categories to which Searle resorts (central/parasitic or marginal, serious/nonserious, literal/metaphoric or sarcastic, etc.).

3. It is Searle himself, as we have seen, who reminds us of the necessity of ideal concepts.

4. I do not believe I said that this "goal of language or of interpretation" reveals itself to be "illusory." If I had used this word, which I find nowhere in my text, it would have been an unfortunate choice. Illusion is so little involved here that indeed the structural idealism of which we have just spoken constitutes the condition of a certain classical value of what is called scientific truth. This much said, if this ideal is, as I think and have just recalled, not illusory but instead rendered inaccessible by the very iterability that *nevertheless produces it and renders its project possible*, then indeed and in two senses, "language and interpretation are in some profound way problematized." They are, first of all, in the manner that the language and interpretation I discuss in "Limited Inc . . . " (represented by Searle) are. But in a much more general fashion, so are *all* language and *all* interpretation. Don't you believe that all language and all interpretation are problematic? More than problematic even, which is to say, perhaps of an order other than problematicity? Isn't this also a stroke of luck? Otherwise, why speak, why discuss? How else would what we call "misunderstanding" be possible? That we may or may not be in agreement on this subject attests by itself to this more than problematic problematicity. I only sought to formalize its law in a more "comprehensive" manner. My formulas are not absolute or absolutely formalizable; they cannot claim to be a metalanguage, for reasons I have already given, here and elsewhere.

Your first question goes on to refer to two examples. First, that of intention. The *telos* of "fulfillment, realization and actualization in a plenitude" is indeed a "metaphysical claim." But "metaphysical claim" does not signify here, or at least not in my mind, a futile or obscure speculation. It is for instance the structure described by Husserl (and I believe that I referred to this) in the *Logical*

Investigations, following the movement of a rigorous phenomenological gesture. Searle is deeply indebted to him, whether he knows it, recognizes it, or not. Husserl distinguishes his phenomenology from speculative metaphysics but not from all metaphysics, and I believe, for my part, that his phenomenology is also, as I have tried to show, a great metaphysics.

Moreover, the *telos* of "fulfillment" (and in this I believe Husserl was right) is not an accidental element, separable from the concept of intentionality. It is not a "metaphysical supplement," as in French one sometimes speaks of a "supplement of soul" [*supplément d'âme*], a residue that need only be eliminated in order finally to speak scientifically (and not metaphysically) about intentionality. This *telos* of "fulfillment" is constitutive of intentionality; it is part of its concept. Intentional movement tends toward this fulfillment. This is the origin or the fatality of that "longing for metaphysical plenitude" which, however, can also be presupposed, described, or lived without the romantic, even mystical pathos sometimes associated with those words.

It is not accurate therefore to suggest that anyone who uses the word "intentionality" "invests intention with the *longing* for metaphysical plenitude." Nor did I ever say so. Nevertheless, if one wishes to speak rigorously of an intentional structure one should take into account, with or without "longing," the *telos* of plenitude that constitutes it. This is moreover what Searle does, whether or not he is "longing for metaphysical plenitude" in this or that mode in the texts I have cited and which for the sake of clarity I shall cite again in an instant. This plenitude (this "fulfillment"), for reasons I have already stated (iterability, structure of the trace and of the mark in general), is already inaccessible in perception or in intuition in general as the experience of a present content. This holds a fortiori for what we are concerned with here, the relation of "meaning" between an intention and a speech act. Now, what does Searle literally say? What does he say about "meaningfulness" in relation to intention? He writes this: ". . . there is no getting away from intentionality, because a *meaningful sentence is just a standing possibility of the corresponding (intentional) speech act*" (p. 202, Searle's emphasis). Or again: "But of course in serious literal speech the sentences are precisely the realizations of the intentions: there need be no *gulf* at all between the illocutionary intention and its expression" (p. 202).

The word "realization," which implies of course achievement or "fulfillment," is thus Searle's word. I should not be accused of having lent him or others what in their work I would like to call into question. I take the liberty of repeating your question here, so that readers may have it before them in all clarity: "For example, in 'Limited Inc . . .' you say that what *Sec* 'questions is not intention or intentionality but their *telos*, which orients and organizes the movement and the possibility of a fulfillment, realization, and *actualization* in a plenitude that would be *present* to and identical with itself' (p. 56). But to what extent do Searle and Austin (or the more 'secularized' tradition of language philosophers since Wittgenstein) invest intention with the longing for metaphysical plenitude?

Could they not object that intention doesn't necessarily imply pure plenitude, that they are treating it merely as a pragmatic concept?"

To this question I reply as follows: for Searle at least (and no doubt for others, but I can hardly speak of them here—things are already complicated enough), "realization" is indeed the *telos* of intentionality in speech acts. "Realization" is his word, as we have just verified. It signifies as much as "actualization" or "fulfillment." The "realization" of intentions is explicitly defined by Searle as the "sentence" itself, as the exemplary "sentence," which is to say, the sentence "in serious literal speech."

I do not therefore have to attribute anything unjustly to Searle. He himself formulates, as seriously and literally as possible, this *telos* of full "realization." Moreover: to say that in "serious and literal" language "the sentences are precisely the realizations of the intentions" amounts not merely to proposing a theoretically and philosophically neutral statement concerning a law held to regulate the relation of the two series (realization of intentions on the one hand, seriousness and literalness of expressions on the other). It is tantamount to stating, in a normative or prescriptive manner, that toward which language *ought to* tend: only a serious and literal language can fully realize an intention, or, reciprocally, the best language is, will be, ought to be serious and literal because only in this way can expression become the "realization" of "intention." It is clear that seriousness and literalness are exemplary qualities for the phrases Searle wishes to study and which form the point of departure for what he calls the "idealization of the analyzed concept." Such phrases are defined precisely in terms of the "realization" of intentions in expression. This prescriptive normativeness is not overtly moralistic. I have already said that I never suspected speech act theoreticians of purely and simply giving us moral lessons and telling us to be serious, to avoid metaphors and ellipses. But often while analyzing a certain ethicity inscribed in language—and this ethicity is a metaphysics (there is nothing pejorative in defining it as such)—they reproduce, under the guise of describing it in its ideal purity, the given ethical conditions of a *given* ethics. They exclude, ignore, relegate to the margins other conditions no less essential to ethics in general, whether of *this given* ethics or of *another*, or of a law that would not answer to Western concepts of ethics, right, or politics. Such conditions, which may be anethical with respect to any given ethics, are not therefore anti-ethical in general. They can even open or recall the opening of another ethics, another right, another "declaration of rights," transformation of constitutions, etc. It is such conditions that interest me when I write of iterability and of all that is tied to this quasi concept in a discourse and in other texts that I cannot reproduce here. The ethical-legal-political implications of all these gestures would be easy enough to show; we will doubtless return to this.

This intentionalist teleology is inseparable, in Searle, from this logic of "all or nothing" that you suspect me of projecting. In fact, not only do I find this logic strong, and, in conceptual language and analysis, *an absolute must [il la faut]*, it must (this "it must" translates the faithfulness of my love for philosophy) be sustained against all empirical confusion, to the point where the same demand of rigor requires the structure of that logic to be transformed or complicated.

Not only, therefore, am I far from frontally assaulting or directly deconstructing this logic of all or nothing with an eye to reducing it to, precisely, nothing, but I never project it unjustly into someone else's discourse, for example, Searle's. It is Searle who is obliged to practice conceptual oppositions dominated by the logic of "all or nothing." And he is right in thinking that phrases can never be *just a little* literal or *more or less* metaphorical. Thus, he writes: "I contrast 'serious' utterances with play acting, teaching a language, reciting poems, practicing pronunciation, etc., and I contrast 'literal' with metaphorical, sarcastic, etc." Previously, he had written—I must cite it again to underscore the way in which this oppositional logic goes together with a teleology of plenitude—". . . I confine my discussion to full blown explicit promises and ignore promises made by elliptical turns of phrase, hints, metaphors . . ."

From the moment that Searle entrusts himself to an oppositional logic, to the "distinction" of concepts by "contrast" or "opposition" (a legitimate demand that I share with him, even if I do not at all elicit the same consequences from it), I have difficulty seeing how he is nevertheless able to write this phrase, cited by you, in which he credits me with the "assumption," "oddly enough derived from logical positivism," "that unless a distinction can be made rigorous and precise, it isn't really a distinction at all."

Among all the accusations that shocked me coming from his pen, and which I will not even try to enumerate, why is it that this one is without a doubt the most stupefying, the most unbelievable? And, I must confess, also the most incomprehensible to me.

1. First of all, if it is an accusation, should it not concern above all the author of the phrases I have just cited ("I contrast, . . . and I contrast," "I ignore . . . ," etc.)? Every one of these prescribes the distinction, in a "rigorous and precise" manner, between so many things: "literal/nonliteral, serious/nonserious, etc." Does this not amount to practicing an "all or nothing choice" and taking as a model an "ideal purity"?

2. How can one dare, resorting to such a worn-out rhetorical procedure, to make the pretense of attributing the demand for "rigorous and precise distinction" to a philosophical doctrine or tendency ("logical positivism") which one ostensibly holds to be very circumscribed, even outmoded, and in any case without any presumed relationship to my philosophical "style," all this in order to discredit the logic of my objections? How can one make the demand for "rigorous and precise" distinction the property of any one school of thought or of any one philosophical style? What philosopher ever since there were philosophers, what logician ever since there were logicians, what theoretician ever renounced this axiom: in the order of concepts (for we are speaking of concepts and not of the colors of clouds or the taste of certain chewing gums), when a distinction cannot be rigorous or precise, it is not a distinction at all. If Searle declares explicitly, seriously, literally that this axiom must be renounced, that he renounces

it (and I will wait for him to do it, a phrase in a newspaper is not enough), then, short of practicing deconstruction with some consistency and of submitting the very rules and regulations of his project to an explicit reworking, his entire philosophical discourse on speech acts will collapse even more rapidly. The entire apparatus of distinctions on which this discourse is based will melt away like snow in the sun. To each word will have to be added "a little," "more or less," "up to a certain point," "rather," and despite all this, the literal will not cease being somewhat metaphorical, "mention" will not stop being tainted by "use," the "intentional" no less slightly "unintentional," etc. Searle knows well that he neither can nor should go in this direction. He has never afforded himself the theoretical means of escaping conceptual opposition without empiricist confusion.

What does he do then? On the one hand, he maintains *at all costs*, in his books, the most rigid and most traditional form of the excluded third, he applies the principle even when it obliges him to practice the most brutal and least motivated exclusions. But on the other hand, when he has to retreat into journalistic polemics, he resorts to denial and pretends to have renounced trenchant distinction. For that, he distinguishes (all the same!) calmly (but this time what is the status of this distinction?) between theoretical concepts on the one hand and "real life" on the other. If the former are inadequate to the latter, from which they purely and simply exclude all phenomena said to be "marginal," which they are not capable of taking into account and in truth are not charged to do so, then this does not seem to bother him for a second. My feeling is that he is wrong and misled in both cases. Or rather, that he is misled in the first case and wishes to mislead us in the second. One can hardly believe one's eyes reading the following assertion in the article to which you refer: "He [Culler] also mistakenly supposes that the theory of speech acts seeks some sort of precise dividing line between what is and what is not a promise." "Mistakenly"? Really? In fact, I supposed exactly what Culler supposes. And I still suppose it. And I believe we are right. And the texts that I have cited here do not seem to me to signify anything different. Unless Searle's writing has all of a sudden become what in his own eyes would be perversely "meaningless" or diabolically "playful," I persist in believing that, with organized perseverance, it "seeks some sort of precise dividing line between what is and what is not a promise," notably when he writes in *Speech Acts* (once again I cite), "Our analysis will be directed at the center of the concept of promising. I am ignoring marginal, fringe, and partially defective promises . . ." Once again this would be perfectly legitimate, in my eyes, had the exclusion of those "marginal" cases not been relegated by him to the obscure corner of that thing obscurely and tranquilly named "real life" (I had already said what I thought of this category in "Limited Inc . . . ," see pp. 89–90), and had he sought to render an accounting, theoretically, of these so-called marginal cases. I cite once again (I like and am obliged to cite frequently, so as not to be suspected of injustice or abuse of language) and re-cite at somewhat greater length this time the article from the *New York Review of Books:* "He [Culler] also mistakenly supposes that the theory of speech acts seeks some sort of precise dividing line between what is and what is not a promise. But *in fact* it is a *consequence of the theory* that in *real life* there can be all sorts of *marginal* cases within each family of speech acts" (my emphasis). I will make an effort to leave my stupefaction at this phrase behind and will raise only one or two questions among the much greater number that it calls for. If the theory of speech acts (and it should always be added: in the form given it by Searle, which is far from being its sole representative, much less exhausting it) does not "seek some sort of precise dividing line between what is and what is not a promise," what exactly does it do? All the more, since this strange affirmation should be valid of *all* speech acts, and not only for the promise, which is here only an example of them. If one does not look for, and hence does not find any "precise dividing line," how will a promise be determined? How will one proceed to the "idealization of the concept analyzed"? How will "the center of the concept of promising" be differentiated from "all sorts of marginal cases"? How will one distinguish between a nonideal promise as a "marginal case" and all sorts of other speech acts which have nothing to do with promises? What is "real life" for Searle? How is the space of theory to be distinguished from this so-called real life where marginal cases proliferate? Of what does speech act theory speak? Of what should it render an accounting? What should it describe and from where does it draw its objects and its examples if not from "real life"? And if it excludes, even provisionally, methodologically, what goes on there ("all sorts of marginal cases . . ."), what is left for it? To what does it refer? Why determine as "marginal" what can always go on in "real life," which is, to my knowledge, the only place from where a theory of language can draw its "facts," its "examples," its "objects"? And in "real life" how are what Searle calls "marginal cases" "within each family of speech acts" to be distinguished? How is "each family" to be determined without some sort of "precise dividing line"? I fear that all that is not really *very* serious. As in philosophy, and as a classical philosopher (which, it is true, I remain as well), I don't see a big difference, here again, between being "just a little serious" and being "not serious at all," all of which, I'm afraid, is not serious at all. No more so than the opportunism of a polemic that drove Searle to deny in an inconsistent manner or to mask precipitately a theoretical weakness.

Indeed, Searle's article in the *New York Review of Books*, an article of unbridled resentment (written *after* "Limited Inc . . ." and without the slightest reference to my discussion of his theses), seems to me to testify both to the incoherence I have just recalled and to a reading of the texts concerned which at the very least is hasty. But I cannot demonstrate this point by point without trying, this time, the patience of readers who can consult this article on their own (and naturally also the texts of which Searle claims to speak) in order to decide for themselves whether my generalization is unfair or not. But I shall return later to the ethical-political dimensions of the behavior I am criticizing here.

Since I have just spoken of inconsistency and lack of consequence, a final question on the same phrase: What do "fact" and "consequence" mean when

Searle writes; "But in fact it is a consequence of the theory that in real life there can be all sorts of marginal cases within each family of speech acts"? Could the "fact" ("in fact") be that the "marginal cases" in "real life" are a "consequence of the theory"? Have I understood correctly? But what exactly is to be understood? That what Searle calls "real life" is, with its marginal cases, a "consequence of the theory"? This itself would be astonishing enough, but at least it would confirm that a theory can never authorize itself, as Searle's does, to "ignore" anything in "real life" and least of all "marginal, fringe and partially defective promises . . .," "promises made by elliptical turns of phrase, hints, metaphors, etc.," "parasitic forms of communication such as telling jokes or acting in a play . . .," "and all sorts of marginal cases within each family of speech acts. . . ." Unless this formula is only a rather clumsy manner (but in that case clumsy indeed for a theoretician of language) of saying that one can only determine marginal cases, and first of all encounter them *as such*, by starting from and consistently following the consequences of theory. If this is indeed what Searle means, then I reiterate my objection: a theory of nonmarginal cases is only possible, interesting, and consistent if it can account, in the structure of those cases said to be nonmarginal, for the essential possibility of cases interpreted as marginal, deviant, parasitical, etc. How are the latter possible? What must the structure called "normal" or "normative" be, what must the structure of the field where it inscribes itself be for the deviant or the parasitical to be possible?

In the face of these same problems and to avoid such inconsistency and confusion, what are the principles to which I subscribe, in "Limited Inc . . ." and elsewhere? In referring to these texts, I must restrict myself here to the most schematic remarks.

1. I confirm it: for me, from the point of view of theory and of the concept, "unless a distinction can be made rigorous and precise it isn't really a distinction." Searle is entirely right, for once, in attributing this "assumption" to me. I feel close to those who share it. I am sufficiently optimistic to believe that they are quite numerous and are not limited, as Searle declares, with rather uncommon condescension, to "audiences of literary critics" before whom he has "lectured."[4] Does Searle seriously think that only "literary theorists" would raise this objection? I had in effect already suspected that this was an assumption that Searle himself did not share continuously, rigorously enough, even before he let it be known in such a highly improvised manner, in the *New York Review of Books*. I regretted it and said to myself that he must feel rather isolated in the community of philosophers and scholars.

2. This being said, for the same reason I do not have confidence in *just any* conceptual distinctions. When this or that conceptual opposition does not operate distinctly, when it functions only by virtue of a too "weak" idealization that pays the price of excluding all phenomena called "marginal" and of being incapable of describing or accounting for anything whatsoever, then, without renouncing either the concept or the distinction, without capitulating to empiricism, for example, to the "a little fictional" or the "somewhat ironic," I believe

one must search to comprehend what is going on, to analyze the presuppositions of discourse, to transform its axiomatics, to propose other conceptual distinctions and even, however troubling that may appear, another general "logic." This logic can be "other" to the point of overturning a good many habits and comforts. It can lead us to complicate—distinctly—the logic of binary oppositions and to a *certain use* of the value of distinction attached to it. The latter has indeed certain limits and a history, which I have precisely tried to question. But that leads neither to "illogic" nor to "indistinction" nor to "indeterminacy." This other "logic" does not authorize, in theoretical discourse *as such*, any kind of approximative statement. It never renounces, as Searle in the haste of a polemic seems to do and to advocate, clear and rigorous distinction.

3. The concept of iterability (which is not simply the concept of repeatability, as Searle repeats in the *New York Review of Books*, repeating the initial confusion that had kept him from understanding anything in *Sec* and in several other related texts—see at least "Limited Inc . . .," p. 62) seems to me indispensable for beginning, at least, to account for all the difficulties that we meet in this field and in others. If these difficulties were not so resilient, how could such an absence of theoretical consensus be explained, such a burgeoning of heterogeneous discourses? Instead of excluding "marginal" or "parasitical" cases, what must be recognized is how a structure called normal or ideal can render possible or necessary all these phenomena, all these "accidents." And to accomplish this task, other concepts must be formed, the habitual logical space transformed (others will say, deformed), etc. Doubtless, this concept of iterability, with all its related concepts, with all its consequences or its implications (nothing less than the open-ended array [*dispositif*] of deconstructive discourse in its present phase), troubles the binary and hierarchical oppositions that authorize the very principle of "distinction," in common parlance no less than in theoretical and philosophical discourse. That is, what it does is less to disturb them than to bring into the open that which is disturbing them and menacing their consistency, their order, their pertinence. But the deconstruction of binary and hierarchical oppositions does not open the way to confusion, to "indistinction," or to the empiricism that Searle all of a sudden seems to make his own, even if it is only in order to object to those benighted "literary theorists" who think, rightly, that a distinction without rigor and without precision is not one at all. As a philosophy, empiricism is still dominated by a logic I deem it necessary to deconstruct. Doubtless the concept of iterability is not a concept like the others (nor is *différance*, nor trace, nor supplement, nor parergon, etc.). That it might belong *without* belonging to the class of concepts of which it must render an accounting, to the theoretical space that it organizes in a (as I often say) "quasi"-transcendental manner, is doubtless a proposition that can appear paradoxical, even contradictory in the eyes of common sense or of a rigid classical logic. It is perhaps unthinkable in the logic of such good sense. It supposes that something happens *by* or *to* set theory: that a term might belong *without* belonging to a set. It is of this too that we are speaking when we say "margin" or "parasite." It is of this as well that an accounting, and a

reason, must be rendered (*rendre compte et raison*), as the enlightened modern thinkers we still want to be, right? But this thought of iterability, if it troubles all exclusion or simple opposition, should not capitulate to confusion, to vague approximations, to indistinction: it leads instead to an extreme complication, multiplication, explication of "precise and rigorous distinctions." I have given several examples in "Limited Inc . . ."; I cannot return to them here.

You write: "Could they not object that intention doesn't necessarily imply pure plenitude, that they are treating it merely as a pragmatic concept?" A very complicated question. There are several ways of determining the "not necessarily" ("doesn't necessarily imply plenitude").

1. First of all, one can think that the point toward which intention necessarily tends (what we called above its *telos*) is plenitude, in the perceptive intuition, in its expression, or in the experience of adequation between intention and expression. Insofar as this *telos* necessarily defines the essence of intention, it is not "necessary" that it be attained. It can happen that for diverse reasons there can be intentional acts without plenitude and, in this sense, yes, "intention doesn't necessarily imply pure plenitude." But if intentionality is to be described in its essence (which implies the *telos*), the movement toward plenitude must be considered essential and must be integrated into the ideal concept of intention. (I say "ideal concept," i.e., also rigorous concept. If by pragmatic concept you mean one that is empirical and approximative, I have trouble seeing how it would be able to found, theoretically, seriously, a theory, Searle's, which is intentionalist through and through, treating intention as the founding principle of all speech acts that are serious, literal, and meaningful.) Nonplenitude will be treated as though it were an extrinsic accident, even if it in fact occurs frequently, even if it takes place everywhere. This I call "fundamental intentionalism"—Searle's. In this case, I do not believe that the concept of "intention" can be treated as a "pragmatic concept," not at least if by that you mean a concept that is empirically useful, provisionally convenient, constructed without great rigor. This is not how one generally wants, how one generally intends to treat it, even if it is, in my eyes, what happens most of the time.

2. To continue, one might also reason that intention is not essential to speech acts or to anything else. Language, and many other things would then have to be questioned without making the intentional structure into a principle. In this case, to be sure, intention "doesn't necessarily imply plenitude," and it lacks, even necessarily, qua finite intention, plenitude. But that is not overly important and one can treat this concept as a pragmatic concept (in the sense of "empirically useful upon occasion, in such and such a context"). This position would be shared by the nonintentionalisms and the empiricisms or pragmatisms of different types. It is not mine.

3. For I am naturally tempted by another analysis, as you have seen in "Limited Inc. . . ." In following the inclination of this temptation, I would say not simply that "intention doesn't necessarily imply pure plenitude," but that it necessarily can and should *not* attain the plenitude toward which it nonetheless inevitably

tends. Plenitude is its *telos*, but the *structure* of this *telos* is such that if it is attained, it as well as intention both disappear, are paralyzed, immobilized, or die. The relation to the *telos* is therefore necessarily dual, divided, split. What is understood as *telos* must therefore be rethought. And it is precisely to the extent that this relation to *telos* is also intricate, complex, split, that there is movement, life, language, intention, etc. Plenitude is the end (the goal), but were it attained, it would be the end (death). This non-end is not an extraneous vestige of the teleological essence of intention, it belongs to it as its most intimate and most irreducible other, as the other itself in it. It lasts as long as there is life, intention, language, or, as I prefer to say in general, the mark (or vice versa). (I take the liberty here of referring to what I say elsewhere of the finite infinite of the *différance,* in *Of Grammatology* and in *Speech and Phenomena.*) If nonplenitude (the non-*telos*) is therefore not an empirical accident of the *telos*, or even a simple negativity, one cannot not take it into account as one might a contingent accident held in the margin out of concern for method or for eidetic purity. Whether it is a question of prediscursive experience or of speech acts, plenitude is at once what *orients and endangers* the intentional movement, whether it is conscious or not. There can be no intention that does not tend toward it, but also no intention that attains it without disappearing with it. This is why, in the phrase you cite, I said that "we are dispossessed of the longed-for presence in the gesture of language by which we attempt to seize it."

What in this context I call iterability is at once that which tends to attain plenitude and that which bars access to it. Through the possibility of repeating every mark as the same it makes way for an idealization that seems to deliver the full presence of ideal objects (not present in the mode of sense perception and beyond all immediate deictics), but this repeatability itself ensures that the full presence of a singularity thus repeated comports in itself the reference to something else, thus rending the full presence that it nevertheless announces. This is why iteration is not simply repetition.

Under this name or others I have tried to describe this structure in numerous texts, and not only in *Sec* and in "Limited Inc. . . ." I cannot elaborate on that here, but I would like to add one clarification. As the condition of possibility and of impossibility, with all the paradoxes to which this last formula constrains us, iterability retains a value of generality that covers the totality of what one can call experience or the relation to something in general (Searle is right to say that "iterability looms large" in all my arguments). It does not cover this alone, but it does cover in particular what is called intentional experience. It is presupposed by all intentionality (conscious or not, human or not). Searle seems to recognize this in the last paragraph of the *Reply.* I cite it to show that "iterability looms large" in the arguments of Searle as well: "Thus the peculiar features of the intentionality that we find in speech acts require an iterability that includes not only the types we have been discussing, the repetition of the same word in different contexts, but also includes an iterability of the application of syntactical rules. Iterability—both as exemplified by the repeated use of the same word type and as exemplified by the recursive character of syntactical rules—is not as Derrida seems to think something in conflict with the intentionality of linguistic acts, spoken or written, it is the necessary presupposition of the forms which that intentionality takes" (p. 208).

In "Limited Inc . . ." (z, p. 105) I explained not only why I was in agreement with this recognition of the "necessary presupposition," but that I myself had formulated and emphasized it previously. And I did not see any "conflict" with intentionality, only a structural limit to the *telos*, to the accomplishment (fulfillment) and to the hegemony of said intentionality. The latter is no more the *telos* (the end) than it is the *arché* (beginning or commandment) of experience.

Here is the announced clarification: if the law of iterability, with all its associated laws, exceeds the intentional structure that it renders possible and whose teleo-archaeology it limits, if it is the law not merely of intentionality (nor for that matter merely of the language or the writing of man), then the question of the specificity of intentionality in this field without limit remains open: what *is* intentionality? What does "intention" properly mean as the *particular* or *original* work (*mise en oeuvre*) of iterability? I admit that this enigma grows increasingly obscure for me. It communicates with the greatest questions of being, of meaning and of the phenomenon, of consciousness, of the relation to the object in general, of transcendence and of appearing *as such*, etc. I cannot elaborate this here as I try to do elsewhere. My frequenting of philosophies and phenomenologies of intentionality, beginning with that of Husserl, has only caused my uncertainty to increase, as well as my distrust of this word or of this figure, I hardly dare to say "concept." And since that time, Searle's book on intentionality (1983) has not helped me, not in the slightest, to dispel these concerns.[5] I did not read it without interest, far from it. I am even ready to admire how the author of a book bearing this title, *Intentionality*, could choose, as he declares at the very outset, in the Introduction, to "pass over in silence" "whole philosophical movements" which "have been built around theories of intentionality," avowing, as one of his reasons, "ignorance of most of the traditional writings on Intentionality" (p. ix). Something that is indeed evident in reading the seven lines devoted to Husserl in this book of three hundred pages.

As it is not possible here to discuss the questions that this book raises for me with each phrase, I will risk instead a remark on the respective relations of certain philosophers to what is called the tradition of philosophy, the philosophical traditions.

Searle had written, "It would be a mistake, I think, to regard Derrida's discussion of Austin as a confrontation between two prominent philosophical traditions." I agree with the letter if not with the intention of this declaration, having made it clear that I sometimes felt, paradoxically, closer to Austin than to a certain Continental tradition from which Searle, on the contrary, has inherited numerous gestures and a logic I try to deconstruct. I now have to add this: it is often because "Searle" ignores this tradition or pretends to take no account of it that he rests blindly imprisoned in it, repeating its most problematic gestures, falling

short of the most elementary critical questions, not to mention the deconstructive ones. It is because in appearance at least "I" am more of a historian that "I"
am a less passive, more attentive and more "deconstructive" heir of that so-called
tradition. And hence, perhaps again paradoxically, more foreign to that tradition.
I put quotation marks around "Searle" and "I" to mark that beyond these indexes, I am aiming at tendencies, types, styles, or situations rather than at persons.

Question.

*At the end of "Limited Inc . . . ," in response to Searle's invocation of speech
act rules, you say that "there is always a police and a tribunal ready to intervene
each time a rule [constitutive or regulative, vertical or not] is invoked in a case
involving signatures, events, or contexts" (p. 105). Could you elaborate on this
statement? It seems to say that any specification of linguistic rules and conventions plays into the hands of the police, or that there is something politically suspect in the very project of attempting to fix the contexts of utterances.*

*Of course social authorities often exploit linguistic rules in repressive ways,
but does this fact implicate the codifiers of those rules? Are there not situations in
which Searle's rules could be invoked by someone who was* contesting *police
power? Can Searle's assumptions legitimately be correlated with a particular politics, repressive or otherwise? How would such a tactic differ from that of those
who attack deconstruction as inherently conservative because it has been appropriated by the American academic publish-or-perish system?*

*Perhaps this objection only invokes the concept of "iterability" developed in
Sec and "Limited Inc . . .," which, if I understand it, suggests that any rule can
serve different political uses, depending on its context.*

Answer.

I will first clarify a little the context of the phrase you cite, in which indeed
"police" and "tribunal" are in question. But as you doubtless also noticed, the
words "politics" and "repressive," which you associate with them in your question, are not drawn from my text.

Why didn't I make use of them and why nonetheless does your question remain necessary? The phrase quoted returned to the question of copyright with
which "Limited Inc . . ." had begun. It is part of a very long parenthesis, of which
at least the beginning and the end have to be reconstituted.

(But first I open *another* parenthesis before "reconstituting" the parenthesis
just evoked. The reconstitution of a context can never be perfect and irreproach-
able even though it is a regulative ideal in the ethics of reading, of interpretation,
or of discussion. But since this ideal is unattainable, for reasons which are essential and to which I will doubtless return, the determination, or even the redeter-
mination, the simple recalling of a context is never a gesture that is neutral, innocent, transparent, disinterested. At this very moment we are experiencing this
dramatically in the discourses that proliferate around the writings of de Man during the war, about which I have written elsewhere.[6] The putative or pretended

[*prétendue*] reconstitution of a context always remains a performative operation and is never purely theoretical. To come back to your formulation, "the very project of attempting to fix the contexts of utterances" may not be "something politically suspect," to be sure, but it also cannot be apolitical or politically neutral. And the analysis of the political dimension of all contextual determination is never a purely theoretical gesture. It always involves a political evaluation, even if the code of this evaluation is overdetermined, resists classifications [such as right/left], and is yet to come—promised—rather than given. I close this parenthesis in order to return to the "very long parenthesis of which at least the beginning and the end have to be reconstituted.")

This parenthesis was destined not to close but instead to reserve for later an open question that you have good reason to recall here: "(I shall leave this question open and not claim the copyright, in the name of the signatories of *Sec*, to the arguments borrowed from it and reproduced, almost literally and with regularity by Sarl, while pretending [and this word "pretending" announces the entire problematic of the two pages that follow, concerning reflexively the speech acts of the debate itself between Searle and myself: this is an example of how the text is written, an example of the examples it provides for speech act analysis while simultaneously provoking the theory to take up the challenge] to pose them as objections. I will not claim the copyright because ultimately [*en dernière instance*] there is always a police and a tribunal ready to intervene each time a rule [constitutive or regulative, vertical or not] is invoked in a case involving signatures, events, or contexts . . .)."[7]

And on the following page, just as the parenthesis is about to be closed and as this is being said—"I close the parenthesis"—I tried to do something other than what I said, that is, to leave the question entirely open: "(. . . I shall therefore not claim a copyright because this entire matter of the police must be reconsidered, and not merely in a theoretical manner, if one does not want the police to be omnipotent: and also because the copyright is the object of *Sec*, its issue [*chose*] and its business, its cause [*Sache, Ursache*] and its trial, process, proceeding [*procès*], albeit one that is impossible to appropriate [*un procès interminable*]. I close the parenthesis.)"

My intention was therefore not primarily to determine the law, the tribunal, or the police as political powers *repressive in themselves*. Moreover, I do not believe that they are that, purely and simply. I do not know what you have in the back of your mind on this point, but I would hesitate before associating the police, directly and necessarily, as you seem to do, even if it is only for the sake of provoking a response on my part, with a determinate politics, and in particular with a repressive politics. We need here to distinguish very carefully if we are not to succumb to the facile solutions and ideological consensus of the *doxai* of right or left. I will return to this in an instant. Every police is not repressive, no more than the law in general, even in its negative, restrictive, or prohibitive prescriptions. A red light is not repressive. If one insists on considering its prohibitive force as being "repressive" (which is not to be absolutely prohibited in a context yet to be determined), then this repressive character must be distinguished from that associated, in an evaluation that is never neutral, with the unjust brutality of a force that most often violates the very law to which it appeals. This distinction is sometimes difficult, but it is indispensable if one is to avoid hastily confounding law and prohibition, law and repression, prohibition and repression. Elsewhere I have tried to mark out what in the essence of the law is not necessarily tied to negativity (prohibition, repression, etc.).[8]

What, then, was my *primary* concern in this passage? Not to denounce a determinate politics or a repressive practice, however implicit they might be. I wanted first of all, in regard to the "general theory" (in the sense of Austin's concept and project), to recall a logical necessity. Which? No one can deny that each time a copyright is invoked, reference is made to a law and to the possibility of its being enforced, if need be, by those representatives of the law which are the judges and the police; at the same time, it must be recognized that rape, theft, perjury, fraud are always possible. No signature is possible without recourse, at least implicitly, to the law. The test of authentification is part of the very structure of the signature. That amounts to saying that "forgery" is always possible, the *possibility* of transgression is always inscribed in speech acts (oral or written).

That is one theoretical consequence or implication that I wanted first of all to recall to Searle, and its effects on his entire discourse are, I believe, nondelimitable. In the description of the structure called "normal," "normative," "central," "ideal," this possibility must be integrated as an *essential* possibility. The possibility cannot be treated as though it were a simple accident—marginal or parasitic. It cannot be, and hence ought not to be, and this passage from *can* to *ought* reflects the entire difficulty. In the analysis of so-called normal cases, one neither can nor ought, in all theoretical rigor, to exclude the possibility of transgression. Not even provisionally, or out of allegedly methodological considerations. It would be a poor method, since this possibility of transgression tells us immediately and indispensably about the structure of the act said to be normal as well as about the structure of law in general. I will not repeat my objection (in **y**) to the order of "logical dependency" invoked by Searle concerning the relation between "nonfiction or standard discourse" and "fiction," defined as its "parasite." But I recall this example here apropos of your question. One cannot subordinate or leave in abeyance the analysis of fiction in order to proceed firstly and "logically" to that of "nonfiction or standard discourse." For part of the most originary essence of the latter is to allow fiction, the simulacrum, parasitism, to take place—and in so doing to "de-essentialize" itself as it were.

The real question, or at any rate in my eyes the indispensable question, would then become: what is "nonfiction standard discourse," what must it be and what does this name evoke, once its fictionality or its fictionalization, its transgressive "parasitism," is always possible (and moreover by virtue of the very same words, the same phrases, the same grammar, etc.)? This question is all the more indispensable since the rules, and even the statements of the rules governing the relations of "nonfiction standard discourse" and its fictional "parasites," are not things found in nature, but laws, symbolic inventions, or conventions, institutions that, in their very normality as well as in their normativity, entail something of the fictional. Not that I assimilate the different regimes of fiction, not that I consider laws, constitutions, the declaration of the rights of man, grammar, or the penal code to be the same as novels.[9] I only want to recall that they are not "natural realities" and that they depend upon the same structural power that allows novelesque fictions or mendacious inventions and the like to take place. This is one of the reasons why literature and the study of literature have much to teach us about right and law. It is also why, it may be said in passing, what Searle calls "literary audiences" are far less naive and often much better prepared to analyze these problems than certain professional philosophers, with a penchant for pontificating, appear to realize. The work currently being done in certain law schools around deconstruction and literary theory seems to me to furnish the best indication of the necessity to which I allude. These projects are doubtless among the most promising and most interesting being undertaken today.

I add very quickly (much too quickly for a problem as serious and difficult as this one, but it's the price to be paid for the genre of the epistolary afterword) that when I speak here of law, of convention or of invention, I would like not to rely, as it might seem I do, upon the classical opposition between nature and law, or between animals alleged not to have language and man, author of speech acts and capable of entering into a relation to the law, be it of obedience or of transgression. It is in order to minimize this risk and to keep in reserve an entire deconstruction of onto-theological humanism (including that of Heidegger) that I prefer always to speak of the iterability of the *mark* beyond all human speech acts. Barring any inconsistency, ineptness, or insufficiently rigorous formalization on my part, my statements on this subject should be valid beyond the marks and society called "human."[10]

This, then, was the principle of my primary concern. It did not aim at condemning a determinate or particularly repressive politics by pointing out the implication of the police and of the tribunal whenever a rule is invoked concerning signatures, events, or contexts. Rather, I sought to recall that in its very generality, which is to say, before all specification, this implication is irreducible. That would not necessarily signify, as you immediately translate, that "any specification of linguistic rules and conventions plays into the hands of the police," if by this expression you want to elicit the image of repressive brutality, in helmet and uniform, to which in fact the theoretician of speech acts would not hesitate to have recourse. But there are, first of all, several ways of invoking or of specifying the rules. There are "theoretical" grammarians, linguists, and jurists who state, describe, explain the norm without insisting upon its application, at least its immediate application, by force (physical or symbolic). Other functions consist in eliciting respect for the law and in disposing of a force deemed legitimate to this end. These two types of function, these two ways of "fixing" rules and also, to take up your expression again, of "fixing" the "contexts of utterances," bring together in a single person the theoretician of right [*droit*], the legislator (the inventor or first signatory of a constitution himself, or those in whose name he claims to act), and the executive power. What is at work here are structures of "performativity," allegedly descriptive or constative, that I have tried to describe elsewhere.[11] Sometimes all these roles are combined and confounded in the same person or the same apparatus [*dispositif*], despite their relative heterogeneity. In its power of sanctioning, evaluating, selecting, and when it insists, for example, upon respect for language, for the cultural patrimony, and for a large number of rules associated with them, theoretical research in its academic form is the privileged place for these functions to be confused. In any case, the "theoretical" duty of every theoretician (for me this is also an "ethical-political duty": a "theoretical *duty*" is never purely theoretical) also consists in describing as lucidly as possible the situation I have just evoked. This is why, on the other hand, there are police and police. There is a police that is brutally and *rather* "physically" repressive (but the police is never purely physical) and there are more sophisticated police that are more "cultural" or "spiritual," more noble. But every institution destined to enforce the law is a police. An academy is a police, whether in the sense of a university or of the Académie Française, whose essential task is to enforce respect for and obedience to [*faire respecter*] the French language, to decide what ought to be considered "good" French, etc. But I never said that the police as such and a priori, or "the very project of attempting to fix the contexts of utterances," is "politically" suspect. There is no society without police even if one can always dream of forms of police that would be more sublime, more refined or less vulgar.

But if the police as such is not politically suspect a priori, it is never politically neutral either, never apolitical. Political evaluation, suspicion for example, will always be formulated in a given context, starting from given forces or interests, against another manner of determining the context and of imposing this determination. This context is not only or always a discursive context. One politics is always being played against another (and perhaps, virtually, one police against another). This political dimension is not always apparent. It often dissimulates itself, articulates or translates itself through mediations that are numerous, differentiated, potential, equivocal, difficult to decipher. It often depends upon codes that are still poorly apprehended, allowing therefore for different possible implementations, given the mobility of contexts that are constantly being reframed. But who can believe that our discourses, which appear to be purely theoretical, on the status of the parasite for instance, are not at the same time highly political in nature? Once it has been demonstrated, as I hope to have done, that the exclusion of the parasite (of divergences, contaminations, impurities, etc.) cannot be justified by purely theoretical-methodological reasons, how can one ignore that this practice of exclusion, or this will to purify, to reappropriate in a manner that would be essential, internal, and ideal in respect to the subject or to its objects, translates necessarily into a politics? Politics of language (which can lead, even if it does not always do so, to violences committed by the state), politics of education, politics of immigration, behavior with regard to the "foreign" in general, etc. This touches all the social institutions—and it is not even indispensable to mobilize the code of class struggle to recall it. More generally, it touches everything, quite simply everything: style of "life," of "speech," of "writing," etc. All that is political through and through, but it is not only political. I would say the same of deconstruction, which is above all and from its beginnings, as I recalled in "Limited Inc . . .," a practical analysis of what is called the parasite and of the axiomatics upon which its interpretation is based.

This being said, I believe that one must be very careful in drawing consequences from these propositions. First of all, to come back to the words of your question after having clarified how "police," "polices," must be understood, I would not say "that there is something politically suspect in the very project of attempting to fix the contexts of utterances." No, not "suspect." But there is always something political "in the very project of attempting to fix the contexts of utterances." This is inevitable; one cannot do anything, least of all speak, without determining (in a manner that is not only theoretical, but practical and performative) a context. Such experience is always political because it implies, insofar as it involves determination, a certain type of non-"natural" relationship to others (and this holds as well for what we call "animals," since, without being able to go into it here, what I am saying implies a rather profound transformation of the concept of the "political" along with several others in order to be able to say that man is not the only political animal). Once this generality and this a priori structure have been recognized, the question can be raised, not whether a politics is implied (it always is), but which politics is implied in such a practice of contextualization. This you can then go on to analyze, but you cannot suspect it, much less denounce it except on the basis of another contextual determination every bit as political. In short, I do not believe that any neutrality is possible in this area. What is called "objectivity," scientific for instance (in which I firmly believe, in a given situation), imposes itself only within a context which is extremely vast, old, powerfully established, stabilized or rooted in a network of conventions (for instance, those of language) and yet which still remains a context. And the emergence of the value of objectivity (and hence of so many others) also belongs to a context. We can call "context" the entire "real-history-of-the-world," if you like, in which this value of objectivity and, even more broadly, that of truth (etc.) have taken on meaning and imposed themselves. That does not in the slightest discredit them. In the name of what, of which other "truth," moreover, would it? One of the definitions of what is called deconstruction would be the effort to take this limitless context into account, to pay the sharpest and broadest attention possible to context, and thus to an·incessant movement of recontextualization. The phrase which for some has become a sort of slogan, in general so badly understood, of deconstruction ("there is nothing outside the text" [*il n'y a pas de hors-texte*]), means nothing else: there is nothing outside context. In this form, which says exactly the same thing, the formula would doubtless have been less shocking. I am not certain that it would have provided more to think about.

Since there is much at stake here, permit me to add three clarifications in the form of reminders.

1. This way of thinking context does not, as such, amount to a relativism, with everything that is sometimes associated with it (skepticism, empiricism, even nihilism). First of all because, as Husserl has shown better than anyone else, relativism, like all its derivatives, remains a philosophical position in contradiction with itself. Second, because this "deconstructive" way of thinking context is neither a philosophical position nor a critique of finite contexts, which it analyzes without claiming any absolute overview. Nevertheless, to the extent to which it—by virtue of its discourse, its socio-institutional situation, its language, the historical inscription of its gestures, etc.—is itself rooted in a given context (but, as always, in one that is differentiated and mobile), it does not renounce (it neither can nor ought do so) the "values" that are dominant in this context (for example, that of truth, etc.).

2. A few moments ago, I insisted on writing, at least in quotation marks, the strange and trivial formula, "real-history-of-the-world," in order to mark clearly that the concept of text or of context which guides me embraces and does not exclude the world, reality, history. Once again (and this probably makes a thousand times I have had to repeat this, but when will it finally be heard, and why this resistance?): as I understand it (and I have explained why), the text is not the book, it is not confined in a volume itself confined to the library. It does not suspend reference—to history, to the world, to reality, to being, and especially not to the other, since to say of history, of the world, of reality, that they always appear in an experience, hence in a movement of interpretation which contextualizes them according to a network of differences and hence of referral to the other, is surely to recall that alterity (difference) is irreducible. *Différance* is a reference and vice versa.

3. There is a supplementary paradox that also must be taken into account and that complicates all of this in a manner that is both terrible and yet nonviolent (for it is perhaps nonviolence itself): as soon as it accommodates reference as difference and inscribes *différance* in presence, this concept of text or of context no longer opposes writing to erasure. The text is not a presence, any more than "remains" (*la restance*) are the same as permanence. I insisted on this in "Limited Inc. . . ." This concept of writing or of trace perturbs every logic of opposition, every dialectic. It de-limits what it limits.

This is why (a) the finiteness of a context is never secured or simple, there is an indefinite opening of every context, an essential nontotalization; (b) whatever there can be of force or of irreducible violence in the attempt "to fix the contexts of utterances," or of anything else, can always communicate, by virtue of the erasure just mentioned, with a certain "weakness," even with an essential nonviolence. It is in this relationship, which is difficult to think through, highly unstable and dangerous, that responsibilities jell, political responsibilities in particular. That will seem surprising or disagreeable only to those for whom things are always clear, easily decipherable, calculable and programmable: in a word, if one wanted to be polemical, to the irresponsible.

I would like now to try to respond as attentively as possible to the second part of your second question, taking as seriously as possible each of your formulations. To begin with, this one: "Of course social authorities often exploit linguistic rules in repressive ways, but does this fact implicate the codifiers of those rules?" I have already uttered my perplexity at this use of the concept of "repression." Do you think that the "rules" or that certain rules might be repressive *in themselves?* Is every prescription or every prohibition repressive or should we introduce here numerous distinctions? Is "Thou shalt not kill" repressive? Perhaps you think that the abusive use of certain rules can be repressive, something that the word "exploit" seems to suggest? If I place myself within this hypothesis, the answer is simple enough: apparently, no, the "codifiers" of these rules are not implicated in this "exploitation." But this concept of the "codifier" in turn remains rather indeterminate: does it refer to those who produce the rules, in a gesture that itself is rather complex (for example, that of the legislators, of whom I have elsewhere recalled just how much they have to resort to tricks with performatives and constatives) and which may be attributed to individuals or to communities that are sometimes easy, sometimes more difficult to determine? Or does it refer to theoreticians who formalize or systematize a code and its implications? Naturally, according to the latter hypothesis (which can never, I believe, attain anything like a rigorous purity), the "codifiers" could never be "implicated," much less judged guilty, each time there is a repressive exploitation of the said rules enabling use and abuse to be distinguished. Nevertheless, and it is doubtless here that the ethical-political responsibility of the theoretician begins, the codification of the rules *ought* to take into account or try to account for the possibility of abuse insofar as the latter is inscribed in the structure of normality itself (see above). With the best intentions in the world (and this is why one must be careful in assigning responsibilities and culpabilities) a "codifying" theoretician can fail in this *duty*. He can do this for different reasons, depending upon the situation. This theoretical failure, this failure to accomplish a theoretical *duty* can, sometimes, be ideologically-politically motivated. Such motivations can sometimes appear almost without mediation, at any rate relatively easily determinable, but only sometimes. This theoretical limit can only be explained, and in any case can only impose itself and ultimately pretend to any measure of legitimacy by virtue of enormous networks of presuppositions. What is called deconstruction endeavors to analyze and if possible to transform this situation.

You ask immediately after: "Are there not situations in which Searle's rules could be invoked by someone who was *contesting* police power?" Yes, why not? But once again, what police are we talking about? And rules always involve police forces. I said before that there are police and police, that the police are not necessarily repressive, that a repressive police can only be opposed by another police, etc. Moreover, I am not sure what you mean by "Searle's rules." There are no Searle's rules, as you well know. There are analyses and formalizations proposed by Searle concerning certain rules, and sometimes concerning rules which constitute right, morality, and politics and are accepted as such by a majority of persons in given communities, for example, ours. To this extent, if a repressive police, that is to say, one which violates these laws, commits abuses, then one can indeed "invoke" these rules to contest police power, thus opposing to it, by virtue of good rules, the reference to a more just police. This I will gladly grant you. Nor did I ever say, or think, that the rules, of which you seem to think that Searle is, in one sense or another, a "codifier," are repressive rules. This is a word which, it seems to me, I have never employed because it is a concept which, out of context, is lacking in rigor.

You then ask: "Can Searle's assumptions legitimately be correlated with a particular politics, repressive or otherwise?" The seriousness of the question does not permit me to respond without numerous precautions. Of which "assumptions" are you speaking? If you mean those I describe in "Limited Inc . . .," my answer is no. In the nucleus of their theoretical structure, if it could be isolated, these "assumptions" do indeed, it seems to me, have a political (as you say) correlative, but not a "particular" political correlative. They would be common to the axiomatics of numerous (and perhaps even all) politics in the West, whether of the right or of the left, as well as to what their codes have in common. From this point of view, the deconstruction of these "assumptions," and hence of these codes, if it also has a political dimension, is engaged in the writing (or if you prefer, in the future production) of a language and of a political practice that can no longer be comprehended, judged, deciphered by these codes.

Having thus responded no in these precise terms to the question you posed, I would try to distinguish as clearly as possible between, *on the one hand*, what I have called the nucleus of the theoretical structure (to which, as you know, I am up to a point even able to subscribe, and of which I have shown that, whenever it answered to the most demanding requirements of traditional philosophy, it coincided, with the exception of a few assumptions, with certain of my statements), and *on the other hand*, certain aspects of the practice of John R. Searle, of his manner of discussing, of arguing, of polemicizing, of his rhetoric and of the forms in which he takes part in social and intellectual life, in short, of the modalities through which the said theoretical nucleus is *put to work* (*mise en oeuvre*). In this regard I certainly do *at times* disapprove of the politics of this practice, of certain of its moments in any case: to insult an author instead of criticizing him through demonstration, to accuse the other of a "distressing penchant for saying things that are obviously false" and of a thousand "confusions" while not taking the trouble to read any of the incriminated writings with the slightest attention (this I have tried to demonstrate and will not repeat; it is the entire object of "Limited Inc . . ."), and above all, to attempt in newspaper articles for instance to turn gossip into an argument in order to accuse me, and with me all those interested in my work, of "terrorist obscurantism."[12] This style, or at least the style of this particular manifestation (and nothing indicates that Searle is always in such a state apart from when he polemicizes against deconstruction, with Culler or with me in a newspaper—although the question remains why deconstruction, Culler, or I cause him to so lose control), seems to me indeed to have broad political implications. *These* gestures imply a politics (you would call it "repressive"), but no one has the right, nor do I ever claim such a right, to generalize and say that it is Searle's politics *in general* or those of the theory he puts to work *in general*.

Moreover, once again, not having much taste for such trials, and however severe my judgment (ethical or political-theoretical) might be concerning Searle's gestures in his answer to *Sec* or in his article in the *New York Review of Books*, I will not resort to your words (police and repression) to describe them in a general fashion, beyond what I have cited in note 12 above. Insults and abusive analogies come all too easily in our milieu these days. I have too many examples in mind. Similarly I will be careful not to extend to all of Searle's work, which deserves respect even if it is open to discussion or to criticism, the judgment which this or that aspect of its socio-academic elaboration [*mise en oeuvre*] seem to me to call for. I shall be even more careful not to extend to every theory of speech acts (of which Searle is only one representative) the same conclusions. Even if this elaboration is never entirely extrinsic with regard to that "theoretical nucleus," even if a consistent elaboration should prohibit such slips or aggressions, it is conceivable that other authors might elaborate the same theoretical nucleus in a very different way, without the violence you call "repressive." I do not exclude this possibility. This or that article of John R. Searle is, let us not forget, only a minor element in a highly determined context, which itself is inscribed in other, much larger and more overdetermined contexts. I do not know the ideological-political "opinions" of John R. Searle. Given all that I have read and understood of him, I am unable to exclude almost any possibility. But the one exception, perhaps, is that of his taking an interest in what I and several others are doing: deconstructing the political codes in whose spectrum his discourse and political practice are situated. Of such an interest, at any rate, there is not the slightest hint, nor does he afford himself the wherewithal with which it might be developed. On the contrary, I even seem to have noticed in him an actively defensive attitude toward any manifestation of such an interest. Perhaps this bears witness to an instinctive but sure sense of what is at stake in deconstruction. I do not exclude this possibility either. For I have come to understand that, *sometimes, certain* bitter and compulsive enemies of deconstruction stand in a more certain and more vital relationship, even if not theorized, to what is in effect at stake in it than do *certain* avowed "deconstructionists." In any case, the field here is unstable and turbulent.

I have more difficulty in comprehending the next phrase of the same question ("How would such a tactic differ from that of those who attack deconstruction as inherently conservative because it has been appropriated by the American academic publish-or-perish system?"). I have just explained why what you qualify as "a tactic" does not bear the slightest resemblance to what I do or want to do. If it were a "tactic" used against deconstruction, it would not be of great interest in my eyes, even if it could, during a certain period, have a certain efficacy. There is no one, single deconstruction. Were there only one, were it homogeneous, it would not be inherently either conservative or revolutionary, or determinable within the code of such oppositions. That is precisely what gets on everyone's nerves. I see very well in what respects certain of my writings, or certain of my practices (for example), have something "conservative" to them and I assume it as such. I am for safeguards, for memory—the jealous conservation—of numerous traditions, for example, but not only in the university and in scientific, philosophical, literary theory. I am actively committed to such safeguards. But at the same time, I could also show how certain of my writings (sometimes the same ones) or certain of my practices (sometimes the same) seem to call into question the foundations of this tradition, and I assume that as well. What does this signify? That to understand what is going on in these texts and practices, the opposition conservative/revolutionary is no longer pertinent. Deconstruction, in the singular, is not "inherently" anything at all that might be determinable on the basis of this code and of its criteria. It is "inherently" nothing at all; the logic of essence (by opposition to accident), of the proper (by opposition to the improper), hence of the "inherent" by opposition to the extrinsic, is precisely what all deconstruction has from the start called into question. As deconstruction is inherently neither "conservative" nor the contrary, the political evaluation of each of the gestures called deconstructive will have to depend, if it is to be rigorous and in proportion to what it is addressing, upon analyses that are very difficult, very minute, very flexible with regard to the stereotypes of political-institutional discourse. Deconstruction does not exist somewhere, pure, proper, self-identical, outside of its inscriptions in conflictual and differentiated contexts; it "is" only what it does and what is done with it, there where it takes place. It is difficult today to give a univocal definition or an adequate description of this "taking place." This absence of univocal definitions is not "obscurantist," it respectfully pays homage to a new, very new *Aufklärung*. This is, in my eyes, a very good sign. To this answer, concerning principles, I will add three more points.

1. Deconstruction in the singular cannot be simply "appropriated" by anyone or by anything. Deconstructions are the movements of what I have called "exappropriation." Anyone who believes they have appropriated or seen appropriated something like deconstruction in the singular is a priori mistaken, and something else is going on. But since deconstruction is always "something else," the error is never total or pure.

2. If nevertheless there is indeed, to a certain extent, still very slight, a certain multiplication of practices that are deconstructive in style (research, writing, reading, teaching, publication, etc.) in the university, it would be necessary, before speaking of appropriation, to know if the system that seems to appropriate something is or is not modified by that which it believes it is appropriating. Even though I do not believe appropriation to be possible in general, I am not opposed to what *you* call "appropriation": it is inevitable that something resembling appropriation take place in order for the university, for example, to be

141

affected by it. Otherwise, the only hope for deconstruction's remaining happily intact and pure would be for it to be utterly ignored, radically excluded or definitively rejected. You know that this is not my foremost concern. It is perhaps the ambiguous wish of those who make opposition to deconstruction their profession.

3. What is "the American publish-or-perish system"? Its definition would require numerous analyses that I cannot attempt here. To remain at a relatively trivial level, I will say that to my knowledge there are in this regard at least as many signs of exclusions or of censorship as of appropriation. In numerous places the war against anything deemed "deconstructionist" closes the doors of universities and of publishers. If works that take into account the deconstructive problematic or make reference to it in one manner or another are on the increase and are above all diversifying themselves in fields that are part not only of philosophy or of literary theory, but also of the social sciences, law, architecture, etc. (and as you seem to believe it, I grant you that this is perhaps a fact), why should it be viewed simply as a sign of appropriation by "the American publish-or-perish system"? Couldn't this be interpreted otherwise? If it were simply a symptom of appropriation, why would it arouse such aggressivity and uncontrolled reactions? Perhaps your allusion to the "publish-or-perish system" implies that in your eyes much, perhaps even too much is being written in a deconstructive style. But even if this were the case and even if these works were published so easily (which I do not believe at all when I consider things from a statistical, i.e., quantitative point of view), why exclude other explanations? For example, that the field of work opened by "deconstructive" questions shows itself to be richer, newer, and that the provocation to research, even to writing is more stimulating?

Question.

In Of Grammatology, *you make it clear that you do not deny the ability of interpreters, for certain purposes, to reproduce a so-called literal meaning of a text. You say that the "moment of doubling commentary should no doubt have its place in a critical reading," and that without "this indispensable guardrail" "critical production would risk developing in any direction at all and authorize itself to say almost anything" (p. 158).*

Could you comment on how this issue of the possibility of a "doubling commentary" may bear on an assertion like the following in "Limited Inc . . .": in breaching and dividing the self-presence of intentions, iterability "leaves us no choice but to mean (to say) something that is (already, always, also) other than what we mean (to say) . . ." (p. 62). If this process of intentions and meanings differing from themselves does not negate the possibility of "doubling commentary," then are its practical implications for interpretation perhaps not so threatening to conventional modes of reading as has been thought—or, perhaps I should ask, are they threatening in a different way than has been thought?

I raise this question not to suggest that the self-divided nature of meaning has no practical consequences for interpretation, but to ask whether those consequences are best described in terms of undecidability and indeterminacy. I ask this from a sense that, in the United States at least, the controversy over your work has often become caught up in somewhat unprofitable disputes over whether words can mean anything determinate (i.e., whether your work eliminates all "guardrails")—something which it seems you've never denied. A possible result is that more-interesting issues you have raised have tended to be overlooked, such as those having to do with your view that meaning is founded on acts of exclusion and repression which leave their traces on it. At least in focusing almost entirely on the issue of determinate reading vs. *undecidability, the popular criticisms of your work seem hardly to recognize this latter issue, which has to do with the way discourse inscribes power relations.*

Of course those who believe in determinate meaning tend to ignore the ways discourse inscribes power relations, but could not one argue that those ways can themselves be quite determinate? In other words, would there not be some advantages for the moment anyway in separating the issue of whether meaning is structured by rhetorical coercion from the issue of whether meaning is determinate?

Answer.

This question is even more difficult. I realize that my answers have already been too long. For contingent reasons of time and of place, and hence without rigorous justification, I will have to pay greater attention to the economy of my responses. They will be shorter and more elliptical. I will shift rhythm and not recite your questions in their entirety each time, all the more easily since they are often accompanied by answers or hypotheses with which I feel myself to be largely in agreement.

I have just finished rereading the chapter of *Of Grammatology* ("The Exorbitant Question of Method") from which the proposition you cite, on "the moment of doubling commentary," is drawn. To economize on what would otherwise be an overly long answer, I propose that the interested reader also reread the chapter. And I will add this clarification: the moment of what I called, perhaps clumsily, "doubling commentary" does not suppose the self-identity of "meaning," but a relative stability of the dominant interpretation (including the "self"-interpretation) of the text being commented upon. With, as I say in this passage, all the "classical exigencies" and the "instruments of traditional criticism" (of which, by the way, I indicate, in a political-institutional proposition, the vital necessity: the university should, I believe, assure the most rigorous transmission and conservation, but the best strategy to this end is never simple), "doubling commentary" is not a moment of simple reflexive recording that would transcribe the originary and true layer of a text's intentional meaning, a meaning that is univocal and self-identical, a layer upon which or after which active interpretation would finally begin.

No, this commentary is *already* an interpretation. Perhaps I should not have called it commentary. I do not believe in the possibility of a pure and simple "doubling commentary." I used these words to designate what, in a very classical and very elementary layer of reading, most resembles what traditionally is called "commentary," even paraphrase. This paraphrastic moment, even if it appeals to a minimal competence (which is less common than is generally believed: for example, familiarity with French, with a certain French, in order to read Rousseau in the original text), is already an interpretive reading. This moment, this layer already concerns interpretations and semantic decisions which have nothing "natural" or "originary" about them and which impose, subject to conditions that require analysis, conventions that henceforth are dominant (I thus gradually approach what, in the course of your question, you describe in terms of "power relations"). Simply, this *quasi*-paraphrastic interpretation bases itself upon that which in a text (for instance, that of Rousseau, of which I was then speaking) constitutes a very profound and very solid zone of implicit "conventions" or "contracts." Not of semantic structures that are absolutely anchored, ahistorical or transtextual, monolithic or self-identical—which moreover would render the most paraphrastic commentary either impossible or useless—but of stratifications that are already differential and of a very great stability with regard to the relations of forces and all the hierarchies or hegemonies they suppose or put into practice: for example, the French language (its grammar and vocabulary), the rhetorical uses of this language in the society and in the literary code of the epoch, etc., but also a whole set of assurances that grant a minimum of intelligibility to whatever we can tell ourselves about these things today or to whatever part of them I can render intelligible, for example in *Of Grammatology*, with whatever limited success. At stake is always a set of determinate and finite possibilities.

Without a solid competence in this domain, the most venturesome interpretations of *Of Grammatology* would have been neither possible nor intelligible, nor even subject to discussion. What must be understood is not what this or that French word means to say *naturally or absolutely*, beyond all possible equivocation, but rather, first, what interpretations are probabilistically dominant and conventionally acknowledged to grant access to what Rousseau thought he meant and to what readers for the most part thought they could understand, in order, second, to analyze the play or relative indetermination that was able to open the space of my interpretation, for example, that of the word *supplément*. And once again, what holds for the context "Rousseau" or the "Essay on the Origin of Languages" also holds for the context in which *we* speak of it today. On the one side, things are the same, a solid tradition assures us of this. But on the other, they are profoundly different. To evaluate the two sides and to get one's bearings, one must be armed, one must understand and write, even translate French as well as possible, know the corpus of Rousseau as well as possible, including all the contexts that determine it (the literary, philosophical, rhetorical traditions, the history of the French language, society, history, which is to say, so many other things as well). Otherwise, one could indeed say just anything at all and I have never accepted saying, or encouraging others to say, just anything at all, nor have I argued for indeterminacy as such.

But I do not believe, as you suggest, that it is opportune to dissociate questions of "power relations" or of "rhetorical coercion" from questions of the determinacy or indeterminacy of "meaning." Without play in and among these questions, there would be no space for conflicts of force. The imposition of a meaning supposes a certain play or latitude in its determination. I shall return to this in a moment.

If I speak of great stability, it is in order to emphasize that this semantic level is neither originary, nor ahistorical, nor simple, nor self-identical in any of its elements, nor even entirely semantic or significant. Such stabilization is relative, even if it is sometimes so great as to seem immutable and permanent. It is the momentary result of a whole history of relations of force (intra- and extrasemantic, intra- and extradiscursive, intra- and extraliterary or -philosophical, intra- and extraacademic, etc.). In order for this history to have taken place, in its turbulence and in its stases, in order for relations of force, of tensions, or of wars to have taken place, in order for hegemonies to have imposed themselves during a determinate period, there must have been a certain play in all these structures, hence a certain instability or non-self-identity, nontransparency. Rhetorical equivocation and mobility, for instance, must have been able to work within "meaning." *Différance* must have been able to affect reference. In short, what I sought to designate under the title of "doubling commentary" is the "minimal" deciphering of the "first" pertinent or competent access to structures that are relatively stable (and hence destabilizable!), and from which the most venturesome questions and interpretations have to start: questions concerning conflicts, tensions, differences of force, hegemonies that have allowed such provisional installations to take place. Once again, that was possible only if a non-self-identity, a *différance* and a relative indeterminacy opened the space of this violent history. What has always interested me the most, what has always seemed to me the most rigorous (theoretically, scientifically, philosophically, but also for a writing that would no longer be only theoretical-scientific-philosophical), is not indeterminacy in itself, but the strictest possible determination of the figures of play, of oscillation, of undecidability, which is to say, of the *différantial* conditions of determinable history, etc. . . . On the other hand, if I have just prudently placed quotation marks around "minimal" and "first," it is because I do not believe in the possibility of an absolute determination of the "minimal" and of the "first." According to contexts (according to this or that national culture, in the university or outside the university, in school or elsewhere, at one level of competence or at another, on television, in the press, or in a specialized colloquium), the conditions of minimal pertinence and of initial access will change. You know that I am thus alluding, in passing, to concrete problems of curriculum, for example, or to the level of requirements in our profession, whether we are talking of students or of teachers.

Once that "minimal" and "first" are understood to have meaning only in

determinate contexts, the concept that I was aiming at with the inadequate expression of "doubling commentary" is the concept of a reading-writing that,
counting on a very strong probability of consensus concerning the intelligibility
of a text, itself the result of the stabilized solidity of numerous contracts, *seems*
only to paraphrase, unveil, reflect, reproduce a text, "commenting" on it without
any other active or risky initiative. This is only an appearance, since this moment
is already actively interpretive and can therefore open the way to all sorts of
strategic ruses in order to have constructions pass as evidences or as constative
observations. But I believe that no research is possible in a community (for example, academic) without the prior search for this minimal consensus and without discussion around this minimal consensus. Whatever the disagreements between Searle and myself may have been, for instance, no one doubted that I had
understood at least the English grammar and vocabulary of his sentences. Without that no debate would have begun. Which does not amount to saying that all
possibility of misunderstandings on my part is excluded a priori, but that they
would have to be, one can hope at least, of another order. Inversely (to take only
one example, which could be multiplied), if Searle had been familiar enough
with the work of Descartes to recognize the parodic reference to a Cartesian title
in my text (cf. what I say about this in **t**), he would have been led to complicate
his reading considerably. Had he been attentive to the neological character of the
French word *restance*—remains—which in my text does not signify permanence, he would have been on the right track and well on the way [*sur la bonne
voie*] to reading me, etc. For of course there is a "right track" [*une "bonne voie"*],
a better way, and let it be said in passing how surprised I have often been, how
amused or discouraged, depending on my humor, by the use or abuse of the
following argument: Since the deconstructionist (which is to say, isn't it, the skep-
tic-relativist-nihilist!) is supposed not to believe in truth, stability, or the unity of
meaning, in intention or "meaning-to-say," how can he demand of us that we
read *him* with pertinence, precision, rigor? How can he demand that his own text
be interpreted correctly? How can he accuse anyone else of having misunderstood, simplified, deformed it, etc.? In other words, how can he discuss, and
discuss the reading of what he writes? The answer is simple enough: this definition of the deconstructionist is *false* (that's right: false, not true) and feeble; it
supposes a bad (that's right: bad, not good) and feeble reading of numerous
texts, first of all mine, which therefore must finally be read or reread. Then perhaps it will be understood that the value of truth (and all those values associated
with it) is never contested or destroyed in my writings, but only reinscribed in
more powerful, larger, more stratified contexts. And that within interpretive contexts (that is, within relations of force that are always differential—for example,
socio-political-institutional—but even beyond these determinations) that are relatively stable, sometimes apparently almost unshakeable, it should be possible to
invoke rules of competence, criteria of discussion and of consensus, good faith,
lucidity, rigor, criticism, and pedagogy. I should thus be able to claim and to
demonstrate, without the slightest "pragmatic contradiction," that Searle, for

example, as I have already demonstrated, was not on the "right track" toward understanding what I wanted to say, etc. May I henceforth however be granted this: he could have been on the wrong track or may still be on it; I am making considerable pedagogical efforts here to correct his errors and that certainly proves that all the positive values to which I have just referred are contextual, essentially limited, unstable, and endangered. And therefore that the essential and irreducible *possibility* of *mis*understanding or of "*in*felicity" must be taken into account in the description of those values said to be positive.

In short, to cite you, not only, as you rightly say, "this process of intentions and meanings differing from themselves does not negate the possibility of 'doubling commentary,' " but this "doubling commentary" and its "guardrails," which are always constructed (and hence deconstructible), would themselves be neither possible nor necessary without this play of *différance*. And you are right in saying that these "practical implications for interpretation" are "not so threatening to conventional modes of reading," since they seem to rejoin the minimal "requirements" of all culture, of all reading, of all research (academic or not). But they are also rightly felt to be "threatening in a different way" by those conservatives who are most paralyzed or most paralyzing, for two reasons.

1. First of all, because the premises of this discourse on "doubling commentary" recall, as I have just done, that the norms of minimal intelligibility are not absolute and ahistorical, but merely more stable than others. They depend upon socio-institutional conditions, hence upon nonnatural relations of power that by essence are mobile and founded upon complex conventional structures that in principle may be analyzed, deconstructed, and transformed; and in fact, these structures are in the process of transforming themselves profoundly and, above all, very rapidly (this is the true source of anxiety in certain circles, which is merely revealed by "deconstruction": for before becoming a discourse, an organized practice that *resembles* a philosophy, a theory, a method, which it *is not*, in regard to those unstable stabilities or this destabilization that it makes its principal theme, "deconstruction" is firstly this destabilization on the move in, if one could speak thus, "the things themselves"; but it is not negative. Destabilization is required for "progress" as well. And the "de-" of *de*construction signifies not the demolition of what is constructing itself, but rather what remains to be thought beyond the constructivist or destructionist scheme).[13] What is at stake here is the entire debate, for instance, on the curriculum, literacy, etc.

2. Following this, if, as I had written, "reading must not be content with doubling the text" (p. 158), the concept corresponding to the inadequate expression "doubling commentary" defines only a layer or a moment, an indispensable implication of reading, of a reading that is itself interpretive, inventive, or "productive," assuming thereby the form of another writing, in a text in transformation in which the possibilities of differential play are increasing *and* at the same time becoming increasingly determined. It is that which doubtless appears most "threatening in a different way."

I take advantage of the occasion to specify that the word "productive," which I use frequently in this passage in *Of Grammatology* to characterize a reading that is "protected" but not "opened" by the "guardrails," can remain equivocal. Such "productivity" ought not signify either "creativity" (for this interpretive reading does not create just any meaning *ex nihilo* and without prior rule)[14] or simply "rendering explicit" (*producere* as setting forth or into the light that which is already there). The concept and the word "production" pose enormous problems which cannot be discussed here (I believe I have dealt with them elsewhere).[15] The same holds for the expression "text, in the infrastructural sense that we now give to that word" (p. 164). By infrastructural, I did not mean a substantial stratum, a substratum present underneath a superstructure (in the conventional Marxist sense of this figure). I wanted to recall that the concept of text I propose is limited neither to the graphic, nor to the book, nor even to discourse, and even less to the semantic, representational, symbolic, ideal, or ideological sphere. What I call "text" implies all the structures called "real," "economic," "historical," socio-institutional, in short: all possible referents. Another way of recalling once again that "there is nothing outside the text." That does not mean that all referents are suspended, denied, or enclosed in a book, as people have claimed, or have been naive enough to believe and to have accused me of believing. But it does mean that every referent, all reality has the structure of a differential trace, and that one cannot refer to this "real" except in an interpretive experience. The latter neither yields meaning nor assumes it except in a movement of differential referring. That's all.

I will only briefly paraphrase the last two paragraphs of your third question on undecidability, indeterminacy, and power relations. These paragraphs very effectively clarify matters and I am prepared to subscribe to them. With two qualifications.

1. I do not believe I have ever spoken of "indeterminacy," whether in regard to "meaning" or anything else. Undecidability is something else again. While referring to what I have said above and elsewhere, I want to recall that undecidability is always a *determinate* oscillation between possibilities (for example, of meaning, but also of acts). These possibilities are themselves highly *determined* in strictly *defined* situations (for example, discursive—syntactical or rhetorical—but also political, ethical, etc.). They are *pragmatically* determined.[16] The analyses that I have devoted to undecidability concern just these determinations and these definitions, not at all some vague "indeterminacy." I say "undecidability" rather than "indeterminacy" because I am interested more in relations of force, in differences of force, in everything that allows, precisely, determinations in given situations to be stabilized through a decision of writing (in the broad sense I give to this word, which also includes political action and experience in general). There would be no indecision or *double bind* were it not between *determined* (semantic, ethical, political) poles, which are upon occasion terribly necessary and always irreplaceably singular. Which is to say that from the point of view of semantics, but also of ethics and politics, "deconstruction" should never lead either to relativism or to any sort of indeterminism.

148

To be sure, in order for structures of undecidability to be possible (and hence structures of decisions and of responsibilities as well), there must be a certain play, *différance*, nonidentity. Not of indetermination, but of *différance* or of nonidentity with oneself in the very process of determination. *Différance* is not indeterminacy. It renders determinacy both possible and necessary. Someone might say: but if it renders determinacy possible, it is because it itself is "indeterminacy." Precisely not, since first of all it "is" in *itself* nothing outside of different determinations; second, and consequently, it never comes to a full stop anywhere, absolutely [*elle ne s'arrête nulle part*], and is neither negativity nor nothingness (as indeterminacy would be). Insofar as it is always determined, undecidability is also not negative in itself.

2. The words "force" and "power" which I have just joined you in using, also pose, as you can well imagine, enormous problems. I never resort to these words without a sense of uneasiness, even if I believe myself obligated to use them in order to designate something irreducible. What worries me is that in them which resembles an obscure substance that could, in a discourse, give rise to a zone of obscurantism and of dogmatism. Even if, as Foucault seems to suggest, one no longer speaks of Power with a capital P, but of a scattered multiplicity of micropowers, the question remains of knowing what the unity of signification is that still permits us to call these decentralized and heterogeneous microphenomena "powers." For my part, without being able to go much further here, I do not believe that one should agree to speak of "force" or of "power" except under three conditions, at least.

A. That one takes account of the fact that there is never any thing called power or force, but only differences of power and of force, and that these differences are as qualitative as they are quantitative. In short, it seems to me that one must start, as Nietzsche doubtless did, from difference in order to accede to force and not vice versa.

B. That, starting from this qualitatively differential thought, one opens oneself, in attempting to account for it, to this apparently perverse or paradoxical possibility: the ostensibly greater force can also be the "lesser" (or the "strongest" force is not "strongest" but "weakest," which supposes the essential possibility of an inversion of meaning, that is to say, a mutation of meaning not limited to the semantics of discourse or the dictionary but which also "produces" itself as history).

C. That one takes into account, consequently, all the paradoxes and ruses of force, of power, of mastery, as traps in which these ruses cannot avoid being caught up.[17] I would be tempted to say analogous things on the subject of "repression." A while back, in responding to your second question, I displayed considerable caution, even reticence concerning the use of the word "repressive" in my discussion with Searle. But I am much less worried about this *other* concept that the *same* word seems to designate in the phrase in which you affirm that "meaning is founded on acts of exclusion and repression." Once there is the exercise of force in the determination and the imposition of meaning, and first of all in the stabilizing determination of a context, it is inevitable that there be some form of repression. Simply, it is not the same as what we spoke of above, not the same level in any case. The repression at the origin of meaning is an irreducible violence. It is difficult to call it "bad" or to condemn it from a moral or political point of view. One can hardly say as much of the repression or of the repressiveness of which we spoke at the outset.

Question.

American commentators have often spoken as if the point of essays like "Signature Event Context" and "Limited Inc . . ." is to put such concepts as truth, reference, and the stability of interpretive contexts radically into question. Yet in a recent discussion of South African apartheid in Critical Inquiry *(vol. 13, Autumn 1986), you speak of the need "to call a thing by its name" and to "be attentive to what links words to concepts and to realities" (p. 163). You speak of the "massively present reality" of apartheid, "one which no historian could seriously put in question" (p. 160). And you chide two of your critics for ignoring "the grammatical, rhetorical, and pragmatic specificity" of your utterance and for not paying "attention to the context and the mode of [your] text" (p. 158).*

I suspect these comments have surprised some of your commentators. Do they contradict the direction of your thought elsewhere, or have the commentators mistaken your implications? Could the apparent discrepancy be an instance of what you have often discussed as "double writing," or different textual strategies addressed to different kinds of situations?

Answer.

I will answer your fourth question even more briefly. The premises of my response are now clear, I hope. I have never "put such concepts as truth, reference, and the stability of interpretive contexts radically into question" if "putting radically into question" means contesting that there *are* and that there *should be* truth, reference, and stable contexts of interpretation. I have—but this is something entirely different—posed questions that I hope are radical concerning the possibility of these things, of these values, of these norms, of this stability (which by essence is always provisional and finite). This questioning and the discourse attuned to its possibility (even the discourse concerning the possibility and the limits of the interrogative attitude in general)[18] evidently no longer belong simply, or homogeneously, to the order of truth, of reference, of contextuality. But they do not destroy it or contradict it. They are themselves neither false, nor nontrue, nor self-reflexive (identical to themselves and transparent), nor context-external or metacontextual. Their "truth" is not of the same order as the truth they question, but in pragmatically determined situations in which this "truth" is set forth they must submit (in large measure: I will explain later this qualification, which may seem strange) to the norms of the context that requires one to prove, to demonstrate, to proceed correctly, to conform to the rules of language and to a great number of other social, ethical, political-institutional rules, etc. The proof that I have not "put . . . the stability of interpretive contexts radically into question" is that I incessantly recall, as I did a short while ago, that I take into account and believe that it is necessary to account for this stability, as well as for all the norms, rules, contractual possibilities, that depend upon it. But what does it mean to account for a stability? On the one hand, it does not necessarily mean to choose or accept or try to conserve the stability for its own sake, no matter what the cost; it is not tantamount to being "conservative." And on the other hand, to account for a certain stability (by essence always provisional and finite) is precisely not to speak of eternity or of absolute solidity; it is to take into account a historicity, a nonnaturalness, of ethics, of politics, of institutionality, etc. If recalling this is to put radically into question the stability of contexts, then, yes, I do that. I say that there is no stability that is absolute, eternal, intangible, natural, etc. But that is implied in the very concept of stability. A stability is not an immutability; it is by definition always destabilizable.

The "commentators" whom you evoke would, as you suggest, have totally "mistaken" the "implications" of my discourse in general and of what I have said of apartheid in the particular context to which you refer. They commit the same "mistakes" as those to whom I respond in *Critical Inquiry*. I consider the context of that discussion, like that of this one, to be very stable and very determined. It constitutes the object of agreements sufficiently confirmed so that one might *count* [*tabler*] on ties that are stable, and hence demonstrable, linking words, concepts and things, as well as on the difference between the true and the false. And hence one is able, in this context, to denounce errors, and even dishonesty and confusions. This "pragmatics" or this programmatology (see n. 16) also entails deontological (or if you prefer, ethical-political) rules of discussion of which I remind my critics when I believe they have failed to observe them. But the very fact that, impelled by this or that interest (subject to analysis—and I analyze it), they can fail in this way, make errors, not understand, read badly, not respect the pragmatic, grammatical, or moral rules, the fact that I have been obliged and able to remind them of it—all this confirms that the context is only relatively stable. The ties between words, concepts, and things, truth and reference, are not *absolutely* and purely guaranteed by some metacontextuality or metadiscursivity. However stabilized, complex, and overdetermined it may be, there is a context and one that is only relatively *firm*, neither absolutely solid [*fermeté*] nor entirely closed [*fermeture*], without being purely and simply identical to itself. In it there is a margin of play, of difference, an opening; in it there is what I have elsewhere called "supplementarity" (*Of Grammatology*) or "parergonality" (*Truth in Painting*). These concepts come close to blurring or dangerously complicating the limits between inside and outside, in a word, the framing of a context. In such cases as this discussion, as well as over there in South Africa, disagreement, equivocation, and "infelicity" are possible, as well as relations of force (see above). Without even looking for other proof, the fact that this discussion took place suffices to attest to this possibility, as does the fact that it takes such efforts to be convincing. So does the fact that, following all the didactic explanations I gave, other examples of confusion or bad faith could have emerged.

To be sure, all this supposes that, according to the specific situation, one resorts, as you yourself emphasize, to "different textual strategies." What I write now responds to a strategy very different from that of "Limited Inc . . .," which itself did not resemble any other text bearing my signature. But in this there is nothing original on my part, neither in the practice of these strategies, nor in what I am saying about them. I simply emphasize that this difference and these strategies *as such* must be thought through, and out of this the greatest number of consequences must be drawn in the most consistent manner possible. Despite the close links, this multiplicity of strategies is not always to be identified, as you seem to suppose, with what I have called "double writing." This last concept, although it speaks of "two" instead of "multiple," remains more general, classically one would say more "fundamental." It designates a sort of irreducible divisibility, "quasi-transcendental," as I have said elsewhere, of "deconstructive" writing. It must inevitably partition itself along two sides of a limit and continue (up to a certain point) to respect the rules of that which it deconstructs or of which it exposes the deconstructibility. Hence, it always makes this dual gesture, apparently contradictory, which consists in accepting, within certain limits—that is to say, in never entirely accepting—the givenness of a context, its closedness and its stubbornness [*sa fermeture et sa fermeté*]. But without this tension or without this apparent contradiction, would anything ever be done? Would anything ever be changed?

This leads me to elaborate rapidly what I suggested above concerning the question of context, of its nonclosure or, if you prefer, of its irreducible opening. I thus return to the question of apartheid. It is exemplary for the questions of responsibility and for the ethical-political stakes that underlie this discussion. In the different texts I have written on (against) apartheid, I have on several occasions spoken of "unconditional" affirmation or of "unconditional" "appeal." This has also happened to me in other "contexts" and each time that I speak of the link between deconstruction and the "yes."[19] Now, the very least that can be said of unconditionality (a word that I use not by accident to recall the character of the categorical imperative in its Kantian form) is that it is independent of every determinate context, even of the determination of a context in general. It announces itself as such only in the *opening* of context. Not that it is simply present (existent) elsewhere, outside of all context; rather, it intervenes in the determination of a context from its very inception, and from an injunction, a law, a responsibility that transcends this or that determination of a given context. Following this, what remains is to articulate this unconditionality with the determinate (Kant would say, hypothetical) conditions of this or that context; and this is the moment of strategies, of rhetorics, of ethics, and of politics. The structure thus described supposes both that there are only contexts, that nothing *exists* outside context, as I have often said, but also that the limit of the frame or the border of the context always entails a clause of nonclosure. The outside penetrates and thus determines the inside. This is what I have analyzed so often, and so long, under the words "supplement," "parergon," and each time that I have said of the trait of writing or of inscription (for instance, that which marks the limit of a corpus or of a context) that it was divisible and that it erased itself in the very process of marking.

This unconditionality also defines the injunction that prescribes deconstructing. Why have I always hesitated to characterize it in Kantian terms, for example, or more generally in ethical or political terms, when that would have been so easy and would have enabled me to avoid so much criticism, itself all too facile as well? Because such characterizations seemed to me essentially associated with philosophemes that themselves call for deconstructive questions. Through these difficulties, another language and other thoughts seek to make their way. This language and these thoughts, which are also new responsibilities, arouse in me a respect which, whatever the cost, I neither can nor will compromise. But this is already too long for a letter that is an afterword, I cannot pursue this direction any further here.

Question.

In the wake of the controversy over de Man's early writings, what would you say about the alleged difficulty deconstructionists must have in appealing to "deniability"[20] or in acknowledging the reality and determinacy of historical events?

Answer.

I do not know to what difficulty or to which "deconstructionists" you are alluding. For my part, I believe I have answered these questions. I have answered them above in their generality (on the subject of reality, determinacy, and historical events). I have responded concerning the example of "de Man's early writings" in a long essay published in *Critical Inquiry*.[21] The most serious question for me, today and tomorrow, is a different one. I would like to say a few words about it. What of deniability in the attacks that have been unleashed in the press against de Man and above all (as though de Man were only a pretext) against "deconstruction" and "deconstructionists"? Why has the press (most often inspired by professors, when they themselves did not write directly) multiplied denials, lies, defamations, insinuations against deconstruction, without taking the time to read and to inform itself, without even taking the trouble to find out for itself what "deconstructive" texts actually say, but instead caricaturing them in a stupid and dishonest manner? Why do such methods often so strikingly resemble what they claim to denounce but also begin to imitate (summary show trials, caricature, denial, falsification, incapacity to acknowledge or to recognize what is said, done, written by those under attack and with whom accounts are to be settled, etc.)? Why so much fear, hate, and denial of deconstruction? Why so much resentment? I am thinking in particular, but this list is far from closed, of the article in *The New York Times* (1 December 1987), that of Jon Wiener in *The*

Nation (9 Jan. 1988), of David Lehman in *Newsweek* (15 Feb. 1988) and in the *Los Angeles Times* (13 Mar. 1988), of Frank Schirrmacher in the *Frankfurter Allgemeine Zeitung* (10 and 24 Feb. 1988) (for the same phenomena are developing in West Germany). In all these cases, the gesticulation of resentment is always spectacular in its ignorance or in its cynicism. It is sinister even if it sometimes assumes an aspect that is jubilatory, frankly comical, or narcissistic (I mean self-referential), as in the article by Walter Kendrick, "De Man That Got Away: Deconstructors on the Barricades," *Village Voice Literary Supplement*, no. 64, Apr. 1988). It is in this direction that I will pose questions of "deniability" or of "acknowledging the reality and determinacy of historical events"—today and tomorrow, and not only concerning what de Man was able to write half a century ago when there was no question, and with good reason, of deconstruction. In the article in *Critical Inquiry*, I have written at length on the complex question of continuity *and* discontinuity in Paul de Man's early and late writings.

And since I have already alluded above to the intervention of the press in the debate with Searle, I would still want to raise the very serious problem of the responsibility of the press in its relations to the intellectuals or in political-intellectual, philosophical, cultural, or ideological debates. And above all the problem of the responsibility of intellectuals in their relations to the press. Not in order to recommend retreating into the interior of the Academy, even less to accuse the press in itself or in general, but on the contrary to call for the maximal development of a press that is freer and more rigorous in the exercise of its duties. In fact, I believe that professional journalists are more demanding in this regard than are those intellectuals who make use of newspapers as instruments of a power that is immediate and subject to few controls.

Again, thank you, dear Gerald Graff, for your initiative, your questions, and your objections. And excuse the schematic and overly charged character of my answers. Once more, their aim is not to close the discussion, but to give it a fresh start.

Jacques Derrida
Translated by Samuel Weber

NOTES

1. They will be cited further on, before each response.

2. Repeatedly, during the course of my answers, it happens that I begin by citing a part of this chain of "words" or "concepts." I do it by economy, and these allusions do not refer to verbal or conceptual units but to long textual chains that I cannot reconstitute here. On the other hand, the list of these words is not closed, by definition, and it is far from limiting itself (currently) to those that I cite here or see often cited (*pharmakon, supplement, hymen, parergon*). To those whom this interests, I indicate that if the list remains indeed open, there are already many others at work. They share a certain functional analogy but remain singular and irreducible to one another, as are the textual chains from which they are inseparable. They are all marked by iterability, which however seems to belong to their series. I take this particular example only because in this context it will be the object of considerable discussion.

3. See the previous note.

4. The entire article would have to be cited, or at the very least its section 5. I will have to be satisfied with this passage, while referring the reader to its context. "When I have lectured to audiences of literary critics, I have found two pervasive philosophical presuppositions in the discussion of literary theory, both oddly enough derived from logical positivism. First there is the assumption that unless a distinction can be made rigorous and precise it isn't really a distinction at all. Many literary theorists fail to see, for example, that it is not an objection to a theory of fiction that it does not sharply divide fiction from nonfiction, or an objection to a theory of metaphor that it does not sharply divide the metaphorical from the nonmetaphorical." The phrase which follows is more reasonable and more interesting. I will therefore cite it as well. "On the contrary, it is a condition of the adequacy of a precise theory of an indeterminate phenomenon that it should precisely characterize that phenomenon as indeterminate; and a distinction is no less a distinction for allowing for a family of related, marginal, diverging cases." I shall return later to the manner in which I treat this problem of determination. But even if I am not far from agreeing with what this last phrase (and it alone) says, I have never seen any evidence of the slightest concern in Searle, not in his *Reply* or elsewhere, with a "precise theory" of what he calls here the "indeterminate phenomenon." And above all, above all I do not believe that phenomena which are marginal, metaphorical, parasitic, etc. are in themselves "indeterminate," even if it is inevitable that there be a certain play in the general space for them to produce and determine themselves, which is quite different from calling them "indeterminate" in themselves. I insist on scrupulously citing this phrase in order never to miss an opportunity of underscoring to what point I might agree with Searle. It is a rule that I try to follow in all discussion. It sometimes

makes things long, unsettling, and complicated. But it must be. I believe that I would not agree with anything else in this article, which I unfortunately cannot cite and criticize here in its entirety.

5. John R. Searle, *Intentionality: An Essay in the Philosophy of Mind* (Cambridge: Cambridge Univ. Press, 1983).

6. Jacques Derrida, "Like the Sound of the Sea Deep within a Shell: Paul de Man's War," trans. Peggy Kamuf, *Critical Inquiry* 14 (Spring 1988): 590–652.

7. Elsewhere I discuss these aspects of relations to the law, for instance in "Living On," trans. J. Hulbert, in *Deconstruction and Criticism* (New York: The Seabury Press, 1979); "The Law of Genre," trans. A. Ronell, *Glyph* 7 (Baltimore: Johns Hopkins Univ. Press, 1980); "Title: To be Specified," trans. Tom Conley, *Sub/Stance* 31 (1981); "Devant la loi," trans. A. Ronell, in *Kafka and the Contemporary Critical Performance* (Bloomington: Indiana Univ. Press, 1987); "Le facteur de la vérité," in *The Post Card: From Socrates to Freud and Beyond*, trans. Alan Bass (Chicago: Univ. of Chicago Press, 1987); "Restitutions of the Truth in Painting," in *The Truth in Painting*, trans. Geoff Bennington and Ian McLeod (Chicago: Univ. of Chicago Press, 1987).

8. See the previous note.

9. These assimilations are attributed to me with an insistence and blindness that would merit prolonged analysis. The mechanism involved is always the same. Old and familiar oppositions are to be protected at all costs, even if their pertinence is limited. And those for whom they are not sufficient and who search to elaborate finer, more complex differences, which are sometimes paradoxical, are then confronted with the accusation of blurring or effacing limits. Of not being sufficiently attentive, in short, to difference! I am not going to recall here, this is not the place for that, the difference that I have always sought to recognize between differences and oppositions. But it may be permissible on this occasion to underscore that I have never assimilated or reduced, as is often said, concept to metaphor (see, e.g., the entire last part of "White Mythology," in *Margins of Philosophy*, trans. Alan Bass [Chicago: Univ. of Chicago Press, 1982], particularly pp. 262–63). Instead, I have sought to deconstruct the concept of metaphor itself and proposed an entirely different "logic," "a new articulation" of the relations between concept and metaphor, which is to say, also between philosophy, science, logic on the one hand, and rhetoric on the other. Deconstruction, as I have practiced it, has always been foreign to rhetoricism—which, as its name indicates, can become another form of logocentrism—and this despite or rather because of the interest I have felt obliged to direct at questions of language and at figures of rhetoric. What is all too quickly forgotten is often what is most massively evident, to wit, that deconstruction, that at least to which I refer, *begins* by deconstructing logocentrism, and hence also that which rhetoricism might owe to it. Also for the same reason I never assimilated philosophy, science, theory, criticism, law, morality, etc., to literary fictions. To take an interest in a certain fictionality in the first series, a fictionality whose conditions are only *shared* by literature (for example), to take an interest in the "formal structure," in the "rhetorical organization," or in "textual types" (*Margins*, pp. 293ff.) of philosophical discourse, to read and discuss those writers who took a similar interest (Nietzsche or Valéry, for instance)—this does not in the slightest signify reducing, leveling, assimilating. On the contrary, it is to endeavor to refine the differences.

The most massive and most recent example of the confusion that consists in attributing confusions to me in places where quite simply I have not been read is furnished by Habermas, precisely concerning the debate with Searle. The second of the two chapters devoted to me in his latest book is entitled "Excursus on Leveling the Genre Distinction between Philosophy and Literature" (in *The Philosophical Discourse of Modernity*, trans. F. Lawrence [Cambridge, Mass.: MIT Press, 1987]). Although *I am not cited a single time*, although not one of my texts is even indicated as a reference in a chapter of twenty-five pages that claims to be a long critique of my work, phrases such as the following can be found: "Derrida is particularly interested in standing the primacy of logic over rhetoric, canonized since Aristotle, on its head" (p. 187); " . . . the deconstructionist can deal with the works of philosophy as works of literature . . . " (p. 188); " . . . in his business of deconstruction, Derrida does not proceed analytically. . . . Instead [he] proceeds by a critique of style . . . " (sic! p. 189).

That is false. I say *false*, as opposed to *true*, and I defy Habermas to prove the presence in my work of that "primacy of rhetoric" which he attributes to me with the three propositions that follow and which he then purports to criticize (pp. 190ff.). With a stupefying tranquillity, here is the philosopher of consensus, of dialogue and of discussion, the philosopher who claims to distinguish between science and literary fiction, between philosopy and literary criticism, daring not only to criticize without citing or giving a reference for twenty-five pages, but, even worse, justifying his nonreading and his atmospheric or hemispheric choices by this incredible alibi: "Since Derrida does not belong to those *philosophers who like to argue* [*argumentationsfreudigen Philosophen*, my emphasis!], it is expedient [*ratsam*] to take a closer look at his disciples in literary criticism within the Anglo-Saxon climate of argument in order to see whether this thesis really can be held" (p. 193). From here, Habermas goes on to intervene in, interpret, arbitrate, conclude my debate with Searle without making the slightest reference to my text. He sides with Searle although in his eyes the "discussion between Derrida and Searle" remains "impenetrable" (*undurchsichtige Diskussion*, trans. p. 194). Without citing me, then, a single time, and abusing citations of Jonathan Culler at points where, it being a question of relations between a generality and its "cases," the latter is occasionally obliged to rigidify my arguments out of pedagogical considerations, Habermas does not hesitate to regularly establish a transition, again without the slightest reference to my texts, by means of phrases such as these (to cite once again): "In his initial argument [sic!!], Derrida posits a not very clear link between quotability and repeatability on the one hand, and fictionality on the other . . . ," or "In this argument [sic], Derrida obviously already presupposes what he wants to prove . . . ," or "Derrida's purposely paradoxical statement [sic] that any interpretation is inevitably a false interpretation, and any understanding a misunderstanding . . . ," or again, "Up to this point, I have criticized Derrida's third and fundamental assumption . . . ," etc.

Such procedures still surprise me, and I have difficulty believing my eyes, in my incorrigible naïveté, in the confidence that I still have, in spite of everything, in the ethics of discussion (in morality, if not in moralism), in the rules of the academy, of the university, and of publicaiton. For if Habermas had taken even the slightest care to read me or made any attempt to cite me, he would have seen that the "links" as well as the distinctions betwen quotability, repeatability and fictionality are abundantly and, I dare to believe, clearly justified in "Limited Inc . . . " (**x**, p. 97–102, and precisely in answer to the confusion of Searle reproduced by Habermas). On the contrary, he would have sought in vain the slightest phrase supporting what he calls my "paradoxical statement": I do not think nor have I ever said that "any interpretation is inevitably a false interpretation, and any understanding a misunderstanding." Why? In what way? This is what I discuss and argue at length (for I am one of those who love "arguing," as can be seen), for instance in *Sec* and in "Limited Inc. . . ." The relation of "mis" (mis-understanding, mis-interpreting, for example) to that which is not "mis-," is not at all that of a general law to cases, but that of a *general possibility inscribed in* the structure of positivity, of normality, of the "standard." All that I recall is that this *structural possibility* must be taken into account when describing so-called ideal normality, or so-called just comprehension or interpretation, and that this possibility can be neither *excluded nor opposed*. An entirely different logic is called for.

If I insist here on the example of Habermas, after that of Searle, it is not only because of the importance of the questions I have just evoked, in their very contents. It is to underscore a situation that is unfortunately typical—and politically very serious—at a juncture that I will not hesitate to qualify as worldwide and historic; which is as much to say that its scope can hardly be exaggerated and that it deserves serious analyses. Everywhere, in particular in the United States and in Europe, the self-declared philosophers, theoreticians, and ideologists of communication, dialogue, and consensus, of univocity and transparency, those who claim ceaselessly to reinstate the classical ethics of proof, discussion, and exchange, are most often those who excuse themselves from attentively reading and listening to the other, who demonstrate precipitation and dogmatism, and who no longer respect the elementary rules of philology and of interpretation, confounding science and chatter as though they had not the slightest taste for communication or rather as though they were afraid of it, at bottom. Fear of what, at bottom? Why? That is the real question. What is going on at this moment, above all around "deconstruction," to explain this fear and this dogmatism? Exposed to the slightest difficulty, the slightest complication, the slightest transformation of the rules, the self-declared advocates of communication denounce the absence of rules and confusion. And they allow themselves then to confuse everything in the most authoritarian manner. They even dare to accuse the adversary, as Habermas does me, of "performative contradiction" (pp. 185–86). Is there a "performative contradiction" more serious than that which consists in claiming to discuss rationally the theses of the other without having made the slightest effort to take cognizance of them, read them, or listen to them? I invite interested readers—or whoever may still have doubts about what I have just said—to read for themselves this chapter by Habermas which claims to criticize me, naming me for twenty-five pages without the slightest reference and without the slightest citation. For what I have been unable to render of all this is the frankly comic aspect such contortions often give to certain passages.

Of course, I am not suggesting that it suffices to cite a few phrases or to mention some titles of books in order to argue seriously, to comprehend and enlighten a thought. To be convinced of this it will be sufficient to read Habermas's preceding chapter ("Beyond a Temporalized Philosophy of Origins: Derrida"), in which the apparatus of several footnotes protects no better against an at least equal confusion. But enough, for this chapter, unlike that which follows, does not concern problems directly related to "Limited Inc. . . ."

10. I have made this explicit often and in various places, notably in my most recent book, which collects numerous references on this subject. See *De l'esprit: Heidegger et la question* (Paris: Galilée, 1988); a translation by Geoff Bennington and Rachel Bowlby is in preparation for the University of Chicago Press.

11. Jacques Derrida, "Declarations of Independence," trans. T. Keenan and T. Pepper, *New Political Science* 15 (Summer 1986).

12. I cite: "Michel Foucault once characterized Derrida's prose style to me as '*obscurantisme terroriste.*' The text is written so obscurely that you can't figure out exactly what the thesis is (hence '*obscurantisme*') and when one criticizes it, the author says, '*Vous m'avez mal compris; vous êtes idiot*' (hence '*terroriste*')."

Why do I cite this? Not just for fun. Nor in order to comment directly on the content of these declarations and of these citations. In my opinion it speaks for (and of) itself here. I just want to raise the question of what precisely a philosopher is doing when, in a newspaper with a large circulation, he finds himself compelled to cite private and unverifiable insults of another philosopher in order to authorize himself to insult in turn and to practice what in French is called a *jugement d'autorité*, that is, the method and preferred practice of all dogmatism. I do not know whether the fact of citing in French suffices to guarantee the authenticity of a citation when it concerns a private opinion. I do not exclude the possibility that Foucault may have said such things, alas! That is a different question, which would have to be treated separately. But as he is dead, I will not in my turn cite the judgment which, as I have been told by those who were close to him, Foucault is supposed to have made concerning the practice of Searle in this case and on the act that consisted in making *this* use of an alleged citation. . . . Since what is involved here is ideology, ethics, and politics (academic politics and politics in general), and since you have led me onto this terrain, I will recall only one other fact. In authorizing herself in turn with the same judgment of authority, and in citing this same unverifiable citation, the Halleck Professor of Philosophy at Yale, member of the International Institute of Philosophy, Fellow of the American Academy of Arts and Sciences, Chairman of the American Philosophical Association (1976–83), President of the Association for Symbolic Logic (1983–), Mrs. Ruth Barcan Marcus wrote to the French government (State Ministry, Ministry of Research and of Technology) 12 March 1984, to protest my nomination (in truth the unanimous election by my colleagues) to the position of Director of the International College of Philosophy. I cite this letter: "To establish an 'International College of Philosophy' under Derrida's charge is something of a joke or, more seriously, raises the question as to whether the Ministère d'Etat is the victim of an intellectual fraud. Most of those informed in philosophy and its interdisciplinary connections would agree with Foucault's description of Derrida as practicing 'obscurantisme terrioriste' " (sic! Professor Marcus's French or memory are less sure than Searle's). This letter was signed with all the titles that I have just mentioned and addressed on the letterhead of Yale University, where at the time I was teaching with the title of Visiting Professor. Outside of several private comments, Yale University never felt it necessary to protest or to make excuses officially. I will not dwell on practices such as these, which call to mind sinister memories. I have cited these facts in order better to delimit certain concepts: in such cases, we certainly are confronted with chains of repressive practices and with the police in its basest form, on the border between alleged academic freedom, the press, and state power. The international dimension of this repressive police (a kind of academic "interpol") is manifest, I could provide other evidence. It is true that in the case I am discussing, the lucidity of a French minister (who immediately understood what was going on and whom was involved) cut short a maneuver to which moreover his respect for academic freedoms prevented him from lending any support. But can one always count on such lucidity and such respect for academic freedoms?

13. On the play or function of the de- in "deconstruction," I refer for example to my "Lettre à un ami japonais" in *Psyché: Inventions de l'autre* (Paris: Galilée, 1987), English translation in *Derrida and Différance*, trans. David Wood and Andrew Benjamin (Evanston, Ill.: Northwestern Univ. Press, 1988), and to "Désistance," in *Psyché*, published in English as the Preface to *Typographies* by Philippe Lacoue-Labarthe (Cambridge, Mass.: Harvard Univ. Press, forthcoming). The *de-* signifies less a negative modality affecting a construction or a "sistance," an "estance," than a demarking with regard to the foundationalist/antifoundationalist scheme, or to the constructivist scheme, or to the ontological scheme of Being as Stance (*histēmi*, etc.). As short as this is, this clarification concerns in principle therefore all the oppositions we accept too quickly, including here that between stability and instability. From this consequences ought to be drawn but this cannot be done here. The scheme of stability, which depends upon that of the stance, of station, of stasis, etc., still depends too much upon what is deconstructed, that is, upon the ontological project itself, in the texts to which I here can only refer.

14. Cf. "Psyché: Invention de l'autre," in *Psyché*.

15. In numerous places, e.g., *Positions*, trans. Alan Bass (Chicago: Univ. of Chicago Press, 1981), pp. 86, 104 n. 31.

16. In "My Chances/*Mes chances:* A Rendezvous with Some Epicurean Stereophonies," trans. Irene Harvey and Avital Ronell, in *Taking Chances*, ed. Joseph H. Smith and William Kerrigan (Baltimore: Johns Hopkins Univ. Press, 1984), I propose calling "programmatological" the space of an indispensable analysis "at the intersection of a pragmatics and a grammatology" (p. 27). Grammatology has always been a sort of pragmatics, but the discipline which bears this name today involve too many presuppositions requiring deconstruction, very much like speech act theory, to be simply homogeneous with that which is announced in *De la grammatologie*. A programmatology (to come) would articulate in a more fruitful and more rigorous manner these two discourses.

17. See in particular my essay "From Restricted to General Economy: A Hegelianism without Reserve," in *Writing and Difference*, trans. Alan Bass (Chicago: Univ. of Chicago Press, 1978), and *The Post Card*, pp. 395ff.

18. Cf., e.g., *De l'esprit*.

19. In numerous places, from *Spurs: Nietzsche's Styles to Ulysse gramophone (*Paris: Galilée, 1986*)*, and *De l'esprit*.

20. Editor's note: The reference is to comments of mine, which were quoted by Jon Wiener in the *Nation* article ("Deconstructing de Man") to which Derrida refers below. I observed that "there is an irony [in the de Man case], since deconstructionists have a problem appealing to what politicians call 'deniability.' One of the themes of deconstruction is that the position you try to separate yourself from tends to reappear as a repressed motif in your own text." I also said that "people who adopt deconstructionist positions have various sorts of politics—including radical feminism and other progres-

sive commitments—so an attempt to smear all de Manian deconstruction with de Man's past is unfair" (p. 23).—G. G.

21. Jacques Derrida, "Like the Sound of the Sea Deep within a Shell: Paul de Man's War."